SY 0027442 9

ST. MARY'S
COLLEGE OF EDUCATION
LIBRARY
920
DOS
31655

D1348813

The Best Times

Books by
John Dos Passos

Historical
Narratives

THE GROUND WE STAND ON
THE HEAD AND HEART OF THOMAS JEFFERSON
THE MEN WHO MADE THE NATION
MR. WILSON'S WAR
THE SHACKLES OF POWER

Contemporary
Chronicles

CHOSEN COUNTRY
THREE SOLDIERS
MANHATTAN TRANSFER
THE 42ND PARALLEL
NINETEEN NINETEEN
THE BIG MONEY
THE MOST LIKELY TO SUCCEED
ADVENTURES OF A YOUNG MAN
NUMBER ONE
THE GRAND DESIGN
THE GREAT DAYS
MIDCENTURY

Rapportage

JOURNEYS BETWEEN WARS
STATE OF THE NATION
TOUR OF DUTY
BRAZIL ON THE MOVE

John Dos Passos

AN INFORMAL MEMOIR

The Best Times

ANDRE DEUTSCH

FIRST PUBLISHED 1968 BY
ANDRE DEUTSCH LIMITED
105 GREAT RUSSELL STREET
LONDON, WC1

PRINTED PHOTOLITHO IN GREAT BRITAIN
BY EBENEZER BAYLIS AND SON LTD
THE TRINITY PRESS
WORCESTER AND LONDON

SBN 233 95978 5

Contents

By Way of Introduction...

We were sitting around one evening at Moskowitz's down on the Lower East Side in New York. It must have been during Prohibition days because we were drinking turnip wine.

An intenselooking pale blackhaired young fellow comes over from another table, plunks himself down in the seat opposite, and announces that he is a high school senior. He gives me a black look through his glasses.

"I've been watching you all evening."

"God forbid."

"What I want to know is why don't you act like a writer?"

"How ought a writer to act?"

"You know just as well as I do how a writer ought to act."

I tried to ease him off. "Suppose I did know," I answered as mildly as I could, "how do you know I'd want to act like a writer?"

He glared at me through his glasses. He was groping for words. He got to his feet. "Let me tell you one thing," he spluttered all out of breath, "meeting you sure is a disappointment."

The Best Times

CHAPTER 1

The Commodore

For years a wooden box full of my father's letters has stood on my mantel at Spence's Point. It is a box I made in a manual training course when I was eleven or twelve maybe. It's not too bad a job; I'm sure I couldn't do anything of the sort now. It's made of pine with bevelled corners, neatly squared and varnished. It even has a little brass latch. I haven't the faintest idea how the box has managed to survive. Time and again I have started reading the letters, but each time it has been as if a great fist squeezed my heart. I just couldn't go on.

These are letters my father wrote me during the last seven or eight years of his life.

Now that I have reached the age he had reached when he wrote them maybe I can summon the fortitude to copy out enough from them to make his figure stand up out of the shades.

As I remember him he was a short broadshouldered man, very bald, with gray mustaches that bristled like the horns of a fighting bull. His skin was so transparent the blue veins stood out on his forehead. When he went out he carried a cherry cane and walked with a springy almost truculent step. There was a happy defiance in the way the curled points of his mustaches bristled. They responded to his mood. The few times I saw them droop I felt sick with dismay.

He got up at six or earlier and charged into each new day like a bull charging into the arena. First he did a half hour of vigorous setting-up exercises. Then he plunged into whatever cold salt water was to be had. Out on his boat on the Potomac he would go overboard. At his house in New York he would put ice cream salt in his tub.

How the smells cling in your memory! Even today his image is associated in my mind with the smell of melons. There lingers somewhere in the back of my head an infantile memory of a table with a white cloth in a sunny window—sunlight through lace curtains—and the sun flashing on his bald head as he leaned over to slice a huge yellow melon. I must have been very small, in a high chair probably, because in the picture everything is very large. The melon is enormous. He was nearsighted and had a way of taking off his pincenez to see something close to. He is leaning over the slices of melon to flick the seeds off. I can see the red places where the pincenez have cut into the skin on either side of his nose. He's laughing about something. Breakfast was a favorite meal. He loved to hold forth at breakfast. The memory is full of good humor.

My mother suffered a series of minor strokes and was a helpless invalid during the last years of her life. A year before she died John R.'s mind must have suddenly filled with thoughts of his own death because he wrote out his instructions, in his bold hand that showed both points of the steel pen in the broad strokes, to his executors as to how he wanted to be buried. The paper only came into my hands after my halfbrother Louis' death. The envelope was addressed to Joe Schmidt, my father's secretary, who worked for him with enthusiastic devotion for many years. There is a notation on the envelope in my cousin Cyril's hand, "not opened until after the funeral," which explains why John R. was buried in New York. As soon as I glanced at it I tucked it away in the wooden box.

"To my Executors" it reads. He does not want to be buried in New York, but wants his body to be buried where he buried my mother a year later, in the churchyard of old Yeocomico Church at Tucker Hill near our place in Virginia.

> As I look upon death to be but an epoch in a perpetual journey and as I am sure to enter into a better and happier life I wish no mourning to be worn by my family. On the contrary I desire them to hail the event with joy and, instead of solemnity, to celebrate it with hilarity and mirth. Man is the meanest thing on earth, the lowest in the scale of animal or vegetable life. He who dies therefore is bound to find something better in the next life. The degree or state which he will occupy in his new existence will depend upon his intellectual and moral culture. I accordingly do not dread death but look upon Him as a fortunate and welcome visitor. If the weather permits I wish to have a funeral festival held at Sandy Point with beer, punch and the eating auxiliaries served. And let those who enjoy the festivities remember that I do not envy them. On the contrary I tender them my sympathies.
>
> New York, June 19, 1914
> John R. Dos Passos

He loved to play the lavish host. Westmoreland County, where he had bought what turned out to be the family farm, was a remote and rural area then. One of his delights was to invite all the neighbors, white and colored alike, to a Christmas barbecue at Sandy Point, or to a foxhunt on his land. Sometimes a steer was roasted whole in a pit. There was an endless supply of oysters shucked out of the barrel or roasted on an iron sheet. Kegs of beer had come down on the boat from Washington or Baltimore. There was punch for the gentry. These were the festivities he was projecting for his funeral.

I was born late in both my father's and my mother's lives. Each had a son some eighteen years older than I was. My mother's people were Marylanders who had chosen the Confederate side in the Civil War. As a little girl Mother went through the siege of Petersburg. Though there was some dispute in the Sprigg family as to which of the children it was, I firmly believed when I was small that it was my mother General Lee had taken up on his white horse, Traveller.

My father was a fervent abolitionist and ran off as a boy to serve in the northern army. I came to know him—through the turbulence of conflicting currents of love and hate that mark so many men's feeling for their fathers—at the end of his lusty climb to wealth and influence.

John R. was born in Philadelphia in 1844. His father, Manoel dos Passos, was an immigrant from the town of Punta do Sol on the island of Madeira, and his mother, Lucy Catell, came from a family of South Jersey Quakers. My father remembered her as attending the Methodist Church.

Manoel dos Passos's baptismal certificate reads 1812. He was born in Punta do Sol, a tiny town buried in a deep gash in the mountain a few miles east of Funchal, which is the capital of Madeira. Fishing boats are hauled up on the shingle beach below and on the slopes above are the vineyards and irrigated and terraced croplands that support the population. While I was growing up I thought of my father's people as tillers of the soil, but they actually seem to have been men of the counting house and the pen, notaries, minor officials. There were priests in the collateral branches. On the central square a solid-looking residence with the seven stars of the Great Bear engraved over the door is still known as the Vila Passos.

My grandfather had to leave Punta do Sol in a hurry as a very young man as a result of some incident involving a stabbing. He shipped out for America and is said to have landed in Baltimore. He worked as a cobbler and later made shoes. Eventually he moved to Philadelphia and married and raised a family. His earnings were skimpy. My grandmother had a hard time keeping the children clothed and fed. A man of exigent tastes, particularly about cookery, my grandfather had a terrible temper. My father used to tell me that if his father didn't like the way a dish was cooked he would raise the window and pitch it out into the street. The hungry children would sit in their chairs wide-eyed with horror at seeing their dinner disappear.

After an attempt to run away to sea, my father went to work as an office boy for a law firm and soon became the chief support of the family. When the Civil War broke out he enlisted as a drummer in some Pennsylvania regiment. So far as I know he never saw combat but was sent home from the reserves back of Antietam with a severe case of dysentery. Working his way according to the apprenticeship system he studied law in the office of an attorney named Price, and took courses at the University of Pennsylvania night school.

When I was a small boy I met Mr. Price. John R. asked him to lunch on his boat. Although he was well over ninety, he came up the gangway of the *Gaivota,* anchored off some Philadelphia yacht club, with a light step. John R., who always said he owed his start in life to Mr. Price's teaching and kindness, treated him with affectionate deference. His daughter, a nice jolly woman with flashing black eyes, came along. They both called my father Jack. That made an impression on me because up to then I'd been the only Jack in the family. I was further impressed by the fact that Mr. Price's daughter smoked small black cigars.

John R. moved to New York at the age of twentythree and hung out his shingle in an office that had once been occupied by Aaron Burr. He first made his mark in the lawcourts by getting the charge against a Frenchman who had shot his wife dead in a fit of jealousy reduced from murder to manslaughter. As a result he was retained by the Stokes family when young Edward S. Stokes was convicted of murder for shooting Jim Fisk.

This was the most sensational criminal trial of the seventies in New York. The Stokes family was rich and prominent in every phase of the city's life. Jim Fisk was a peddler from Vermont who had made a fortune in cotton during the Civil War. He owned a brokerage house and had won a garish sort of fame by joining with Jay Gould in the plundering of the Erie Railroad and in an attempt to corner the gold market which brought about the Black Friday panic on Wall Street in 1869. He owned a hotel and an opera house and called himself Admiral of the Fall River Line and was the flashiest of the financial buccaneers of the day. Stokes shot him before a number of witnesses in the lobby of the Grand Central Hotel on Broadway. The quarrel was over the favors of a wellknown actress. John R. was asked to join the counsel for the defense after Stokes was convicted of murder in his first trial and was generally credited with getting the verdict set aside.

His success in the Stokes case left him at twentyseven one of the leading attorneys at the New York bar. He married a lady of means and social standing and moved into a new office in the Mills Building across the street from the Stock Exchange. There he made himself an expert in the law as it pertained to brokerage practices. He took in his younger brother Benjamin as partner. Though other partners came and went the firm, even after my uncle Benjamin's early death, was known through the years as Dos Passos Brothers.

Since John R. had an acutely analytical mind he synthesized his practice in *Treatise on the Law of Stock-Brokers and Stock-Exchanges,* which soon became the principal textbook on the subject in the country's lawschools.

Stock Exchange law led to corporation law. It was the heyday of mergers and trusts. John R. combined legal learning with a knack for getting along with people and for cajoling other men into getting along with each other. Soon his advice was required on every difficult problem of incorporation. He worked on the reorganization of the Erie Railroad and on the Reading and the Texas Pacific. His fee for his advice to the Havemeyer interests on forming the Sugar Trust was reputed to be the largest on record. Again, deducing theory from practice he compiled a treatise: *Commercial Trusts.*

From close contact with financiers came opportunities for investment. John R. never could develop the wholehearted devotion to profit necessary to build up a fortune. His speculations were picturesque but they often proved unwise or, to say the least, before their time. He was full of grandiose schemes for Mexican railroads and plunged into a realestate speculation in the region of Chapultepec Park in Mexico City. He early saw the possibilities of Diesel motors. During the eighties he devoted a great deal of time and money to a project to build tubes under the Hudson River. In his autobiography William Gibbs McAdoo, who finally accomplished what New Yorkers had considered a whimsical dream, gave John R. credit for much help and advice. Like many a good lawyer John R. was more adept at building other men's fortunes than his own.

He was a lavish spender. He was known as among the gayest of gay entertainers in a period when social life in New York still had a little of the cordiality of the small town. He was an accomblished public speaker. His fine singing voice was an asset in those days when singing was an afterdinner accomplishment. *Larboard Watch Ahoy* was his favorite, but he could remember almost any number out of *Pinafore* or *The Mikado* or Offenbach's *La Belle Hélène* or *Les Cloches de Corneville.* He was known for his ability to recite whole scenes out of Shakespeare's plays. He had a great flow of conversation and rarely lost his sense of humor.

He was a warmhearted man besides. He supported needy relatives and was always ready to bail out an unfortunate friend. Passionately fond of the sea, he liked to talk of being descended from a mythical Portuguese pirate. He was a powerful swimmer. He loved sailing. For some years he owned a fast Gloucester schooner converted into a yacht, named the *Mary Wentworth.* In my time it was a hundred-foot steam yacht named the *Gaivota.* All this cost a great deal of money. One of his partners once told me that, though Jack Dos Passos pulled in larger fees than anyone in the firm, every year's end found him in the red.

It was natural that he should be always on the edge of taking the plunge into politics. Having educated himself, he was profoundly read in English and American constitutional law. He steeped himself in the political writing of the English seventeenth and eighteenth centuries. He always kept sets of Bacon and Montesquieu close at hand. An immigrant's son, he cherished the dream of the perfect republic based on the Anglo-Saxon tradition of individual liberty with justice for rich and poor. This was the dream that had brought so many to the American shore. He was far too outspoken in his opinions to be a successful politician. He used to tell me with a laugh that, thinking as he did, he couldn't be elected dogcatcher in any precinct in the land.

I believe he was originally a gold Democrat of the Grover Cleveland stripe, but in 1896 he came out for McKinley, whom he personally admired and whose position on the gold standard he approved. He was profoundly moved by the Cuban struggle for independence and helped raise loans for the Cuban republic. Although he later had some qualms about the war against Spain, he defended McKinley's action against Aguinaldo in the Philippines from attacks by the anti-imperialists. He couldn't abide T.R.

In 1904 he brought out a pamphlet denouncing the Republican party for the whole course of its history. He blamed it for the reversal of Lincoln's policy of conciliation toward the South; for the impeachment of Andrew Johnson; for unconstitutional tampering with the currency; for the packing of the Supreme Court and the skulduggeries that cheated Tilden out of the presidency; and, most recently, for the theft of Panama from the Republic of Colombia. He blamed the Republicans for overcentralizing the government and for turning Congress into an oligarchy where the lawmaking power was in the hands of the eight Senators and ten members of the House of Representatives who headed the important committees. He campaigned vigorously for Judge Parker in 1904.

The Roosevelt-Parker campaign remained vivid in my mind as the occasion of my first fist fight. My father considered English education much better than American. Since his tenderly affectionate relations with my mother remained technically irregular so long as his first wife lived, it was only in Europe that they could travel openly together. As a result I was sent to school at Peterborough Lodge in Hampstead in the northern suburbs of London. For a while I was the only American there. Then, in the fall of 1904, another American appeared. We were introduced by one of the masters who expected us to fall on each other's neck. Quite the contrary. The new boy walked up to me with a suspicious look and asked me who I was for for President. I was taller than he was but he was older and stockier. When I said Judge Parker he promptly punched me in the nose. I flailed around helplessly. The scene was humiliating. It was forty years before I could properly appreciate Theodore Roosevelt.

It must have been around this time that I was taken to Madeira to recuperate from a hernia operation. We stayed at Reid's Hotel on a magnificent headland overlooking Funchal. The garden was full of lizards. I already had a passion for small animals and set about catching lizards to keep for pets. It was tantalizing how they would run off leaving their tails in your hand when you tried to catch them.

Again it is the smells of Funchal that have stayed in my head. Public transport was by sledges drawn by oxen over the cobbled roads. The barefoot driver trotted alongside occasionally greasing the runners with a long rag dipped in a curiously scented oil. The same smell, mixed a little with heliotrope and roses, pervaded the little basketwork cars we coasted on down the steep cobbled slope that wound down from the church on the mountain to the city square.

I've always remembered Dr. Vergil as coming to see us at Reid's Hotel, but a letter of my father's reporting his death speaks of him as living in Lisbon. Anyway I was already studying Latin in school, and my father, determined I should not lose anything by the enforced vacation, induced this cousin of ours to tutor me every day. I remember a sallow, bearded little gentleman in a dusty frock coat who appeared every morning with a bunch of tightly packed roses for my mother. We called him Dr. Vergil because he knew the entire *Aeneid* by heart. *Arma virumque cano* is about all I retained from his lessons.

John R. got along very well with the British. Although proud of his Portuguese extraction he never ceased to believe that the Anglo-Saxon tradition of law and representative government was the only possible basis for the development of a worldwide Christian civilization. He admired the personal uprightness of the Spaniards and Portuguese he knew, but when they tried to work together in a political framework he found them hopeless. Only the English had the principles of practical statesmanship bred into their bones.

In 1903 he had published the only one of his books that found much of an audience outside of the legal profession. *The Anglo-Saxon Century* was the result of years of conversations with Ted McFadden, a Philadelphia lawyer who was his most intimate friend. McFadden wrote a verse play and Addisonian essays and shared John R.'s enthusiasm for the classical culture of the British ruling gentry.

The book was a plea for an immediate customs union among all English-speaking peoples. The Canadian provinces should vote themselves into the Union as states. An arbitration court should immediately be set up to adjudge disputes. Currencies should be standardized and citizenship made interchangeable between the United States and Great Britain and her colonies. He saw such a union as the only way of countering the Russian expansion which he already saw as a threat to free institutions. The political union of the Anglo-Saxon peoples would insure a century of peace.

The book was possibly better received in England than in the United States. John R. found himself quite a lion in the West End of London.

In that connection an odd little memory remains in my mind. I'm in a room in a London hotel, possibly the Langham, where he usually stayed. My mother and I have come to see him in his court uniform before he goes to be presented to King Edward. There is an English valet in attendance. The air is saturated with cologne and the bayrummy smell of the bearsgrease he used to point up the tips of his mustache. He's wearing short pants just like I am, and a frilled shirt and black silk stockings and strutting up and down in front of the tall rainstreaked windows reciting Othello's address to the Venetian senate. I am eyeing him with mixed feelings.

To me the court dress seemed final. Here Dedi is on the edge of becoming an Englishman and I have been making a desperate plea to be allowed to go home to America to school. I didn't mind the hard study and I don't remember any particular fagging or bullying but I was an American and my entire small frame revolted at going to school in England. I can't remember what the upshot was right then but eventually I won my point.

It was a great disappointment to John R. He believed English education was much better than American. He had hoped I would go on through some public school to Oxford or Cambridge. His culture, though he had gotten it all himself out of books, was very much the same classical culture his English friends had imbibed from their schooling. Here he found men who would talk about Cicero and Demosthenes without affectation. Julius Caesar and Lord Bacon were part of their world, and not oddities dreamed up by an eccentric lawyer of foreign extraction. He found English conversation sound and durable like English tailoring.

How much of this seeped into my childish mind I don't know. One is always retinting one's childhood memories. What I really remember, with lithographic vividness, of life with my father in England is sitting on the roof of a coach and four being driven with jingle of harness through green lanes, and the footman in livery tootling on the brass horn; and a great hamper being opened for a picnic under a royal oak in a park full of grazing deer. There's a gentleman who looks very much like King Edward; same little beard, everybody tells him so. His answer is that his name is a lot older in England than the royal house. Even I recognize it has a Norman sound: Sir William Vavasour. I didn't like him. And there's a very pretty lady in a fruitbasket hat and leg of mutton sleeves, named Mrs. Bonheur, but I don't remember anyone else. I did like her until she asked so many questions. Corks popped in tiny champagne bottles and I had so many little cheesecakes called Maids of Honor that I felt a bit sick. Sounds like something I read in a book, but the fragments of the remembered scene stand out quite clear.

Then there's an even sharper image of my father's hands, with the blue veins standing out, as he pulls on the oars of a boat. We are fishing for salmon on a Scottish lake. A storm of rain and wind has come up and the boat is half swamped and I'm only a tiny bit scared because his hands look so quiet and powerful as he pulls for the shore.

The spring Halley's comet appeared I was at the Choate School in Wallingford, Connecticut. I remember gazing at the great comet, which looked like a bright segment of the Milky Way and filled a huge stretch of sky, with some awe through the attic skylight in the house I roomed in. John R. wrote me from Virginia that he had gotten up before day to see the comet and found it indeed magnificent. He wondered whether comets were female. The newspapers were full of scare stories about what might happen to people on earth when we passed through the possibly noxious gases of the comet's tail. John R. added that it would be funny if she set everybody to sneezing.

Under the leadership of a slightly older boy (I was always the youngest everywhere in those days) named Skinny Nordhoff, I was at the height of the taxidermist period every American youngster seems to go through. Since I was useless in athletics on account of rapidly increasing myopia, when my father furnished a canoe, Skinny and I were allowed to go paddling on the Quinnipiac and even to camp out some weekends. I was allowed to keep a pet raccoon in a chicken wire pen.

We dreamed of exploring the Mackenzie River. We trapped small rodents and tanned their hides. We caught bullfrogs and skinned them and cooked their legs over an open fire in a secret spot in the woods below the pond. We kept gartersnakes in our pockets. We studied with passionate interest the egglaying habits of the hoptoads that shrilled so loud about the pond in the spring.

To John R.'s delight I had taken up Greek with Mrs. St. John, the headmaster's wife whom I found adorable. As the daughter of Professor Seymour at Yale she had grown up with the language. Dedi was planning to start on Greek himself; said he'd never had time before. Eventually, a Greek grammar joined the little blue paperback manual called *French Verbs at a Glance* he kept by his bed to study when he woke up at night. In one of his letters he wrote, "I hope you are making good progress with Homer and that you feed the coon a little Greek for a change of diet now and then."

❧❧❧

During this period Mother was living in her house at 1201 19th Street in Washington. She was driven out every day in a livery stable victoria by an Irish coachman named Pat. Her more fashionable friends came to see her in electric broughams. I didn't spend much time there as most vacations we all went to Sandy Point. John R. would have me down to New York for an occasional weekend besides when he had tickets to some Shakespeare production, or his favorite Gilbert and Sullivan, or once it was Sarah Bernhardt on one of her many farewell tours. He would put me up at the Murray Hill Hotel on Park Avenue just below the gleaming new Grand Central Station.

He would insist on my dressing for dinner and we would sit together in state at Delmonico's over meals that seemed to me endless. There is a time in childhood when you are embarrassed by everything your parents do. I'd huddle in acute misery while he joshed with the waiters or indulged in boastful talk with some friend who would sit down for a moment at his table.

Once I have a dim recollection of getting the floor away from him. There were several people at the table. Somebody asked a question about beavers. Beavers were something I knew about. Though I was fearfully shy, before I knew what I was doing, I had launched into a disquisition on beavers, their lodges and dams, their habits and virtues. John R.'s friends stared at me in astonishment, but he listened carefully and kept drawing me out —like a witness in court—until I'd told all I knew.

When we parted, though he knew I'd brought along books of my own—I was a furious reader in those days—he'd slip me a book "to read on the train." It was only many years later, by remembering back, that I discovered how well my father directed my reading.

He had a habit of reading *Paradise Lost* Sunday mornings at breakfast, said it was better than going to church. Milton didn't take with me much at that time, though I could recite long passages from "L'Allegro" and "Il Penseroso" quite volubly. In fact it was only in middle age, after a lot of reading in the Commonwealth period in preparation for a book I was writing, that I awoke to the magnificence of *Samson Agonistes*. Maybe the seed was sown at those breakfast tables in Washington or on the *Gaivota* or at the Sandy Point house. John R. was wont to say that the mind was like a big old trunk in the attic. Nothing you put in was ever lost. Often you couldn't find things but eventually they turned up.

The first book I remember his giving me was Captain Marryat's *Mr. Midshipman Easy* when I was eight. I read it through again and again; then Ballantyne's *The Coral Island*, and every sea story I could lay my hands on. A few yachting trips and sailing a canoe off the Sandy Point shore whetted my taste for the sea. Until it was obvious that I was too nearsighted to pass the physical I planned to work for an appointment to Annapolis and to follow the sea as a career.

Of Dickens, of course he read *The Christmas Carol* aloud every Christmas; then there was the blue paperback set of Dumas. All his life John R. worked for a mastery of French. He insisted we write to each other in French, which he wrote fluently if ungrammatically. Since I'd learned French as a child in Brussels he sometimes asked me to correct his mistakes. Wherever he went he left a trail of Dumas Père's* historical romances, which he read at night when he couldn't sleep and tired of the French verbs. I read them right after him.

He abhorred magazines and bestseller novels. No use reading a book you couldn't learn something from. The taste for history he implanted in me as a child surely did take root.

By the time I came along, the men he'd known, like his friend McFadden, whom he considered really firstrate, were most of them dead. He did introduce me to Mark Twain as we were walking down Fifth Avenue one blustery morning, but all I remember was his flowing hair and white suit, which seemed incongruous on such a cold day, and the fact that his name wasn't really Mark Twain at all.

This was on one of John R.'s early morning walks. To the end of his life he walked down from his house on 56th Street to his office in the Commercial Cable Building on Broad Street. Times I walked with him I was astonished by the variety of people he knew—cops on the beat, cabdrivers, whitewings, lawclerks. He always remembered some personal thing to ask them about: Was the sick wife better? How were the boys doing in school?

Among his letters to me while I was in boardingschool was one about Thomas Edison:

> I had a very interesting episode today. I went out to see the great electrician Edison at his laboratory at Orange. I know him very well, and he is both a good friend and an interesting man. . . . He has been working on a storage battery for years and he now claims he has the best in existence. He is a wonderful personage for, in this age where money seems to be the "be all and the end all" of human ambition he, although very rich, relegates wealth to the second rank and looks upon his work as his first love. He works 18 hours a day & says, calculating his age on that basis, he is at least 100—He is there at the factory all the time working like an ordinary laborer. He is a man after my own style—I wish you had been along to have met him.

Since I hated boardingschool—being called Frenchy and Foureyes and the class grind—I was in a hurry to get to college. When I passed the Harvard entrance exams everybody thought I was too young to go, so I was shipped abroad for a tour in charge of a young man named Jones, who had some classical attainments and was planning to become a Dominican monk.

Although he'd made his career in nineteenth-century finance and law, John R. had an eighteenth-century mind. His religion was the Deism of Thomas Jefferson and John Adams; he told me he had run away from home once when his father threatened to make him a priest. He was managing to give me an eighteenth-century education.

So Mr. Jones and I took the Grand Tour. We visited art galleries, stared up at cathedrals—I already had a passion for architecture—and quoted Gibbon in the Roman Forum; read Thucydides (from the trot) in Athens and evoked Julius Caesar and Napoleon while brushing off the baksheesh-seekers in front of the Sphinx.

My father had a strong predilection for Caesar. After reading Froude's essay, Caesar became my private idol. In my daydreams I often sat in my tent and dictated five letters at a time to rule the known world. As much as any eighteenth-century Etonian I was living in the Roman Forum and the Attic Stoa. I sent home a long Plutarchian disquisition on Alcibiades, his faults and follies.

My letters got so stilted John R. included in several of his answers a humorous plea "to forego dogmatism." I must have been a prime little prig. At home when I came out with some illfounded opinion he had a way—which I found profoundly irritating to the budding ego—of taking off his glasses and staring at me blandly and asking: "Is that remark the result of experience or observation?"

In the course of our travels Mr. Jones and I kept running into a congenial family of New Zealanders engaged on a similar expedition. I did not say a word in my letters about how helplessly smitten I was with the younger daughter or the mortification I felt when I caught her, on the forward deck of the steamer, one moonlight night on the Aegean, flirting in French with a young Turk named Talaat Bey.

Back in Washington from Europe in the spring of 1912 I found John R. spending more time than usual at 1201 19th Street. Unless I'm mistaken he was arguing a case before the Supreme Court. His marriage to my mother had been made public and they were living together as man and wife. I don't remember exactly how I felt about having my civil status regularized; historical novels had filled my head with the romance of the bar sinister.

John R. remained a political maverick. In 1908 he had campaigned for Taft.

He was trying to use his friendships among the politicians to further his scheme for law reform. He was convinced that the time had come to revise and simplify the whole legal code. Years of practice had convinced him that the complications and obfuscations of state and Federal law gave the rich an enormous advantage over the poor in civil cases. They could hire better lawyers. In criminal cases he thought the accused should testify. At the same time he advocated a system of public defenders for the impecunious. Law reform became the forlorn hope of his later years.

By June, 1912, he was putting in all his time on his campaign. The Democratic National Convention was assembling to pick a

Presidential candidate. The Metropolitan Club buzzed with bigbug politicians. Reform was in the air in both parties. The Governor of New Jersey, ex-Professor Wilson of Princeton, hailed as a probable Democratic nominee, was the incarnation of civic virtue. It seemed a propitious moment for any kind of reform. Carrying a fat little leather handbag, shaped rather like a dachshund, which was stuffed with closely written legal cap, John R. went off hopefully to Baltimore on the B&O.

I was left in charge of the household. Poor Mother had to be cared for like a child. I had to do the marketing and pay the household bills. The cook, named Lizzie, kept getting drunk and had to be fired. There was nobody but me left to clean up after she vomited all over the maid's room before departing.

That June was fearfully hot. There seemed to be no oxygen in the Washington air. Mother was very poorly and I wanted to get her down to the farm. I wanted to be there myself. There I could ride and swim and work in the garden and sail my canoe. In Washington there was nothing in the world to do; my cousins, who were the only people of my age I knew there, had gone to Bay Head for the summer.

Restless as only a sixteen-year-old can be, stifling more with boredom than with the heat, I kept rushing out-of-doors for short desperate walks through brick streets stale with stewing foliage. Though there was a nurse in attendance, I could never go very far for fear Mother might need me for something.

Reading became a sort of anesthesia. I devoured *The War of the Worlds* and the whole series of H. G. Wells' tales of the marvelous I found in a pile of back numbers of *The Strand Magazine* up in the attic. Though they seemed as tedious as the Washington streets, I plowed through the novels of George Eliot. I read a lot of Poe: I was thinking of myself as the victim of one of Poe's horror stories, chained to a gridiron of tiny chores while from Baltimore came the tantalizing rumble of the great world. Even through the dull columns of the newspapers I could detect the distant din of political oratory, the clash of arms of stalwarts hacking and hewing over the platform. I saw them in breastplates and helmets. I was so steeped in Homer I couldn't help picturing the platform as a wooden structure something like the Trojan horse.

A letter of John R.'s to his lawyer friend Eliot Norton, also interested in law reform, which turned up in the Norton papers at the Houghton Library at Harvard, gives glimpses of what was really going on in the sweltering armory. It was dated Baltimore, June 29, 1912:

> . . . The outlook is altogether uncertain. If Bryan combines with Murphy the trick is done. If the Champ Clarks make the same Bryan will go under. It is a good game of chess now where everything is in the hands of very few men—and the people sacrificed. There is not enough of real patriotism present to dance on the point of a fine cambric needle that yr mother was wont to make your shirts with. The scene in the convention is truly spectacular. Filled as it always is with about fifteen thousand persons it is most impressive. But the whole affair is governed by emotion, the audience deadens or stimulates. The politicians play to the galleries. The speeches from beginning to end have been lower than commonplace. The amphitheatre is so large that one has to yell to fill it & all those beautiful intonations and histrionic features are wanting—*in necessitate rei*. If an orator wishes to make a statement—a mere statement of fact—he yells it and adds fierce gesticulation even to an announcement that it is time to adjourn. We are crushing out oratory—I mean that we are in the last stages of it—we are standing at the grave. But let it go—a real convention should exclude the public. Exclude the public! Good God man what are you saying?

When John R. came home I was bitterly disappointed. Not a word would he say about the convention. He was no man to admit defeat. All he would talk about was how late they had kept him up nights. We had an old tomcat at that time who amused John R. by what he called his reprehensible habits. The tomcat would be out on the town for days and then, when we had decided he was gone for good, we would find him curled up asleep on a rug in the parlor. John R. said he felt like that old tomcat, he was going to sleep and sleep; and he certainly did.

It was about this time that Mrs. Harris appeared in our lives as Mother's trained nurse. Mrs. Harris made everything easier for all of us. She was not only a competent nurse but she took over the duties of housekeeper. She played the piano and knew a lot of what we called "college songs" in those days. She was good company and soon became a member of the family. She was with us when we went aboard the *Gaivota.* We took along a box of Fourth of July fireworks big as a coffin to set off on the beach at Sandy Point.

John R. had the knack of leaving his troubles behind him as soon as he stepped aboard his boat at the Washington dock. It's hard for the young to interest themselves in the troubles of the old—their own seem so much more urgent—but I did have inklings of his money worries, of his daily struggle to raise funds to protect speculations he believed would at any moment bring in the fortune he needed to assure a comfortable retirement. I knew he dreamed of settling down at Sandy Point and putting all his time in on farming and writing up law reform. Better than anyone I understood the tragic frustration of Mother's illness. I thought I understood it. Romantic love was something I thought I knew about. It used to annoy me no end when my father would insist that no man under forty could understand what love meant. During all the painful years of their long love affair my mother and father had looked forward to a peaceful family life together and now . . . I never remember hearing the slightest whisper of complaint.

The moment he stepped aboard the boat and put on his yachting cap he was known as the Commodore. Mother he referred to as the Princess. My monicker was Monsieur Singe. For attendants we had Tom, the cook, a tall lean very black man whose corn muffins I can taste in recollection to this day, and Old Ben, who was my father's valet ashore and officiated gravely as steward afloat. I was fond of Old Ben. Ben's kinky hair was gray. His broad brown face wore the smile of unction of a deacon greeting the congregation at the church door. On the *Gaivota* he wore gleaming white starched jackets. Since he was about the Commodore's size he wore his castoff suits and particularly his old derby hats when he was off duty. The four of us formed the cast of characters in a sort of charade the Commodore conducted with Mrs. Harris as the indulgent audience.

We had a Victor talking machine aboard, one of those with a big horn the fox terrier used to listen to so raptly in the ads: "His Master's Voice." Cruising downriver we would set it up on a table on the afterdeck. Monsieur Singe would wind up the clockwork and change the records: the Princess would lie back in a deck chair, weak and vague, but with a sweet lost look of loveliness she never lost, while the Commodore performed a private tap dance of his own to whatever music came along. *Pinafore* was his favorite.

Once we got past Indian Head everything pleased him. He knew and loved every creek and every sandtipped point of pines on the Potomac River. He delighted in catching or not catching fish when we went out with handlines in the dinghy; in the scream of gulls; in the rustling noise a flock of coots made when they took off from some glassy bay; in the sight of an eagle bullying a fishhawk out of his dinner; in the cawing of the crows circling some riverside oak.

He was particularly fond of crows. He said their caw-caw was really ha-ha. They were laughing at us. He would dance his little dance and pace the deck of the *Gaivota* with his bantam swagger and laugh back at the laughing crows: "Ha haha."

Since he was away so much things were always going wrong on the farm. He took crop failures and such misadventures as the mysterious disappearance of turkeys from the flock or pigs from the pen with imperturbable good humor. He got entertainment from the country people's sly ways; he loved the Negro farmhands because he could always make them laugh.

The Northern Neck farmers were isolated from the world by bad roads in those days. Communication was entirely by water. To reach the state capital from Sandy Point you had to take a day's drive through beds of sand and sloughs of mud over to the Rappahannock River, wait for the steamboat; overnight to Fredericksburg; and then spend four hours on the train to Richmond.

The Commodore helped get the first telephone lines introduced. Sometimes he wondered if it hadn't been a mistake. News and gossip now traveled almost too fast. He used to say that his friend Mrs. Griffith, five miles away at the Hague, knew what he was going to have for lunch before he'd written down the menu.

A case in point was the story of the naked duke. I think it was in that same summer of 1912 that the Commodore brought a Frenchman along on one of his trips down on the *Gaivota.* This was a client, a tanned young man of unpretentious manners. His name, le duc de Richelieu, stirred up all the Dumas romances my head was stuffed with. They were involved together in some sort of international enterprise concerning Mexico. It would never have occurred to me to ask the Commodore a question about business matters, so I could only guess. Anyway the duke caused a scandal. He turned out to be an early nudist. He would ask to be put ashore and would roam about the Sandy Point beach stark naked. He felt that when he left our little group of houses and barns up near the cannery on the point he was entering virgin wilderness.

He was oblivious of the fact that there was a family of Taliaferros living in an unpainted frame structure farther down the beach. The brothers were watermen who furnished us with a daily bunch of fish, but the sister, Miss Mary, was a spinster.

Miss Mary saw everything and heard everything without ever leaving her dooryard. Though the family had fallen on evil days, she still had some beautiful old furniture and no uncertain pride in the glories of her name. When she caught sight of the naked duke strolling past the windows she threatened to call the sheriff.

The Commodore was quite a crony of hers and liked to stop, on his walks down the deeply wooded road toward Lynch's Point, to pass the time of day with her—a scrawny figure in gingham with a sunbonnet tied under her chin—across the unpainted pickets that enclosed her weedy little garden. Their talk was mostly about the crowned heads of Europe. Even the Commodore had trouble talking her out of sending for the sheriff. The fact that the naked man was a nobleman of high degree made no impression at all. The story traveled in one continuous snicker throughout the whole end of the county.

❦❦❦

That fall I went to college. The Commodore traveled to Boston with me on the pretext that he had business there. We had a last lunch together off his favorite codfish tongues and broiled honeycomb tripe at Young's Hotel. Then I set off with my baggage for Cambridge in a cab. Preoccupied as I was with the chills and fevers of a young person plunging into a new environment, I was painfully aware of his loneliness.

It was the loneliness of a man who has outlived his generation. More and more he found himself on the unpopular side of political questions. He opposed votes for women and President Wilson's putting through legislation for an eight-hour day. He was suspicious of the direct primary. He made speeches and circulated a pamphlet against the election of United States Senators by popular vote, which he felt would upset the balance of powers set up under the Constitution.

In his late sixties his health was still robust, though he did suffer from fits of the gout. He was vain about his health and tried to keep his gout a secret. "Do not say anything about my attack," he wrote once after confiding in me that he had spent a miserable week. "Though like Achilles I am invulnerable except in the heel, I am not anxious for the world to know that an arrow can penetrate there."

I was staying in a lobstermen's boardinghouse at Placentia Bay during the heavy early August days when news came of the outbreak of war in Europe. War on such a scale hardly seemed believable. Back at Sandy Point I found the Commodore of two minds about the business. He admired the British and the industrious qualities of the Germans. He loved to read French but he didn't care too much about the French people or their Russian allies. He cried out with admiration at the courage the Germans showed in taking on half the world. He hoped for a stalemate and a negotiated peace. He thanked God for the broad Atlantic.

He was working on his last book, *Commercial Mortmain,* in which he tried to distinguish between monopolies which were socially desirable and those that weren't. In any case he argued that the Sherman antitrust law was promoting the monopolistic practices it was supposed to do away with. He traced the history of legislation against mortmain in England through Blackstone and Coke and showed how laws often produce results opposite to what had been intended by the legislators. He saw the labor unions growing up to counterbalance the great corporations and proposed that government should, in the public interest, impose similar restraints on both.

Ever since they had first known each other the Commodore had written a letter a day to my mother whenever they were parted. After her death he told me, in his jocose way, that I was now to be the unfortunate target of his daily epistles. Sometimes I read them and sometimes I didn't. Senior year in college I considered myself a very busy fellow. I had laid out an enormous program of reading and writing and besides I was helping edit the *Harvard Monthly*. He dutifully read every word I wrote in it. Occasionally he complained of the lack of humor in the pages of our magazine. The Harvard esthetes were deadly serious young men. I think he would have liked it better if I had made the *Lampoon* instead of the *Monthly*.

When I graduated from college in 1916 the European War was the great national preoccupation. Teddy Roosevelt's boys were whooping it up for preparedness. Franco-British propaganda was beating the drums for American intervention. The professors were losing their minds; hating the Huns became a mania.

The sound of marching feet came dimly through the walls of the sanctum upstairs in the Harvard Union where we edited the *Monthly*. Except for Cummings who was deep in Greek (he had graduated *summa cum laude* in Greek the year before) and in the invention of his special poetic typography, many of us chose to live in the eighteen-nineties. The *Yellow Book* and *The Hound of Heaven* and Machen's *Hill of Dreams* seemed more important, somehow, than the massacres round Verdun.

As for myself I was already breaking off from the esthetes. Cummings and I were both friends with Edward Nagel, who was the stepson of the sculptor Gaston Lachaise, and had been mostly brought up in Paris. Nagel introduced us to the world of "the modern." He got me to reading the Russian novelists in yellow-backed French editions. Dostoevski combined with D. H. Lawrence's *Sons and Lovers* set me to panting for "real life."

It was Nagel who infected both Cummings and me with the

excitements and the experiments of the school of Paris. In the arts everything was abolished. Everything must be reinvented from scratch. It was in Nagel's room I saw my first copies of BLAST, with Eliot's early poems. Diaghilev's Ballet and the novelties at the Boston opera and the Armory Show did the rest.

Esthetes or "realists" we were one in our scorn of our poor classmates who were getting ready to go out into the world to sell bonds. We were proclaiming to all and sundry that poetry was more important than submarines or war guilt or brave little Belgium or the big board on the New York Stock Exchange.

My first project on leaving Cambridge was to find a publisher for a thin anthology of what we considered the *Harvard Monthly*'s best. When I cruised down the Potomac with the Commodore in late June I found him harassed with money worries. There were new wrinkles round his eyes. His mustache was almost white. It had never occurred to me before that he was an old man.

As always he caught fire at any sign of initiative in the young. He was never too preoccupied to listen with interest to my plans. When we eventually found an Englishman named Lawrence Gomme who was willing, for a consideration, to risk publication of *Eight Harvard Poets* the Commodore put up part of the guarantee.

The breathless July days, the dusty roads, the cornfields curling in the drought seemed hideous to me that hot Virginia summer. I wanted to see the war, to paddle up undiscovered rivers, to climb unmapped mountains. Greedily gulping Romain Rolland's *Jean Christophe,* volume by volume, my head filled for a while with "youth against the world" enthusiasm. That and Walt Whitman's *Song of the Open Road.* I was frantic to be gone.

The Commodore observed these adolescent ardors with amused understanding. It pleased him to see I was industrious to boot. Every time he came down to Sandy Point I was working on some new article. Always against something, always the voice crying in the wilderness. He was delighted to have me write my head off, but with patient humor he kept insisting that literature wasn't any way to make a living. He had dropped the idea of putting me through law school, finding me dead set against it, but when I showed interest in architecture he kindled to my taking it up as a career. I was all for an architecture course, but first I wanted to see the world. The world was the war.

No sooner had I finished *Jean Christophe* than I turned against the book and started on an essay to demolish the *Jean Christophe* cult. I penned a diatribe on the subject to a college friend, Arthur McComb, who was still in Cambridge.

Arthur was a very cosmopolitan young man, born in Paris a British subject. His father was a roving Episcopal minister; he had lived much in Italy. He was a convinced pacifist, a selfproclaimed reactionary who already admired Metternich: I thought of Arthur as a living exemplar of the nineteenth-century civilization I saw bleeding to death in the nomanslands of France and Flanders. He had set me to reading Lowes Dickinson and the pacifist declarations of Bertrand Russell, who was proving the sincerity of his convictions by going to jail as a conscientious objector.

"I am trying," I wrote Arthur from Sandy Point, "among other cakes baking, to get out an article on 'Shelley and the Modern Age,' deploring the strange sanity of American young men, their lack of idealism, their 'redbloodness'—also a philippic against *Jean Christophe* as an institution." I kept mounting my fiery steed and riding off in all directions.

Already I had applied for a job with Herbert Hoover's Belgian Relief. "I am dying to get to Belgium to exhaust surplus energy," I wrote Arthur again in August, "by going to and fro in the earth and walking up and down in it. Really, Arthur, I am darned serious, the forces of reason must get together, must make a fuss—we want a new Enlightenment, new Byrons, new Shelleys, new Voltaires before whom the 19th Century stodginess on the one hand and the 20th Century reaction on the other shall vanish and be utterly routed, 'like souls from an enchanter fleeing.'"

In spite of my telling them how well I knew French, the Belgian Relief turned me down as too young.

In New York John R.'s friend Eliot Norton was enlisting recruits for his brother Dick's volunteer ambulance. The idea of serving with the French army appealed to me. The French were the underdog defending their homes against the invader. When the Commodore learned that I'd written Eliot Norton to offer my services, he put in a demurrer. He didn't want me to get killed quite yet. After I was twentyone it would be my own business.

We reached a compromise. He knew I was too restless to settle down to anything; and I think he vaguely surmised that, particularly after Mother's death, it was only to please him I'd stayed on in college. If I would put off the ambulance service, he would set me up for a winter in Spain. In Madrid I'd learn Spanish and take courses at the university preparatory to entering some architectural school. He found a Spanish friend, Juan Riaño, who taught Spanish at West Point, to give me a set of letters.

I guess Arthur also deplored my eagerness to get mixed up in the war—which we agreed in disapproving on ethical grounds—because there exists an expostulating letter of mine to him, written from New York, where I was getting my passport and going to the dentist and attending to various details before leaving for Spain: "War is a human phenomenon which you can't argue out of existence. You people are like Christian Scientists with the yellow fever. All your praying and all your ought nots won't change the present fact. They may change the future but only through frank and sympathetic understanding of reality which is not got by closing doors." I must have realized I was getting too didactic because I concluded the sentence with: "spoken hath the oracle and Pythia can go home to her soup of leeks and her *vin ordinaire* . . ."

"I forgot to tell you my news," I added in a burst of vainglory. "I have become a moneygrubber, a barterer of my soul, an intellectual courtesan . . . I have been paid thirty dollars for an essay! (I admit that to me at present, though I have already spent it on riotous living, it seems a titanic sum) . . . and my head is swelled as the throat of a caroling canary . . ."

The day *The New Republic* published my article, which was the first piece of writing I'd been actually paid for, I sailed for

Bordeaux on the *Espagne*. The Commodore wrote me that afternoon. From the window of his office on Broad Street he saw the steamer's red stacks as she nosed down the inner bay toward the Narrows. There had been a new submarine scare. Though people in the know insisted that steamers of the French Line were immune to torpedoing because the Austrian imperial family owned stock in it, eighty passengers had canceled their reservations at the last moment. He gathered I'd have a cabin to myself.

While he was writing me I was pacing about deliriously happy, alone in what seemed to me an enormous and luxurious stateroom. My letters of introduction and my letter of credit and my passport were laid out on the berth for inspection.

"I have letters to three poets and other amusing people," I wrote Arthur. "I shall live at the Residencia des Estudientes (however one spells it) and study architecture and the Bible like mad—also Cervantes, Calderon, Homer and Vergil's Georgics . . . then in the spring I shall go to Paris and make every endeavor to go to the front by hook or by crook . . . let's hope it'll be the Rhine . . . Plans subject to change without notice," I added, to take the curse off this boastful talk. But there I was bound for Europe with the world before me, sniffing delightedly the special Compagnie Générale Transatlantique smell of bilgewater and moldy mattresses, and the aroma of fresh bread and garlic that seeped up from the galley, and the rankness of sailors' pipes on the bay wind when I opened the porthole.

"Now I am alone," the Commodore wrote me in his own private French. He had found a little squib in a *Tribune* column provoked by my article. "It's odd to see a critique the day after the article was published . . . I miss you a great deal. Nobody to pull my leg except Louis [my halfbrother] who's a veteran at it. Nobody to scold except Louis who's a veteran again."

The sixteenth he wrote he had received a letter of mine mailed with the pilotboat. I'd evidently written in a fit of penitence at being such an ungrateful brat because he explained at length that he hadn't been annoyed at me, never in the world. If he had seemed irritable during the last few days it was that his disposition (which as I knew was generally of the sweetest) had been embittered by business matters that had gone wrong. He had sent me a message via the Cape Race wireless saying "Haha." That was what the Commodore and the crows said to each other. He hoped I'd received the Marconi. Haha between us was a whole full dictionary.

Another day he writes from the Manhattan Club that he has just finished a plea before the New York Supreme Court "which was received with visible approbation." A few days later he has heard from the French Line that the *Espagne* is well on her way across the Atlantic. He is busy writing a speech to deliver for Hughes in the Presidential campaign then in its last two weeks. (If I remember right I was violently for Wilson. "He kept us out of war.")

Next day he writes from the Washington house that his latest fit of gout has almost subsided. He and Mrs. Harris (she had stayed on as housekeeper after Mother's death to take care of the Sandy Point and the Washington houses) have lunched off oysters and an excellent lobster. It's a marvelous autumn day. He's been lazy and goodfornothing and hasn't written a word. Organized labor has endorsed Wilson. Maybe that will be enough to elect Hughes. He sees Labor lining up in a block against Capital, a situation, he thinks, full of peril.

In late October he writes that he has received my cable. He wants to know everything about the trip. He thinks he could get a short article about wartime Bordeaux into the *World* if I mailed it right away. He doesn't like the way the campaign is going. He encloses another clipping about *The New Republic* article. "It's funny," he writes, "how a phrase will flit around like a bird."

He's been reading Lord Brougham's essay on the importance of Greek literature. He's sick to death of business. He wants to settle down quietly to study Greek. Maybe I think he is foolish, but didn't Cato learn Greek when he was eighty?

The first of November he writes from the *Gaivota,* opposite Blackiston's Island. After an exquisite afternoon there is moonlight from a tiny new moon. It's seven o'clock. For his solitary supper he has an omelette, country sausage, wellcooked, and grilled potatoes. He's working on the speech.

He is going to debate with Samuel Untermeyer on the eight-hour law before the New York County Bar Association. I learned years later that oldtimers of the New York Bar liked to compare John R.'s career with Untermeyer's. Their careers in corporation law had run parallel, but Untermeyer ended up several times a millionaire and John R. was always in financial difficulties. Always kicking against the pricks—now he is against the eight-hour law and Untermeyer is for it.

John R. has explained to me often enough that he is not opposed to people working eight hours instead of ten; he is opposed to the government's setting hours and wages. Now he's expecting a rough contest; he writes that Untermeyer is a very clever gentleman experienced in making two plus two equal five.

The note that follows is from the house—the Casa Blanca the Commodore has taken to calling it—at Sandy Point. ". . . The season of the murder of the birds has arrived. Poor little quail. It's a shame to kill them. They are so aristocratic, so pretty . . . No frost. Red tomatoes everywhere in great quantity. The cannery hasn't closed down yet. The wheat is almost all sowed . . ."

He remarks jocosely on the rise in the cost of living. If the price of paper keeps going up he'll have to stop writing. If the price of food keeps going up he'll have to stop eating. Oh well he's eaten plenty all his life. He'll just give up the habit.

November 7. The great day has arrived. It is six-thirty in the evening. The polls are closed. He is awaiting the result phlegmatically. He doesn't find any real sentiments of patriotism in either side. The spirit of demagogy everywhere. It is hard for a thinking man and a man who knows the history of our Constitution to drum up much sympathy for either party. Women are voting for the first time in Illinois and it is thought they will go for Wilson on account of Wilson's peace talk.

The eighth he wrote that he went to bed thinking Hughes was elected. "Imagine my horror to wake up this morning and find the election undecided." Both sides claim victory. He hopes it won't end in a dispute like that between Tilden and Hayes. He has answered a letter about the anthology. "See what a good secretary I am." A letter has come from Eliot Norton thanking me for a copy of *The New Republic.*

He has replied to Norton that Jack has already left for Madrid. "I am his amanuensis and secretary here, occupying these responsible positions, which in classical ages would entitle me to a good social rank & a liberal salary." He replied to Norton's criticism that the article didn't go deep enough, in the words of Mercutio: that it was not deep as a well or wide as a church door but that it would do. He spoofs Norton for not having come out to hear him discuss the eight-hour law: "to show you how badly it was done the meeting enthusiastically ordered my remarks to be printed." Facetiously he signs the letter Dos Passos Sr.

Meanwhile Dos Passos Jr. is established at the Pension Boston right off the Puerta del Sol in Madrid. He finds everything delightful, Spanish civility, the watchmen with lanterns in great cloaks who open the street door at night, the raucous sounds and harsh smells of the city.

The letters Juan Riaño furnished my father couldn't have been better chosen. They were to journalists and literary people of what was then known as the generation of 1898. In spite of my immense bashfulness I found myself having tea with Juan Ramón Jiménez, who already looked as if he had just been painted by El Greco, and being introduced to the formidable spadebearded Valle Inclán at three in the morning in a drafty café.

A husky lawstudent named Carlos Posada took me mountain-climbing in the Sierra de Guadarrama. The Sierra delighted me more than any set of mountains I'd ever seen. A blackbearded little man named José Giner, a nephew of Giner de los Rios, the great educator who was the apostle of the Spanish liberals, turned out to know every sacristan and every forgotten masterpiece in the villages tucked away in the rolling lands of Castile. He was a great walker and so was I. We became firm friends and before long were calling each other "tu."

Right away I started in a magnificent course on the Spanish language under Tomás Navarro Tomás at the Centro de Estúdios Históricos. I found a drawing instructor who bored me half to death by setting me to copy a Florentine bust. I exchanged lessons in Spanish and English with a budding sociologist who was translating a book by John Dewey. How we struggled over that text, three times a week for an hour in the afternoon. I couldn't understand John Dewey in English, much less find Spanish for his interminably tangled phrases.

Pepe Giner was my cicerone. Sometimes in the afternoon we would walk out past the lovely little round Goya church that Jefferson's phrase "spherical architecture" fitted so well, through the rolling country of liveoaks that was the background of Velasquez's portraits, to the old royal hunting lodge of El Pardo. Pepe's father, a retired physician, lived there as custodian. Like Juan Ramón Jiménez he looked as if he had been painted by Greco. Pepe's mother, always in black, was one of the devout ladies in a painting of nuns by Zurbarán. We would eat a sort of high tea with them and walk back through the gloaming. The Madrid we saw rising in silhouette against the evening sky was still the city Goya painted.

Sundays we got up early to catch a six-thirty morning train to the Sierra. I had become one of a close knit group of mountain climbers. Pepe, who was unpretentiously devout, would have been up an hour before to go to Mass.

"My chief joy," I wrote Arthur, "is the Sierra Guadarrama; the long range of brown mountains to the North and West. Behind them the sun sets with numbing glory. I've never seen such sunsets; they stir up your soul the way a cook stirs a pot of broth but with what a golden spoon. Every Sunday, in company of a charming Spanish gentleman and All Madrid, dressed in Alpine costume, knapsacks and the rest, I betake myself to them and there climb. The most wonderful views are everywhere. From the summit you can see the two plains of Old and New Castile, the north a ruddy yellow, the other straw yellow to the south until it is lost in the mists at the foot of the mountains behind Toledo. The snow on the peaks is blown into the most wonderful shapes, feathers, knives, and when the sky is a crushing blue overhead and the rocks sparkle in the sun with their edgings of snow and you can see from Segovia to Toledo . . . No wonder the muse had fled. Embarras de richesses."

Already I was reading Pío Baroja's revival of the picaresque. *Mala Hierba, La Busca, Aurora Roja.* Impressions poured in so fast that no one day was long enough to contain them. Spanish was a continual challenge. I was suffering all the comical mystifications of a new language. Everything amused me. As I learned a little of the language, tabletalk at the Pension Boston, where I stayed on while waiting for a vacancy in the Residencia de Estudiantes, became more and more entertaining. It was a polyglot assembly. "While Don Lorenzo the proprietor-waiter produces course after course of delicious Spanish foods, a perfect bevy of conversations jostle each other around the table. The Lady Authoress and the Danish Gentleman speak German. I speak bad Spanish to the Danish Gentleman who answers in kind, English to the Americans, French to the Portuguese ladies who in turn speak Portuguese among themselves, French to me, Spanish to the Spaniards, who toss a variety of dialects back and forth." I couldn't get over the food. The sharp wintry air gave me a perpetual appetite. I wrote home that the meals went on and on; Spaniards spent all their time eating, except the ones who were starving to death.

What I read and what I saw was all part of the same scene. Toledo was still the Toledo of Cervantes' *Novelas Ejemplares.* Street scenes on the Puerta del Sol were written by Lope de Vega.

This was a time of life when a man makes friends. On the third class coach coming back from Toledo one day I found myself talking with a student from the university who wanted to improve his English. We got along so well that we remained fast friends until his death. Pepe Robles had a sharper tongue than my educationist and liberal acquaintances. He laughed at everything. His talk was more like Pío Baroja's tart writing.

I boasted to Arthur of having one friend he would approve of at the Pension Boston. "Don José Castillejo, a man after your inmost heart . . . He is an oldfashioned nineteenth-century liberal, the leader of part of the Educational Party in Spain, a very brilliant man and the enemy of all forms of darkness, also a Pacifist of Lowes Dickinson brand . . . He also has," I added teasingly, "that subtle humanitarian snobbery of all Lovers of Mankind (I mean one has to hate a little to be human) . . ."

Pepe Robles and I made other trips together. His cynical tales were a tonic after the dogoodism of the liberals. At that time of his life he was an *aficionado* of bullfights and drew pictures of *toreros*. Among my educationist acquaintances bullfights were taboo.

In early December my days were made much more amusing by the unexpected appearance of Lowell Downes and Roland Jackson. Downes had been my good friend Robert Hillyer's best friend at college. I'd known him as a cheerful and congenial drinker. Roly was a classmate, the son of a Colorado judge, who wanted to compose music instead of selling bonds.

Part of Roly's revolt against his father and the business world was that he insisted on wearing sneakers everywhere. Roly's grubby sneakers were embarrassing, because in Spain in those days no matter how ragged a man was, he managed to wear good shoes and a good hat. When we went to cafés, the waiters eyed Roly's sneakers with undisguised disgust. At concerts they were viewed with horror by the welldressed *madrileñas*.

One of the pleasures of Roly's company and Downes' was that they liked to drink. None of my Spanish friends would drink more than one glass of wine and many of them drank only water. The greatest night we had was at a German beerhall called El Oro del Rhin. We ate and drank a great deal for supper and afterward I took them to see Pastora Império. I had seen her before. I thought her the greatest dancer ever. We were all carried away. Feverish with *lo flamenco* we went back to El Oro del Rhin.

In those days I was carrying a volume of Jorge Manrique's poems around in my pocket. I started reading Manrique's poem on his father's death. The snapping of Pastora's fingers was inevitable as death, we shouted over steins of beer. That poem and Pastora, I was proclaiming, were the two great experiences of my life.

Suddenly we couldn't stand the treacly German music any more. Roly went home to bed, but, as it was a brilliant cold moonlight night, Downes and I decided it would be amusing to walk to Toledo. We set off down the arcaded Calle de Toledo and out the gate and along the white road. The road was merry with the jingling of huge twowheeled carts, each drawn by three or four or sometimes five hulking mules. Always in the lead was a little donkey trotting along with mincing steps. We talked with the *arrieros*. They gave us drinks out of their leather winebottles. It wasn't today, we kept telling each other. This was el Quijote's and Sancho Panza's Spain.

I made a rapt entry in my notebook, already crammed with *olés* to Pastora: "A most wonderful night with dim stars and the long sweeping hillsides of Castile brownish under the cold moon. Cocks crew and dogs barked in the distance and you seemed to hear the rustling of the stars' skirts as they did their ceremonial dance about the heavens. In the lower places there was a mist and everything was blurred brownsilver. At last the moon set like a wrinkled and rotten orange just as the first steely glow started in the east."

We walked on and on through lowlying mists that looked like lakes in the hollows until the sun warmed our cheeks.

Of course we never did get to Toledo. At Torrejón we went into the railroad station to sit down for a rest. Our feet were sore and we were monstrously sleepy. Should we keep on? The last *arriero* we had talked to told us it was twentyseven leagues, but strongly advised us to keep walking. Think of all the money we'd save by not taking the train . . .

Then I remembered I had an engagement for dinner in Madrid. At the Embassy of all places. My father had furnished me with a letter to the American ambassador and had insisted I present it. One of the secretaries had invited me, much against my will, to dinner. Tonight was the fatal night. We rode the train back to Madrid, but for all of that the walk left an imperishable glow.

On November 14 John R. acknowledges the arrival of two postal cards. I'm bubbling over with the paintings of the Prado. "They are pretty. Velasquez. What a name! What pictures, and now I'm waiting for your letters. What letters! 'Letters from Madrid' by Monsieur Singe. De luxe edition, price five dollars. Handsome that. Another book 'Reflections of a Young Man in Madrid' by the same author. Another book: 'An Architect's Impressions of the Buildings of Madrid' by a student. That will be enough for the first three months. Otherwise you'll produce more books than Voltaire . . . I've finished my speech on the eight hour law and it has gone to the printers'. Shall I send you a copy? No. It is useless for you to waste your time reading political discussions."

He's sending a great mass of letters, and one printed in *The New Republic* about the article which he thinks will please me.

Next day he's on the train to Washington on the way to the farm. He's reading Cicero and Demosthenes to compare their mentalities. Cicero's always the lawyer, Demosthenes more the statesman. "It's a shame I can't read the world's greatest orator in the original. I find very little satisfaction in the condition of our country. The election of Wilson raises grave questions. We have abandoned the Constitution and are approaching paternalism where all private and domestic business is regulated by the government . . . But we can live here on the farm and form our own little government, our own little despotism."

Next day he writes again of the beauty of the weather. The Casa Blanca is closed up till next summer. "I hated to do it because the last few days here have been marvelous. I've slept well, eaten well, and walked well." He's taking eighteen quail back to New York with him. Jim Franklin has discovered some enormous oysters in Parker's Creek, the kind of oysters Thackeray wrote about; when you swallowed one it was like swallowing a baby. "Large and delicious. I wish you were here to eat them with us. Where are you? Here it is nearly half past six and it is half past eleven where you are. No answer. . . ."

December 4: "I am very tired this evening and I feel a great detestation of the world as it appears in New York. I'm tired of this kind of life and I wish from the bottom of my heart I was at the farm, talking to nature, the cows, the trees, the water and all the things that speak without speaking. Indeed I have passed a tough day but the day is finished and I am alone in my library and I'll soon forget all the frustrations of the day."

In the next letter he still feels a little low, but he'll have a good sleep tonight and be fine in the morning. He feels sad about the fall of Roumania. Another surprise: the bombardment of Funchal. "As you know I have many friends and relatives there and I am very anxious to learn the details."

December 14 he writes from New York. He is cabling a hundred dollars as a Christmas present. "Everybody's talking peace . . . the world is sick and tired of war but it would be a great mistake to settle for a peace that would last only a few months or years to be followed by a worse war . . . It's difficult to make a permanent peace among nations with arms in their hands. And how to restore the small states?"

December 20 he writes that a manuscript has arrived consigned to *The New Republic.* He'll get it copied. "This evening we are busy reading Lloyd George's reply to the German peace proposition. It is a vigorous reply and I think it represents the feelings of our country too. The Germans will now have to show their hand . . . I don't expect peace very soon. In my opinion the Germans will have to be worn out first . . . It is still cold and the cold is expected to last a long while. Since weather, like women, is changeable maybe we'll have some Indian summer again."

December 21. "Mr. Lansing, the Secretary of State, made a very bellicose proclamation today which caused great excitement on the Stock Exchange, producing a semi-panic, almost a Krack, but this evening Mr. Lansing corrected his statement in a more conservative direction. I can't imagine by what rule of international diplomacy Mr. Wilson makes this declaration to the belligerents because the time is not ripe for anything like that . . . The evening papers are full of it."

"My dear Jack," he wrote December 23, "I am your amanuensis, Secretary and alter ego for I write all the replies to your letters and take care to keep you 'en regle' in these things. In other words we have an association; John R. Dos Passos Jr. and Father . . . tonight I'm alone with my books. I'm not reading aloud because I have no audience to listen. Pickwick is dead. Mrs. Harris is in Philadelphia with her mother. The little house in Washington is closed. The Casa Blanca is not open. No fox hunt."

Those foxhunts! Everybody at Sandy Point would have been busy preparing food and drink for days. Beer and frankfurters would have come down on the boat. Salt herring would have been brought in tubs from Mundy Point . . . Christmas day would dawn to the yelping of hounds and the tootle of the little brass horn. A fox had been started. After gulping big breakfasts we would all set off. I'd be riding Rattler, a little sorrel gelding that was hitched to the springwagon weekdays. Rattler had a white streak down his nose that we claimed was a sure sign of Arabian blood. He was a pleasant little horse with an easy canter but he stumbled. He would fall and spill me over his head at embarrassing moments, such as when I was riding gallantly up to greet that goodlooking girl from the other side of Hague. Otherwise neither one of us ever was hurt in Rattler's falls. There weren't too many riding horses in the Northern Neck in those days. Nobody had ever heard of a pink coat. The bulk of the crowd followed the hunt in buggies or little gigs or sulkies. There was many a springwagon and even an occasional oxcart. There was no jumping because the fences were all barbed wire, but such hooting and yodling to the music of the hounds as you never heard, and men and boys scrambling afoot through hedgerows and wet ditches and bramblepatches in the deep pine woods.

The Commodore always took the side of the fox. Wearing woolen stockings and tweed breeches with his felt hat at an angle and brandishing his cherry cane he would walk off briskly in the direction of the music of the hounds. Once he met the fox back of Lynch's Point while the silly hounds were yelping and whining through the shucks of corn at Hominy Hall. The Commodore claimed with a sparkle in his eye to have had a long philosophical discussion with the fox that day.

". . . and worst of all you are on the other side of the Atlantic," he wrote. "It is a sad situation but I am not sad. On the contrary I am gay."

"The year 1916 is almost finished," he wrote on Christmas Eve. "I'm glad enough to see it disappear. I've had poor luck through all the 365 days. Let us hope that 1917 will be better. But in any case I shall be satisfied because, except for gout now and then, my health is perfect. I find myself very solitary. Nobody to read Gabriel Grubb to."

Christmas: "Noël sans Master Jack. Noël sans arbre de Noël

. . . I ate my turkey alone—Louis was sick—and tonight I shall remain alone with my books—par excellence, les compagnons bien intéressants."

Next day he writes: "Christmas is over laus Deo. There is no Christmas sentiment left here. All thoughts are on the gifts. It's disgusting. If you don't give, you are a skinflint, if you don't give a large sum you are worse. Christmas is the birthday of the founder of our Christianity as you well know, but out of our sixty million inhabitants perhaps a hundred thousand remember the meaning of the day. I detest the season. It is worse here in New York than in any other city."

On the twenty-seventh Dedi writes he is off to Washington. Although his library is in New York he feels more at home in the Washington house. He is working on a little critique of Monsieur Wilson's last letter to the belligerents. It is a weak letter and it's a shame to have him intervene just when the Allies were on the point of replying to the communication of the Germans and the Central Powers. "But your friend the President is not guided by the rules of international law. He does what he likes. As in the case of Mexico everything he does aggravates the war instead of working against it. We'll see in six months."

January 5 he is back at 56th Street in pretty good health except that his feet are swollen and hurt when he walks. He's been at the office all day and naturally he feels better when he is at work. Everything looks quiet around the world but he's expecting military and naval operations on a grand scale very soon. Meanwhile peace talks go on.

January 7: "I've passed a stupid day without doing anything except read the newspapers. I expected to get through a good stint of work but little uncontrollable things kept coming up . . . If I'd laid out a programme this morning I would have accomplished something . . . How many hours do we waste each week? But 'not heaven itself o'er the past has power.'" The ninth he has called in a doctor to go into the causes of his gout. "Didn't seem too intelligent. He's examined the heart, stomach and blood pressure and found it satisfactory. I tried to stir his ambition and perhaps he'll know more at the next session."

He is at work on a speech he is to make in February. He wants to go down to the farm but this morning there's a blizzard from out of the northwest. "The world is going gradually to the devil, as you know, being his advocate."

On Saturday January 13 he wrote, "Tomorrow will be your twentyfirst birthday. You will be able to wear the *toga virilis*. You are a man . . . Now you have to wait for fifty. It will come soon because it is indeed true that *tempus fugit* . . . I sent you a cable this afternoon. I imagine you'll receive it Sunday. 'Wear your birthday coat Sunday.' I wrote *toga virilis* but I thought the Commercial Cable company wouldn't accept it, fearing the censor."

The fourteenth he wrote: "The great day has come. My Jack is his own master. He is free. He is free from enslavement to his father. He's free to climb a tree and to do anything, even to pay his own bills. I salute you. When will you come home? Not before you've completed your Spanish . . . Another question entangled with this: When will the war be over? I think not for another year . . . Certainly not before February 1918. The Allies and their enemies are beginning the most enormous preparations . . . unless they meet an unexpected event: lack of money perhaps, or an epidemic, or a great victory that makes further struggle useless, the war will go on. I don't expect any great movements either in the east or the west before spring. In your next letter give me a detailed account of your studies and of the progress you have made in each . . ."

January 17 he's received a bulky manuscript but no instructions as to what to do with it. He hates to say it but my letters are horribly badly written, half in pencil and half in pen, parts in English and parts in French. Almost impossible to read. I must write my letters with more care. He's anxious for me to start the architecture course. At least I'm making progress in drawing. That's the first step. He's not worried about the Spanish. "You are a Latin and your ears will quickly get accustomed to the Spanish sounds." Though it is only 8:15 he feels very sleepy. He's going to read a story by Dumas. Good Night.

"Where are you today?" he wrote on the eighteenth. "How are you? Unfortunately there is no way of getting an answer to these questions before seven or eight weeks. I got home a little tired this evening and I'm not going to do anything except read *Les Mys-*

tères de Paris, a letter or two of Voltaire's and Saint Amand's *Marie Antoinette aux Tuileries.*" He wants to know what I'm reading in Spanish.

He comments on the excellent style of Balfour's communication to Wilson. "But suppose the Allies do destroy German militarism, what next? Another power or syndicate of nations stronger than the Germans will be born from the ashes of Prussia!"

January 19 he writes that he has not been able to get much accomplished during the past week. "It seems impossible to concentrate my ideas, in spite of the fact that I have a great deal to do. Next week I'm hoping to get some proper work done."

Eight days later he was taken ill. He was found unconscious one morning on the bathroom floor. Pneumonia, the doctors said. He died January 27, 1917.

While I read the cable at the cable office all I could think of was the Commodore's voice calling back at the crows on the Sandy Point beach: "Ha haha!"

CHAPTER 2

Twentyfour Hours on and Twentyfour Hours off

The first time I really set out to try to write a novel was in collaboration with Robert Hillyer. Robert in those days was a cherubic fellow with curly hair and dark blue eyes that had a way of popping out from his face when he got excited. At Harvard he had been one of what we called the *cercle littéraire*, mad for Elizabethan lyrics, a violent opponent of free verse. Portraits of the

Virgin Queen hung on his walls. He toasted the great Elizabeth in season and out.

By what seemed to us the devil's own good luck, Robert and Frederik van den Arend and I found ourselves assigned to the same Section 60 when we went to France with the Norton-Harjes Volunteer Ambulance. Robert and I had both liked Van in college. He was one of a cozy group who lived in the same rooming house and called themselves the Family. Though they weren't rearing tearing esthetes we found them congenial in many ways. Van was contrary, irascible and comical when he wanted to be as any blue-eyed Dutchman you ever saw. Immediately the three of us became Athos, Porthos and d'Artagnan, known to ourselves—from our common pursuit of victuals above and beyond the military rations—as the three omeletteers.

When we moved up to the front our duty was twentyfour hours on and twentyfour hours off. At a place called Récicourt on the Voie Sacrée, as journalists called the battered road that supplied Verdun, we took refuge in our hours off duty in the abandoned garden of what had once been a country villa. The house had suffered a direct hit and had completely vanished. Whatever furnishings might have survived had long since been carried off, but by some miracle the place had not been trampled by the troops. The gravel paths were neat as if some gardener had recently swept them with a birchtwig broom. White roses and tall phlox bloomed in the weedy beds. Beautiful brown and white snails crawled among the twining honeysuckle. Under the fragrance of honeysuckle and roses there was just a hint of poison gas from the last barrage. Best of all the backhouse was intact.

It was a beautiful old backhouse, pale pink stucco with a tile roof overgrown with vines. Inside the earth closet with scrubbed deal seats was still clean. There were even a few squares of old newspaper neatly stowed in a box.

We had found the latrines the most hideous feature of the wartime scene, slippery planks over stinking pits. The Boche seemed to have an evil intuition about them: as soon as you squatted with your pants down, he would start to shell.

There was no need to swear each other to secrecy when we discovered the beautiful backhouse. To sit there, looking out, quietly and reflectively, into the weedy garden was a halcyon contrast with the crowded choking scramble of our lives on duty. Not rack nor thumbscrew could have torn its location from us.

Our garden had another charm. When shells came a little too close we could take shelter in the nice little dry concrete fountain in the middle. This was not a region under heavy shellfire, like the crossroads and concentration points, but the Boche, in his methodical way, scattered a few salvoes of artillery over the back country from time to time, just to keep the poilus on their toes.

At that point Robert and Van and I had reason to be pleased with ourselves and with each other. We had been under fire enough to discover that we weren't any more scared than the next man. We were still tingling with that great moment of a man's life when he finds that he can take fright and danger and somehow shrug it off. We hadn't been in danger enough to have it wear us down.

We had even found that by putting our minds to the problem we could keep the damn little model T motors of our Ford ambulances in a fair state of repair. In a letter to Arthur McComb, who was back in Cambridge living in the same frame rooming house Van had recently emerged from, I described with some gusto Bobby, the lyric poet, "on his back in the mud under his car, garbed in blue overalls, a gob of grease on his nose, and a black and grimy bolt uplifted in his hand . . . In the evenings we sit in the arbors and drink a mixture of strong white wine and grenadine. Most delicious!"

This habit, noisome in retrospect, earned us the nickname among our sectionmates of the "the grenadine guards." At the moment I wrote this letter to Arthur we were being organized into a section at Châlons-sur-Marne. There were the usual delays. When we weren't swimming in the Marne wearing funny striped French trunks, I whiled away the time writing letters and confiding in my journal: "I'm sitting in the old beergarden of the erstwhile inn we're using as a barracks—in an arbor. How many pleasant drinks have been drunk here—how many wedding parties flushed with champagne have laughed and giggled and blushed and felt the world soft and warm with the phallic glow." The French cooks were getting dinner at the popote behind me. I was delighted with their enthusiasm for their work. I noted that they had "the inimitable air of Savarins cooking for Henri Quatre."

I was trying to divide all humanity into the useful people like cooks and farmhands and woodworkers and architects and engineers, who were always building up mankind, and the destructive people like politicians and bankers and college presidents and national propagandists, who spread illusions and caused wars and destroyed civilization as fast as the producers built it up. Black was black and white was white. Producers were good, exploiters were evil. Myself and my friends I classed with the producers: "The fellows in the section are frightfully decent—all young men are frightfully decent. If we only governed the world instead of the swagbellied old fogies that do . . . Down with the middle-aged!"

I was absorbed in the problem of how to write clearly. "All my past attempts are on the wrong track. I've closed the book on them." For years I'd been reading Flaubert: letters, short stories, novels. I caught his obsession for the *mot juste.*

On the *Espagne* going home from Bordeaux the past February I read Barbusse's *Le Feu.* The book moved me to frenzy, but already I'd seen enough of wartime France to discover other sides to the story. War was the theme of the time. I was in a passion to put down everything, immediately it happened, exactly as I saw it.

The chance of death sharpened the senses. The sweetness of the white roses, the shape and striping of a snail shell, the taste of an omelet, the most casual sight or sound appeared desperately intense against the background of the great massacres.

"I've not been so happy for months," I wrote Arthur, "there's a rollickingness about it all that suits me. Glorious Dumas rises in a chant of wine and women and death amid the dull stupidity—Poor humans—how damned adaptable we are—you can't down us . . . Hell, by God, is a stimulus."

In this frame of mind Robert and I got together some copybooks from a store in one of the villages that still had school supplies and began to pen alternate chapters of a novel motivated of course by the divine revolt of youth misunderstood. We had both been avid readers of Compton Mackenzie's *Sinister Street* in Cambridge. In spite of all I could do Jean Christophe would not down. Barbusse was rampaging in the background. Under these auspices we made up a sensitive small boy and unrolled his adventures in a world of unfeeling grownups. We added new characters from day to day. The G.N. as we called it kept us from the feeling of dryrot on the brain that's one of the dreariest features of war for the thoughtful young.

Nobody but Van knew of our secret occupation. We would have been razzed to hell and back if any of our sectionmates, who spent their days off playing poker and singing "God help Kaiser Bill," had caught on to what we were up to.

Everything had seemed to me pretty horrible during the months since I left Madrid after the cables came reporting first my father's illness and then his death. It was a nightmare to be back in New York, though my relatives were kind and I had some friends there.

Wright McCormick, who had been a crony in college, had a job as a reporter on I've forgotten which paper. He was going around with a terribly nice girl named Elsie Rizer who was trying to make a name on the stage. I began to appreciate my father's claim that women were always more worthwhile than men. We trooped around with her to studios and theatrical boardinghouses visiting weird acquaintances. One night we were in an apartment where an odd gent was reading Omar Khayyám in a pipeorgan voice while a stout lady danced the dance of the seven veils. In response to a call from a neighbor the police raided the place, though the performance was innocent enough, and we would have all been packed into the paddywagon if somebody hadn't remembered that the District Attorney was a friend and called him on the phone.

This little adventure helped feed our feeling of being outcasts from respectable society. As pacifists we had seceded. We were convinced that America's entrance into the war would only prolong the futile massacre. American troops would be used to quell the social revolution which was about to overturn the corrupt old regimes that had brought on the ruin of civilization. Wright and I spent our spare time going to radical meetings.

Elsie wouldn't go. She said she was a patriotic American. Anyway she insisted that theater and politics didn't mix.

We protested night and day. We were carried away by a brilliant speech of Max Eastman's at a mass meeting in Stanford White's Madison Square Garden; we approved the shrill denunciations of Emma Goldman. We read each issue of *The Masses* damp from the press. My admiration for Woodrow Wilson had turned to virulent hatred. Conscription seemed a personal betrayal. The new freedom had become the new servitude. We signed petitions. We protested the declaration of war. We protested conscription. Bob LaFollette, Gene Debs, Max Eastman were our heroes.

The only part of New York where we felt at home was the Jewish East Side. It was the East Side that first felt the gale of revolution that had set in from St. Petersburg. For the Russian Jews the dreams of fifty years of exile were about to come true. Throughout Europe the rising masses would refuse to be led to the slaughter. In Russia revolution had put an end to war. It was the red dawn of an era of peace, freedom and justice.

The Russians were socialists. It was socialists who had taken action to stop the butchery. Suddenly I believed I was a socialist. Even then I think I marveled a little at the suddenness with which passionate convictions develop in the youthful mind. It was a contagion. In the spring of 1917 some people caught socialism the way others caught the flu.

In an effort to shake up Arthur McComb, whom I considered an imperturbable reactionary, I wrote him that I felt like Saul on the road to Damascus.

All the while I was waiting with desperate impatience for my turn to come to join the ambulance service. While the weeks dragged by I couldn't put my mind on anything, not even on the lessons in driving and repairing cars I was taking at an automobile school on 12th Avenue. The executors of my father's estate tried to interest me in various propositions. But what use was an income to a man who expected to get killed within the year? Even if I did survive, the Revolution would sweep away stocks and bonds, landed interests, property rights. I signed a contract of sale on my mother's house in Washington, which had come to me direct, to raise some needed cash, and let it go at that. "Naked I came into the world" was to be my motto.

From the S. S. *Chicago* I sent Arthur a cartoon by the pilotboat, captioned "A la lanterne," of warmongers, among them Elihu Root and Theodore Roosevelt, hanging from the arclights on Fifth Avenue, while two stickmen, labeled Harvard intellectuals, danced the carmagnole in the foreground.

Being aboard ship, headed for action at last, after all those frustrating years in what then seemed to me the airless hothouse of college life, changed my mood completely. Everything was fun.

A week later I was writing that I had never enjoyed a passage so much. "Until yesterday I neither thought a think nor cracked a book." I reported the rowdy singing in the bar. I found the ship's company a three ring circus. "There are five Socialists on the boat. Imagine, among what the steward tells me are *jeunes gens des meilleures familles américaines; et les allemands aimeraient bien les torpiller* . . . five Socialists and there may be more! Glory Hallelujah!"

One "socialist" who greatly added to the vivacity of the scene on the *Chicago* was John Howard Lawson, an extraordinarily diverting fellow, recently out of Williams, with bright brown eyes, untidy hair and a great beak of a nose that made you think of Cyrano de Bergerac. There was a lot of the Gascon in him at that. He was a voluble and comical talker. He had drastic ideas on every subject under the sun. He was never away from you for ten minutes that he didn't come back with some tale of abracadabrating adventures that had happened in the meanwhile.

He was already writing plays. I'd had a certain introduction to the theater through my friend Ed Massey, who took a Baker course at Harvard and who was already involved in directing. It wasn't long before Jack and I were telling each other how, when we got home from the wars, we would turn the New York theater inside out.

My recollections of that crossing are all set to music, beginning with arriving at Hoboken to find a band playing and people dancing to a Hawaiian hula among the packingcases on the pier. The minute we sat down in the bar we started to sing.

The *Chicago* was stuffed with ambulance men and a few army officers, including Theodore Jr. and Archie Roosevelt on advance missions for the A.E.F. From out of my newborn socialism I regarded them with a baleful eye. Imperialists, militarists. Merchants of death.

The trip was one long party. Our favorite song was:

Oh we're bound for the Hamburg Show
To see the elephant and the wild kangaroo
And we'll all stick together
In fair or foul weather
For we're going to see the damn show through.

We gobbled up the good old French line cuisine. We sang every song anybody knew. We drank the bar dry, and arrived in due time, quite untorpedoed but somewhat overhung, at the mouth of the Gironde.

There we had a chill reminder that war was a serious business: floating debris, the spars of a recently sunk steamer standing up out of the water and redfunneled launches towing boatloads of survivors into the estuary.

While we walked with our duffle through Bordeaux from the dock to the station people cheered us. Pretty women clapped. A Frenchman came running up and put his own hat on the head of a boy who had none. My, we puffed out our chests.

The slow trainride to Paris was a delight. Under the wan European sky the fields of ripening grain smoldered with poppies. Avenues of poplars led to hunched villages. Every village with its steeple and mossy tiles was a picture out of a book of old fairy tales. The hills and woodlots were green green green. Since I spoke more fluent French than anyone else in the crowd I was kept busy buying wine and crusty rolls in the station *buvettes*.

The French people seemed wonderful in those days. The pressure of disaster had brought out the best in them. "Les américains" were highly thought of since President Wilson's declaration of war. From each little errand I came back delighted with the civility I'd met and with the knowing remarks of the elderly men and women who were carrying on all the trades since every young man and even the middleaged were in uniform.

"En voiture, messieurs mesdames." I found enchantment in the twang of the brakeman's little horn.

If I remember right we got into Paris late at the small station on the Quai D'Orsay. We distributed ourselves and our baggage into open cabs. The streets were dark. Everything was very quiet. There was a vague hint of moonlight overhead. Buildings I'd known as a child loomed out of the faint blue lights at streetcorners. The horses' hooves went cloppety clop on the woodblock pavements. Entering the assigned hotel through felt curtains to keep in the light was walking into a mystery melodrama. I was in seventh heaven.

Next morning at the Norton-Harjes headquarters on the rue François Premier who should I run into but Robert Hillyer and Van. They reported that Dudley Poore, another friend from the *cercle littéraire,* who had contributed what we considered the best verse to *Eight Harvard Poets,* had arrived with the Field Service and that Cummings was somewhere in France. We began planning a trip south down the Rhone we would take on our first leave.

The immediate thing we had to do was get ourselves uniforms. Young men out of uniform were liable to arrest on sight and to be put through embarrassing interrogatories. Equipped with ambulance service passes that proved we were not *embusqués* we roamed around Paris while our uniforms were being fitted.

We followed the quais along the Seine to Notre Dame. We peeked through the sandbags into the Sainte Chapelle. We came back through the courtyards of the Louvre and the flowerbeds of the Tuileries. In spite of the war the Punch and Judy shows were still going on and the thin wafflelike *galettes* I remembered from when I was a child were still on sale in the kiosks.

The old gray buildings moved us like music. I caught my first glimpse of the slender dome that soared above the arches linking the pedimented wings of the Institut de France, which for years was to be my favorite building in the world.

When we were so tired we couldn't put one foot before the other we engaged a victoria by the hour and drove and drove. Robert made a poem about "My petite voiture de Paris." Dusk found us on the boulevards. We were astonished by the crowds of prostitutes. Many were young and some were pretty. In the cafés there was an atmosphere of desperate wassail. "For tomorrow we die." We ran into Englishmen and Canadians who declared they were raising the last hell in their lives. I wrote Arthur that men seemed to take a strange sinister joy in the certainty of death.

Within a week I found myself separated from my friends in a bunch of American college boys I didn't know at a Norton-Harjes training camp in the erstwhile hunting preserve of a Marquis de Sandricourt, whoever he was. Since there were no cars to work on they kept us busy drilling. Mostly we learned to cuss. "One swears and filthifies largely and joyfully," I wrote. "Military discipline plus greasy soup remove all joy of life—one waits with faint hope for the moment of release."

Release came soon. I was given travel orders to Châlons-sur-Marne. There I was immediately impressed by the lean tall blond man in an impeccably tailored uniform who was the Chef de Section. From the first moment it was obvious that Fred Singer had the leadership knack. It was delightful to find that Bobby and Van were of the party.

My partner on the Ford ambulance, Jim Parshall, was not only a good fellow but a firstrate driver. This was damn fortunate because at that time I was one of the world's worst. I had a propensity for getting mired in shellholes. He claimed he felt better at the wheel so I let him drive during the tough sessions toward the front and only took over on the quiet roads into the base hospitals. I tried to make it up to him by keeping him supplied with wine and victuals from the French. Section 60 proved a congenial outfit. We were all proud of being part of it.

"Imagine me now in uniform with my hair clipped entirely and a flea bite on my cheek," I wrote Arthur, "seated in the sodden rain-lisping garden of an erstwhile inn . . . Life here consists in waiting until *They* send orders. *They* are strange invisible creatures, gods or demons, that move behind the scenes—inventing futilities and 'flapping from out their condor wings Invisible woe.' "

Soon "They" moved us into the rear of the Verdun sector. Latrine rumors accumulated of a French offensive about to be launched. August 10 I wrote Arthur from a pinewood above a ruined village on a hill overlooking what I described for fear of the censor as "a very famous road." Already we could hear "the deep measured snoring of the big guns at the front." I spoke of "building myself a snail shell of hysterical laughter against the hideousness of war. We have been having a wonderful time. So far we have done nothing more strenuous than take our cars from place to place holding them at the disposition of various army corps who don't want either them or us—and invariably send us traveling again en convoy (twenty cars follow each other like elephants marching into Barnum and Bailey's) down pleasant French roads to spend nights in pleasant villages."

"France has manifold advantages over America, even in these distressful times," I added. "You hear nobody jabber about the glory of war; everybody is quite frank about things. Of Nagel in France—remember what I told you—there are increasing indications . . ."

I was using poor Nagel's name as a codeword for revolution. Indeed there were indications. Mutinies had swept through the French forces that spring. Whenever we got drunk with the poilus in some café behind the lines I would pick up stories of petitions and complaints; of gendarmes, hated because they were used to hunt down deserters, strung up on meat hooks in some abattoir; of regiments shooting their officers and marching on Paris. The summer of 1917 was a ticklish time for the rulers of France.

I was privately developing the theory that the British, more than either the French or the Germans, were keeping the war going. The secret aim of American intervention was to quench the European revolution.

I dreamed of finding some way of countering war propaganda with propaganda for peace. "Bobs and Van and I," I wrote Arthur, "talk most excitedly of going home to Junius letters and that sort of thing—seriously and *à outrance*. Would you chuck reason to the winds and join?"

The latrine rumors were confirmed. The Verdun offensive was on. The same letter told of the three of us sitting in a tiny garden back of a buttressed wall that overlooked the through street in a village and seeing the attacking corps go through. This was the *Voie Sacrée.*

We had struck up an acquaintance with the local schoolmaster on a little stream to which Robert and I had retired in a moment of leisure to sail paper boats. I called mine *le bateau ivre:* I was saturated with Rimbaud that week and never went anywhere without a volume of his verse in my pocket. The schoolmaster was quietly fishing for trout. He showed us how to find helgramites under the stones. The incongruity of finding a man troutfishing under shellfire carried us away. We decided he was a natural philosopher, a Jean-Jacques Rousseau *de nos jours*. When he invited us to drink *un verre de vin blanc* with him we eagerly accepted.

The same evening, with our faces freshwashed and our hair plastered down, Van and Robert and I knocked on his door. He ushered us into his small terraced garden that hung over the street. His wife was charming, a pale woman with huge shining black eyes. She had in her arms a winsome little cat, with eyes, oddly enough, of a luminous brown. We sat at a round marble table perched above the street among the roses and balsams.

We had hardly taken our first sip of wine before the truck convoys began rumbling through. Our faces were on a level with the faces of the men joggling through the narrow street. They were piled thick in the gray jolting trucks. Some were drunk and shouting and waving their canteens. Others stood silent and sullen. Many of them shook their fists at the gendarmes in the sentry box at the corner. "*Mort aux vaches,*" they kept yelling. All looked as ghastly as dead men in their shroud of white dust. The convoy seemed endless. Gears grinding, the trucks roared past. They churned up the dust in the narrow street. The dust coated our table and our hair and the flowers in the little garden. We sat there trying to make polite French conversation while anguish clutched at our throats.

Through the metallic clatter and the clamor of drunken voices we could hear our hosts whispering to each other. "It wasn't like that in '16," the schoolmaster would groan. I began to think of him as the schoolmaster of "La Dernière Classe," Daudet's story that brought such patriotic tears to the eyes of generations of French schoolchildren. "Poor little devils," his wife would answer, "they know they are going to their death." Then she would hug the cat convulsively to her and kiss it all over its face. "It was not like that in '16. There's no discipline any more. Look, they are tearing the canvas covers off the trucks."

They said the same things over and over again. The trucks kept roaring past. There were beardless boys and sturdy youths and middleaged men with mustaches. Faces merged into a blur. All we could see in the dim light was the desperation in their eyes. We tried to say comforting things to the schoolmaster and his wife, but our mouths were stopped with dust. With a "Merci, bonsoir," we slunk away. We felt as if we had been whipped. The memory obsessed me for years.

After our part of the offensive began in the Bois d'Avocourt we were too busy for anguish.

There was the night Jim Parshall and I spent in a deep dugout during a gas attack. We lay down on the bunks after the claxon sounded the warning. Nobody said anything. My face felt strangely slimy under the flimsy oldfashioned French gasmask. Outside shellfragments lashed the shelter like somebody flailing about with a whip. I heard the comforting sound of snoring from some Frenchmen, old hands, who were sleeping quietly in their gasmasks. To pass the time I recited every poem I knew and the Lord's Prayer and "Now I lay me down to sleep" again and again.

Suddenly daylight was filtering in under the blanket that covered the door. The *breloque,* a funny little noisemaker that went hee-honk, like wild geese in the spring, sounded the all clear. We stumbled out to get our motor running while the stretcherbearers brought up our wounded. It made me feel good for some reason to find my cap, which I'd left on the seat, chewed up by a bit of shrapnel as if rats had been at it. There were perforations in the body but our tires and motor were whole. The cream of the jest was that the damage came from a battery of our own guns that had shelled P2 during part of the night through one of those slight military miscalculations.

It must have rained because the mud was worse. While Jim drove I shoved from behind to get her started. The road was nothing but deep ruts. At every lurch the wounded groaned horribly. We wallowed toward the rear through a puttycolored river of mud. One of the worst things was the gassed horses hitched to a row of seventyfives stalled on the road, heaving and gasping with popping eyes and bloody nostrils. Though the gas did us no permanent harm, every few miles we had to get out to puke miserably into the ditch.

One marvelous sight cheered me no end. On the parapet of the third line of trenches the French cooks were already out, gas or no gas, whirling the salad around in wire saladbaskets to dry it.

In late August the weather improved. We were told the offensive had been successful. Sunday afternoons of our days off we squatted in our garden, munching notquiteripe pears and occasionally glancing up apprehensively at a sausageshaped observation balloon hanging in the blue sky overhead, which occasionally attracted white cotton blobs of shrapnel that might well shower down éclats on our heads. There Bobby and I industriously piled chapter on chapter.

P2 became known in Section 60 as "Hell's Half Acre." It was right under a battery of big guns. Every time they fired it was like being hit on the head with a club. Most times we were ordered up there we got pinned down by a bombardment. It was damn disagreeable even when there was no gas attack. I would stretch out on one of the bunks in the deep dugout, and fill my notebook with twentyone-year-old rhetoric: "The guns roar, fart and spit their venom, & here I lie spitting my venom . . .

". . . But gosh I want to be able to express later all of this, all the tragedy and hideous excitement of it. I have seen so very little. I must experience more of it and more—the grey crooked fingers of the dead, the dark look of dirty mangled bodies, their groans and joltings in the ambulances, the vast tomtom of the guns, the ripping tearing sound shells make when they explode, the song of shells outgoing like vast woodcocks, their contented whirr as they near their mark—the twang of fragments like a harp broken in the air & the rattle of stones and mud on your helmet . . . And through everything the vast despair of unavoidable death, of lives wrenched out of their channels—of all the ludicrous tomfoolery of governments . . ."

Dissecting the sensations of danger and fear was my way of making them tolerable: "In myself," I noted on August 26, "I find the nervous reaction to be a curious hankering after danger that takes hold of me. When one shell comes I want another, nearer, nearer. I constantly feel the need of the drunken excitement of a good bombardment. I want to throw the dice at every turn with the old roysterer Death . . . and through it all I feel more alive than ever before . . . I have never lived yet. You can still see the marks of the swaddling clothes. Tomorrow I shall live to the dregs or today I shall die."

You get used to anything. In some ways the high point for me of the Avocourt offensive was the day I caught myself quietly opening a can of sardines for my lunch in the rear of a dressing-station while some poor devil of a poilu was having his leg sawed off on the operating table up front. God knows I was still morbidly sensitive to other people's pain, but I had learned to live in the world and stand it.

Driving an ambulance was a de luxe way of seeing the warfare of those days. You had moments of delightful respite and hot meals back at the base hospitals. Except when you had the bad luck to spend a night under shellfire you always had a dry place to sleep in your ambulance. In three weeks the offensive was over. We were pulled out of the line with what was left of our division and enjoyed pumpkin soup in a lovely little town named Ste. Menehould on the edge of the Argonne Forest.

All too soon Section 60 was taken over by the Medical Corps of the burgeoning A.E.F. "Picture the scene," I wrote. "An automobile full of gentlemen with large jowls and U.S. Army uniforms—Richard Norton, courtly in a monocle—in front a large crowd of ambulance drivers—behind them a much shrapnel-holed barnlike structure, our cantonment. The section dog, by name P2 [a rather mangy policedog Fred Singer had picked up somewhere and named for the abri where Jim and I waited out the gas attack], wanders about uneasily. An occasional shell screeches overhead, makes the fatjowled gentlemen duck and blink and crashes on the riverbank opposite, making much dust fly but causing no apparent damage. Mr. Norton has just finished his very modest speech ending with, 'As gentlemen volunteers you enlisted in this service and as gentlemen volunteers I bid you farewell . . .' What a wonderful phrase, 'gentlemen volunteers,'" I wrote, "particularly if punctuated as it was, by a shell bursting thirty feet away which made everyone clap on their helmets and crouch like scared puppies under a shower of pebbles and dust."

We had the immense satisfaction of seeing the jowly ones in army uniforms bolt for the dugout while Dick Norton, his monocle gleaming in his eye, walked calmly up the ranks shaking hands with every man in turn.

I had sluffed off Harvard indifference, but Harvard snobbery still hung on. I wrote Arthur that I had sworn by all that was holy to remain for the rest of my days a gentleman volunteer. (Looking back on it, it seems a not too disreputable ambition. I have come to see a certain value in snobbery.) I added that I was already trying to wangle admission to a Red Cross section about to be sent to Italy. At the bottom of the page I inserted a drawing of my stickman self paddling a Red Cross gondola across an Italian lake.

With the end of Norton-Harjes came the end of Robert Hillyer's and my collaboration on the G.N. Poor Martin Howe, our hero, was barely out of prepschool when Robert had to go home on pressing family business. Van and I were left alone while the section dawdled *en repos* in a lovely Argonne village named Remicourt.

"I am sitting beside Van at a board table—by the aid of an intensely smoky lamp I am writing you and he is reading Georg Brandes, *The World at War*—a chapter entitled Belgium–Persia —a significant connection of names!" This was a sober evaluation by the great Danish critic of the situation of Europe, which we all read with enthusiasm at the time. Van particularly made it his bible.

I described as "unborn Camemberts" the delicious cheeses, "chaste and tender and reeking with an ozone of clover and cows and placid contemplation," that were a specialty of the place. "In the evening we go to the café in the next town and drink infinities of café au lait or white wine with *sirop de groseille* while poilus about us sing and mutter revolt or shrug their shoulders or say *on les aura* (according to their mental complexion) and we are all very angry and hurt and surprised when at 8:30 by military law the café closes and turns us out into the starlight. Then we wander home and watch the reflections of starshells on the front behind the horizon—or hear the guns popping at a Boche avion that's bombarding a certain unfortunate railway station behind us."

Van and I were accepted for the Red Cross in Italy. There followed a period of waiting in Paris, long walks in search of architecture and *petites femmes . . . rigajig, coucher avec* (alas the remorseful prophylaxis that followed). The quest on the crowded boulevards infinitely romantic under the blue lights. The magnificent spectacle of airraids seen from the steps of the concrete basilica on top of Montmartre. The undulant rumble of Boche motors, the moonlit sky streaked with searchlights and flickering with little sparks of shrapnel, the red flare and the growl of bursting bombs in the distance.

Paris was already filling up with Americans. It was a time of sudden friendships. This must have been when I first met Tom Cope, a lanky Philadelphia Quaker, who had come overseas with a Friends' reconstruction detachment. Tom and I argued endlessly about whether the morally decent thing to do wasn't to go to jail as conscientious objectors instead of playing hide and seek with the problem on the fringes of the great butchery.

But it was all such fun we couldn't stay ethical long. I was seeing everything in terms of gargantuan comedy. I had recently finished the five books of Rabelais and was deep in the Satiricon with the help of a French translation. Petronius I interspersed with Dante's *La Vita Nuova* in preparation for Italy. Over breakfasts of bread and huge bowls of café au lait we confided in each other our incongruous adventures.

Van and Tom and I roamed endlessly around Paris. We discovered the Place des Vosges. We went to concerts and looked at paintings on the rue de la Boëtie. We traveled up and down the Seine on the *bateaux mouches*. We ate fried gudgeons in the treehouse restaurant at Sceaux-Robinson. It was, I think, during those days that we found Mme. Leconte's Rendezvous des Mariniers on the Quai d'Anjou.

Mme. Leconte was a ruddy cheeked countrywoman who kept the best little plain restaurant any of us had ever imagined. She was hearty, hardworking, keenwitted and never too tired for a joke. Monsieur was a dour pale man who had been invalided out of the army with some inexplicable internal malady, which he alleviated by a succession of little glasses of *calvados*. There was a cheerful chubby fifteen-year-old niece named Madeleine whom they worked like a horse. I rented a room upstairs and became almost a member of the family.

My first recollection of Section I of the American Red Cross was of ranks of Ford ambulances in the square in front of the palace at Fontainebleau. Van and I slept under champagne-colored quilts in a magnificent room at the Hôtel François Premier. I could hardly attend to my business for the intoxication of history and the heady ferment of fallen leaves in the russet October woods.

Among the crowd of ambulance drivers we found Jack Lawson, as full of tall tales as ever, in the company of a war correspondent who was making the trip with us. Gouverneur Morris was, I believe, a direct descendant of the original. Though he seemed incredibly elderly to us—he may have turned fifty—he proved a most congenial person. He listened philosophically to our callow diatribes against war and capitalism and the Morgan banks. We took him in tow when we parleyed our meals, and enjoyed his jokes, and took care of him when he drank too much. Our boast was that we never drank enough. He had a special quizzical way of saying, "Have anuzzer one," that became a watchword of the trip.

Our convoy of ambulances, amid every conceivable sort of comic misadventure, proceeded by slow stages to Nevers, then up the Loire, and across the wine country to Mâcon and Lyon, and down the Saône to Valence. Every gray castle and turreted church was a revelation. It was marvelous to come out from under the leaden sky of northern France into the valley of the Rhone and sunlight and the pollarded planetrees of the Midi. We almost lost our minds at the sight of the first Roman arches. We kept straying away from our ambulances to see the sights and guzzle the vintages.

My chief recollections of Marseilles were of denting my fender and the next man's with a horrible crash, which drew unfavorable comment from the management, while trying to back my ambulance into line; and of a macabre dockside dive where the girls picked up coins with their private parts if you set their tips on the corner of the table.

The Italians were trying to boost public morale which had hit bottom after their smashing defeat at Caporetto. A great deal was made of our entrance into Ventimiglia. The newspapers tried to give the impression that our little Section I was the vanguard of a great American army. We were greeted by crowds and flagwaving and singing schoolchildren. People pitched flowers and oranges into the ambulances. One man came near having his eye put out when somebody skimmed a palmfrond into his face.

December 3 we stopped for the night in a dreary industrial suburb named Pontedecimo. After everybody was supposed to be asleep Jack Lawson and I sneaked off and went into Genoa on the trolley.

An oilship was burning in the harbor. The place seemed incredibly dramatic.

Whenever we sat down I made feverish notes. ". . . a pearly glow lights up the pedimented facades of the houses on the hills and the square pointed church that rises above them, etching them curiously against the dark hills behind the town, where the lights, dotted with new constellations, match those in the brilliant night sky . . ."

"This sentence," I added in a mood of revulsion against my flowery writing, "has haunted me for days. I used to think it was good. Now I know it's bad."

At a café on the main square I wrote in high romantic vein that there was "a mad lilting tune coming out from the orchestra . . . Offenbach. I am supposed to be sleeping in car 5. We are in Genoa—mad tinkling Shakespearean Genoa—and the tune is rising in shrill silver rhythms, twining in the blood with all the mystery and flair of Genoa—castellated battlements in the dark, cafés full of quarreling sailors, mosaic-paved streets slippery with the feet of generations—everywhere a hint of old glories, of Orient, of old greedy merchant hoards—of murder in dark streets and people's velvetclad sides slit to red with stillettos . . . We have drunk Strega in bars, we have walked the smooth streets of Genoa —and stared at the intricate marblework of doorways. We have stared in the eyes of the great stone lion before the barred black and white duomo . . . We came on the tram through a dull endless tunnel and burst suddenly into the sky of stars thick as the lights of a city—and Genoa starred like the sky—and old Orion patron of nocturnal adventure."

When closing time came we found that the streetcars had stopped running. We had to walk fifteen kilometers back to our convoy.

In Milan we holed up for a month in a luxurious but unheated hotel while *They* tried to decide what to do with us. The weather was sleety and raw, always on the edge of freezing. Sidney Fairbanks and I had been assigned to a Fiat ambulance. Fairbanks was a Harvard man who I seem to recollect was a Rhodes scholar. He wore a little beard, could dance the old English sword dance, and knew all the words of "The raggletaggle gypsies oh!" There was something wrong with our Fiat. After the rest of the section left for the front we spent frustrating days hanging around an Italian army garage where they worked on it.

I kept entering jingles in my notebook:

Fiat 4, Fiat 4
O mecanician of Milano
When will she roll my Fiat 4?
Piano signore va piano—

There's always been more ennui than action in war. It took years and the reading of *La Chartreuse de Parme* and of Hemingway's lovely descriptions of the city in *A Farewell to Arms* before I learned to appreciate Milan.

In spite of the misadventures of Fiat 4 and the eternal hatred I professed for the internal combustion engine, I came to admire a certain classical simplicity in the Fiat motor. Italy I liked and disliked. I was plunging into Italian with the help of my friends' pickups and the mechanics at the garage and phrase books and a pocket dictionary and the futurist poetry I bought at a bookstall in the Galleria. Boccaccio was my mainstay.

When we left Milan, skirting the Italian lakes where the place names brought back Catullus, we thought we were headed for the Piave, where the Italians, stiffened by some Frenchmen and Britishers, were said to be putting up a resistance at last. Instead we found ourselves stalled again at a place called Dolo in an eighteenth-century villa beside a canal on the Venetian plain.

"Hear the growl of a gasoline stove cooking water for tea in a curious aluminum cannikin," I wrote Arthur on the last day of 1917, "and see seated about a pink lacecovered table that once belonged in somebody's boudoir, Van, with a grouchy air in a T shirt, a certain Jack Lawson, a dramatist, smoking a pipe of unexampled stench, and myself, with a bland air and a bronchial cough. The stove whose name is Hope-Deferred-Maketh-the-Heart-Sick is also warming faintly the cold air of a dingy untidy room, with sheetless beds and a confusion of cots and dufflebags . . . Van is reading *Anna Karenina* in French, Lawson is writing a future Broadway success, I am reading 'Julian and Maddalo.' "

I had already had the news that Estlin Cummings and his friend Slater Brown, who were serving in France in the American Field Service, had been arrested for reasons undisclosed. No one knew what had become of them. The mutinies of the spring of 1917 had lashed every Allied intelligence service into a fever. Censorship of news was redoubled. I wrote Arthur that I was trying to do what I could from a distance. "I have written all sorts of people and I know a man in Paris who is trying to find out all he can." For the life of me I can't remember who that was, unless it was Dick Norton, who, so long as he lived, took a friendly interest in the subsequent fates of his "gentlemen volunteers."

As usual I complained of boredom. "The Italian government considers the A.R.C. ornamental but not useful so here we languish, well treated, wellfed, gazing sentimentally at the Eugeanean Hills and wandering to the border of the lagoon to look at Venice—where we are not allowed to go for some subtle reason . . . A wild air raid last night with the brilliant sky full of throbbing aeroplane motors and shrapnel bursting like rockets and in the distance the crashing snort of exploding bombs rather cheered me up."

Looking back on them, the things I saw during that month on the Venetian plain were a real eyeful. Our villa was near Padua. There I had my first sight of Giotto's frescos of the life of Christ in the Arena chapel. It seemed the finest painting ever. Like many callow youths I'd made a point of irreligion in college. Never having been baptized I claimed I had nothing more to do with Christianity than Anatole France's penguins. Now, seen through Giotto's eyes, the story of Jesus assumed a reality it has never lost. To this day I picture the gospels in the simple sweet stately terms of Giotto's figures.

There was the added poignancy of peeping through protective sandbags at the paintings that gave such enormous scale to the small chapel—the feeling that our mortal eyes might be the last to see them. There were air raids on Mestre and Padua every moonlight night. My last memory of wartime Padua is of seeing, the morning after a particularly noisy night, a column of black smoke coiling up slowly into the wintry air from one of the great domed churches.

"It's hours later but the gasoline stoves are still roaring for tea—and the same company sits writing," I wrote Arthur in my New Year's Eve epistle. Since parting with Robert Hillyer I was carrying on the G.N. all by myself—"in an hour or so the seventeenth abortion of an abortive century will have passed into the musty storehouse of history where all the bales of stupidity and greed and misery are finally bundled away—for the edification of that golden future that is always behind the curve of time—The water's boiling over—a cup o'tay to you!"

New Year's Day our mess was graced by two Red Cross majors, one of them a Boston architect whose work I had rather admired.

They rubbed me the wrong way by declaring in a fit of winey candor that we were at the Italian front only as a propaganda gesture to help keep the Italians in the war. I knew that well enough, but it brought up the painful question of duty, somewhat exacerbated by Tom Cope's righteous Quakerisms in Paris. What I liked to think I was doing was dragging the poor wounded wops out from under fire, not jollying them into dying in a war that didn't concern them.

These qualms were forgotten in the excitement of wangling a trip to Venice. Our mess was out of condensed milk. Somehow I managed to convince the lieutenant that in Venice and Venice alone could condensed milk be bought. Fairbanks and I were furnished with passes and boarded the little steamboat at Fusina. It was a hoarfrosty day of faint rosy sunlight. From the north came the distant thudding of a barrage. The steamboat cut through the scrim of ice on the lagoon with a twanging noise. Roofs and domes and campaniles rose out of the dovecolored surface into a dovecolored sky. It was Venice as Whistler painted it. When the barrage slackened we could hear the sound of churchbells coming across the lagoon. By some miracle we found two boxes of condensed milk in a grocery. We stole a little time to scamper around the Piazza San Marco and the Doge's palace. Most of the great paintings had been hidden away, along with the Roman horses, but though I was much too dedicated to Giotto to appreciate the cloudy pomp of the ceilings of the Venetian school, I took immense pleasure in the mosaic work that appeared behind the sandbags and in every mark of the Romanesque chisel on the creamgray stone.

In Bassano, where the River Brenta flows from out of the Dolomites round the flanks of Monte Grappa, we saw some service. Our advance posts were in picturesque spots in steep mountain valleys. The roads were occasionally shelled by the vicious Austrian eighty-eights, but neither army had stomach for combat. Most of our cases were dysentery and frostbite.

At the dressing stations and field hospitals we messed with the Italian medical officers. Our hackles rose at their treatment of the enlisted men. At a post called Roda there was a halfwitted little redfaced orderly that it was considered great fun to kick around the room after dinner. We didn't like the way they treated the peasant girls. At mountain dressing stations we talked to infantrymen who had had no leave for months and years. They were a haggard halfstarved crew. They claimed that the officers sold their victuals instead of sending them up to the front lines. Cooks we talked to, canny fellows who had been to America and spoke broken English, told the same story. I began to remark in my letters on the sorry treatment of the Italian rank and file.

We were quartered in a great fine building with frescoed walls on the river bank. Dudley Poore turned up in his quiet way and greatly added to the pleasure of our social evenings. Our gang had a fine room, which Fairbanks dubbed "the poets' corner," with a balcony and a view of a handsome covered bridge, and of the towers and battlements of the old walled town. Dudley and I immediately started giving each other a course in drawing during our free time. Whenever it stopped raining we roamed about sketching the bridge and the churchtowers and the wop soldiery and the washerwomen on the riverbank.

Van and I took long walks up toward the front lines. Once we were just stopped by a sentry in time to keep us from walking into an Austrian position on a mountain road where we were admiring the view. I was still jotting down observations of the anatomy of fear. On March 13 the entry was: "A little shelling of Bassano to liven things up—was sitting drawing by the river—the second shell scared me green—for some unknown reason. It wasn't very near either—had a nasty whistle that travelled down one's spine—there was a bitter taste in the mouth for a moment and a strange feeling of lightness in the stomach—like the feeling before you are seasick. Then after a second it was gone except for a slight tremble in the fingers as I went on drawing. Other shells came in without any effect except for the cocktaillike exhilaration I used to feel at Récicourt. I'd never noticed the taste in the mouth as one of the sensations of terror before—rather like the taste of an electric battery."

When we weren't sketching we were writing. I had reached the second chapter of Part III of the G.N. When we weren't sketching or writing or taking long walks we read the Bible aloud. We were all agog with the magnificence of the King James English. Toward evening we drank marsala, a foul beverage but the strongest drink available. Even so, time hung heavy.

When we read of the death of the Empress Taitu of Abyssinia we thought it would be amusing to hold a wake in her honor. Memorial verses were read and a great many bottles of marsala went down the red lane. The result was a scandal. It wasn't so much the drinking or the whooping and singing, or even the writing and sketching, but there was something about the Empress Taitu that stuck in the craw. Our sectionmates began to look at us with a queasy eye.

There was a rumor going around that three members of the section were under suspicion of being pro-German: compromising letters had been intercepted. Already a boy named Heyne had been sent home merely because, so far as we could discover, he had a German name.

While these threats were brewing our licenza came up. Van and Dudley and Jack Lawson and I set off for the south. Our travel orders read Paris but when the conductor came around not a word of Italian could we understand. We were poor ignorant Americans who had gotten on the wrong train.

Our first stop was Bologna, city of green shutters and drunken towers. After a rich meal of spaghetti and some kind of little birds washed down with dark dark wine we found a kindly stationmaster who put us on the Paris express.

We slipped out the other side into the train marked Rome. We tore through Rome, taking in the Forum and the early churches and the Christian paintings in the catacombs. We walked miles out the Appian Way, gazing in astonishment at the bourgeois faces on the Roman tombs and drinking white wine at the trattorias as we went.

We entrained for Naples. There the museums were open. No hint of war. The city was a carnival. Jack Lawson found the Neapolitan ladies so fascinating we had to leave him behind when we started out on foot to Pompeii. Our goal was Paestum. We would walk to Paestum.

The sky was blue. The sunlight was marvelous after the sleet and frostbite of Monte Grappa. Vesuvius was smoking a great black cigar. We walked all day in a sort of enchantment, our musette bags tugging at our shoulders. We might be in wrong but we were having our hour. As we walked along we hummed our theme song for that spring:

Oh Sinbad was in bad
In Tokyo and Rome
In bad in Trinidad
And twice as bad at home.

When our feet began to get sore we hired a cab. The skinny horse had a long nodding feather on his head. ". . . And called it macaroni."

That first view of Pompeii was not to be forgotten. The last days of . . . A thousand years dropped away. We scoured our heads for half-forgotten Latin. We were Roman citizens flitting from wineshop to wineshop. In fact we had taken the precaution of bringing along a fiasco. Not a tourist in sight, not a guide. When the bell rang for closing we paid no attention. After a gaudy sunset the moon rose. We scampered through the lava-paved streets by moonlight. At last hunger drove us out. We climbed a wall and scrambled through the brambles of a dusty embankment.

Next morning we continued on by some sort of trolley to Sorrento. From there we walked the whole magnificent drive, looking out from the cliffs over the sheening Mediterranean, to Positano and Ravello and Amalfi. In Salerno we found we could get a train to Paestum.

There was no station in Paestum in those days. The conductor let us off on a dusty trail that led us not to the ruins but to the beach. After a swim in the delicious crystalline water we arrived at the ruins, like the old voyagers did, from the sea. No living thing in sight but a few sheep grazing among the temples. We scrambled over the fallen stones and gazed our fill at the great honeycolored colonnades with their broad Doric capitals.

It was coming on to rain. We were lamenting the fact that Jack Lawson had missed this most magnificent spectacle on our whole expedition when a horse cab drove up at a gallop. There he was, chipper and shaved and bursting with a whole Arabian Night's entertainment (Burton's translation) of Neapolitan adventures. We laughed our heads off while we stumbled about the ruins. When the rain began really to pour we all piled into the cab and were driven weary miles to a solitary trattoria where we drank a heavy blackish wine and ate up everything they had in the house. For the life of me I can't remember how we got back to Salerno. Paestum was the triumph of that trip.

Back in Bassano I found a welcome letter from Cummings. I was afraid he had been shot. He wrote in French from his father's house in Cambridge. Another case of *"lettres compromettantes."* Cummings and his friend Slater Brown had been arrested when their section was in Ollézy in the past September. They were placed in jail, where they were given the third degree, at Noyan. They were then sent to a concentration camp at la Ferté Macé. After eleven weeks Cummings was released. His father, who was pastor of the Park Street Church and a wellknown lecturer and a mighty man among Boston Unitarians, had shaken up Washington to the point of getting the embassy to intervene; so that Cummings had found himself at the end of the year sailing for America on my old familiar liner the *Espagne.* In his letter he begged me to try to get cigarettes or food packages sent to poor Brown, whom he feared was incarcerated for the duration of the war. Cummings added that he'd been pretty sick after his emprisonment but that he was now better. *"Que je m'ennuie pour la Ville Immense, la Femme superbe et subtile qui s'appelle—tu le sais—Paris."*

Soon I was much too busy with my own scandal to do anything about sending packages to Brown. For a couple of months the threat merely smoldered. There were hints but nothing more as to the nature of the charges against us. Our enlistments expired at the end of May. We were advised to go to Rome to talk to the Red Cross authorities there as to the possibility of further assignments.

June 1 we set out, Van and Dudley and Lawson and I. We had already attained a certain skill in the use of travel orders. We were much too excited about painting and architecture to worry about the complaints of the Italian Intelligence. On the way to Rome we managed to take in Orcagna's frescos at the Campo Santo in Pisa; Siena; and Signorelli's eternal Last Judgment, which we washed down with the magnificent white wine of Orvieto.

"On our way down from the front," I wrote Arthur from a café table across from the Forum where we were drinking tea after another walk out the Appian Way, "we managed to stop off at Pistoja, Lucca, Pisa, San Gimignano, Siena and Orvieto—my ardor for early Italian frescowork has been fanned to fury. I find it unbelievably wonderful."

I told him we were in Rome "under the ridiculous accusation of being proGerman . . . but I think we are managing to prove our innocence to the Red Cross officials." I found the whole thing absurd and "rather diverting." I liked Italy—away from the front —particularly the peasants and working people. "They do things with their hands wonderfully—to this day they make superb ironwork and the best automobiles in the world—at the front their engineering performances are worthy of the Romans."

I filled the rest of the page with a sketch of "St. Fino's town of the beautiful towers" and told him to compare it with Toledo. Arthur, who was a British subject, had in some mysterious way found himself a job in the American consulate in Madrid. "Burn a candle for me in the church where the Conde de Orgaz lives." Much as I enjoyed Italy I insisted that Spain was my meat.

"The authorities" turned out to be the Boston architect who had made such an unpleasant impression on me at Dolo. He was pleasant enough when I went to see him, but intimated that I'd better go home as fast as I could. There was a black mark on my record. "What for?" I asked. He became very mum.

I tried to explain that while I was cheerfully giving what service I could, I felt that as an American citizen I had a right to my own ideas. He muttered something about letters. He seemed embarrassed to have to tell me that he wasn't at liberty to explain anything further. I confided in him that I might have written injudiciously to Arthur McComb in Madrid, or to Pepe Giner, who was of the pro-Allied faction in Spain. I'd written Pepe that if he wanted to serve the cause of civilization he would work to keep his country neutral. Then there were the letters in behalf of Cummings and Brown. Mr. Boston Architect seemed to find these revelations more damaging than not. We agreed that I should return to Paris to seek an enquiry from the Red Cross higher command.

The other three were similarly attainted, but to a lesser degree. They finally talked themselves out of it and Jack Lawson got himself a Red Cross publicity job that kept him in Rome in some splendor during the rest of the war. So far as I remember, after sending a melodramatic telegram to my poor Aunt Mamie in New York, beginning "Falsely accused" and begging her to pull what strings she could to find me a job at the front, I set out alone for Paris.

The people of Paris seemed magnificent to me in the summer of 1918. Airplanes or zeppelins were raiding every clear night and Big Bertha was bombarding the city by day. The scared cats and the fat cats had all left and those who remained seemed determined to show the Germans they wouldn't be disturbed by a little bombing and shelling. Besides they were bucked up at every turn by the sight of newly arrived freshfaced Americans.

While I plodded around from Red Cross headquarters to A.E.F. headquarters, trying to explain my position and getting myself deeper in Dutch every time I opened my face, I saw marvelous scenes. Though a few people were killed and a few houses demolished the Parisians insisted on treating Bertha as a joke. They laughed cynically when little President Poincaré turned up promptly after each explosion to congratulate the survivors. While browsing in the bookstalls I happened to see one shell explode in the Seine. Before the smoke cleared fishermen were out in boats enthusiastically scooping the stunned fish out with their handnets. In the *boîtes de nuit* they sang a song "*'Suis dans l'axe, 'suis dans l'axe du gros canon.*"

I was now as anxious to get into the A.E.F. as I had once been anxious to keep out of it. I wanted to see the war through at any cost. I tried to enlist in all sorts of units. In every case I was turned down for my eyesight or on account of the never explained but always merely hinted-at Italian scandal. An old college friend in an intelligence agency told me in no uncertain terms people like me weren't fit to be in the A.E.F.

"The extreme lack of decency, of small obvious humanness in people comes out more every day," I complained to Arthur. "They are preposterous. I refuse to take them seriously . . . I want to retire to a village among high mountains—Shelley's Caucasus will do—and there live among paintpots and white paper and work in a vineyard for a farthing a day . . . If monasteries were the thing nowadays I should have been in one long ago . . . Let's found one on the end of Finisterre."

Of all the people I tried to interest in my cause Dick Norton was the only man who seemed to understand what I meant, but he was not in any too good odor himself. The word volunteer had gone out of fashion.

Looking back on it, it's surprising that I didn't get myself shot. College-trained Americans, the people who considered themselves the ruling elite, had closed their minds to anything except the most rudimentary "hate the hun" propaganda. Any other attitude was pro-German on the face of it.

Nothing to it but to go home and get myself drafted. A few days before sailing I got my last sight of the bloody side of war. There had been an American offensive. I guess it was Château Thierry. The wounded were being evacuated directly on Paris. An urgent call was sent out from the rue Ste. Anne for Americans on leave or on duty in the city to volunteer for service in a nearby base hospital. The night I particularly remember it was my job to carry off buckets full of amputated arms and hands and legs from an operating room.

Who could hold on to dogmatic opinions in the face of these pathetic remnants of shattered humanity? The world, somehow, never seemed quite so divided into black and white to me after that night.

I sailed home on the good old *Espagne*. The ship was empty. I sat in my cabin and wrote and wrote. To get my feelings off my chest, to tell my side of the story I picked Martin Howe out of the unfinished novel and put him through everything I had seen and heard that summer on the Voie Sacrée. By the time we reached Ambrose Light I'd finished the first draft of *One Man's Initiation: 1917*. That was all that ever really came of Robert Hillyer's and my Great Novel.

I was traveling first class. Since I had changed to civilian clothes none of the passengers suspected I was a pacifist ambulance driver in disgrace. Before I knew what I was doing I found myself chatting with an elderly two-star American general who read French: the highest point of his literary experience was when Quasimodo rescued Esmeralda from the scaffold in *The Hunchback of Notre Dame*. I noted that in spite of being a general, he was "an old dear." I found myself listening carefully to what a Y.M.C.A. man had to say about the triumph of democracy and became so cozy with an Episcopal chaplain that he asked me to pass the plate at his Sunday service in the saloon. I never could keep the world properly divided into gods and demons for very long.

October, 1918, while the triumphant Allies were pushing back the Germans on every front, I spent washing windows at Camp Crane. After a great deal of effort and pestering of relatives and friends I had managed to achieve the position of buck private in the rear rank of a medical corps casuals company billeted in an erstwhile fairground near Allentown, Pennsylvania—known as Syphilis Valley to the troops. The buildings still had signs on them: POULTRY AND RABBITS, FAT STEERS or just HOGS.

Characters whom other outfits found indigestible tended to sift down into the Medical Corps. That casuals company at Camp Crane was the trash can of the Medical Corps. Some were half-witted. All were misfits and oddballs of various kinds. I kept talking to men who had been there eighteen months and seemed reconciled to spending the rest of their lives there. To make things worse Camp Crane was quarantined for the flu. My chances of getting back overseas seemed nil. I was in the deep dumps.

It had taken me six weeks to wangle the promise of a waiver of eyesight requirements from the draft board in New York where I reported for induction. The officials, one of them a politician friend of my uncle's, were friendly, though they could hardly conceal their mirth at my desperate efforts to squirm into the army when everybody else was trying to squirm out of it. The man who examined my eyes gave me plenty of time to memorize the chart. But now, after all this struggle, here I was high and dry in a damn casuals company, in quarantine at that, and with my waiver lost somewhere in the morass of army paper work.

The sergeants found us too awkward to drill so they set us to washing windows. When the windows were washed, we swept out the barracks. When the barracks were swept we swept the autumn leaves off the desolate spaces of the old fairground.

A friend of my aunt's had showed understanding about my Italian scandal. This was James Brown Scott, who was president of the Carnegie Peace Foundation in Washington. He had come out for making the world safe for democracy, was a fervent League of Nations man and a close adviser of Woodrow Wilson's, but in spite of these commitments he was helpful and kind and I hope I showed myself grateful. I can still remember how he screwed up his round pink face under his skimpy gray hair and made clucking noises when I poured my sad tale into his ears.

He said he wanted me to have a nice quiet literary career.

At the time my idea of a literary career was neither nice nor quiet, but I nodded and smiled. For the purposes of the war he was a Major in the Judge Advocate Corps. I sent him a desperate wire from Camp Crane and he replied that he would do what he could.

To pass the time I began to study German. I got a friend to send me Heine's *Harzreise*. It gave me a certain perverse satisfaction to be studying German when the newspapers were full of the banning of German operas and German newspapers. German clover lost its name and even German measles had to be referred to as Liberty measles.

The Y.M.C.A. had a good library. Nobody else used it. I read through their set of Jane Austen, renewed my acquaintance with old man Gibbon's *Roman Empire*, and, with mingled disgust and sympathy, read every word of a dogeared yellowbacked copy of Rousseau's *Confessions* I had brought along in my musette.

Sitting at a table in the empty Y.M.C.A. shack, I planned plays and a novel. The notebook I kept in the pocket of my uniform is full of scribblings about a play—supposed to be written by the romantic uncle Bobby Hillyer and I invented for the G.N.—about a young man who drums on the moon. There is even a rough sketch of what later became the stagesetting for *Garbage Man.* I was jotting down notes on how my buddies talked. A farm boy from Indiana and a little wop from somewhere out west gave me the first intimations of the characters in *Three Soldiers.*

Misery can be damned instructive. I was beginning to take real satisfaction from rubbing elbows with the debris and the jetsom.

"My luck as always is with the unclassified," I wrote Arthur. As I swept I kept whispering to myself, "organization is death."

> . . . as I sweep acres of floorspace and wash windows —as many as the sands of the Lybian Sertes—I repeat the words over and over again—in anagrams, in French, in Latin, in Greek, in Italian, in all the distortions that language can be put to. Like a mumbled Ave Maria they give me comfort . . . I'm glad I'm here even if I seem to grumble. I've always wanted to divest myself of class and the moneyed background—the army seemed the best way. From the bottom, thought I, one can see clear . . .

"You can't imagine the sublime and simple amiability of the average American soldier," I wrote again. "Here is clay for almost any molding. Who is to be the potter?"

When I'd about lost my mind, there was a sudden transformation scene. The waiver appeared. I ran into a jolly Top Sergeant named O'Reilly who was getting together ambulance Section 541 to sail immediately overseas. He too was a veteran of the gentlemen volunteers. Learning that I could type with two fingers he made me acting Quartermaster Sergeant and there we were, off to Camp Merritt in a highly exhilarated state for embarkation. We were so shut in by security at Camp Merritt we never heard of the false armistice. The day of the real armistice we sailed for France.

It was the old White Star liner *Cedric* converted into a troopship. For my sins our company, with me at the head, was put in charge of a messhall. It was somewhere down in the bowels near the stokehole. We served three meals a day to three sets of seasick doughboys. Nine meals in twelve hours. The place was airless. We never stopped sweating. Up to then I'd sometimes been a wee mite squeamish in heavy weather. Now I was too busy fighting for the proper rations for my doughboys with the damned limey stewards who were holding back jam and butter and bacon and stuff to sell on the side, to feel a single qualm. The only time we got up on deck was when we toted the sour garbage pails up pitching companionways—rosies we called them—to dump over the side, me cussing and swearing and bawling out the poor devils of privates if they spilt something on the way—and the officers strutting around looking for trouble with their necks stuck out and their eyes at pinpoint like roosters looking for worms in a barnyard. We had a good bunch of guys and I was eternally grateful to them for the way they worked to get our men fed. When it was over, it was like your first shell fire, you felt better for having been able to take it.

England was gruesome in the dull autumn drizzle. On the transport there was an outbreak of flu. Men died every day. Now at a place called Camp Winnal Downs—I never knew how you spelt it; it was on a rainswept moor in sight of Winchester Cathedral—the flu hit our company.

I was convinced that if you went to the hospital you would never come back. As acting Quartermaster Sergeant I had to sit there at a little deal table making out hospitalization orders for those poor feverish guys. We never saw any of them again. I was determined I wouldn't go to any hospital. The minute I began to feel the symptoms I bought a bottle of rum from a grubby Englishman who was pimping for some women he said he had in a sandpit just outside of camp. I always thought that bottle saved my life. We had orders for France. I kept drinking the rum. On the steamboat crossing the channel I was dizzy with fever but when we disembarked in Havre, where we were housed in icy French barracks with cobbled floors, I felt skinny and weak, but perfectly fit.

Sergeant O'Reilly was another natural leader. He kidded the pants off everybody, but never lost his temper. The boys enjoyed serving under him. Calling ourselves O'Reilly's Traveling Circus, we drove across France to spend a couple of pleasant winter months in Saussheim in Alsace. As interpreter-in-chief I was allowed to do pretty much what I pleased.

I never did get my sergeancy confirmed. Our headquarters was in an old Merovingian town called Ferrières-en-Gatinais. Orders came from Pershing's G.H.Q. that everybody had to drill. Close order drill was like poker to me: I never could keep the hands in my head. I used to march my company out of town to an apple orchard with a nice high wall. There we sat around under the trees if the weather was good and told stories and smoked *caporal ordinaire*. One day an unexpected Colonel turned up. He ordered me to put my boys through their drill. Friends tried to whisper the orders, but I got everything balled up and ended by marching the company head on into the stone wall. The guys couldn't help giggling. The Colonel blew up like a land mine and that was the end of my career as a noncom.

Luckily I had already signed up for the Sorbonne Detachment. College students, if they gave up their priority for repatriation, were to be allowed to study that spring of 1919 in European universities. I picked the University of Paris and was soon foregathering with a number of cronies at Mme. Leconte's on the Quai d'Anjou.

I took courses at the School of Anthropology in Greek and Roman religions, and in Mayan culture, and listened to an excellent lecture on *Aucassin and Nicolette*. Since it was near the tail end of the semester, and I had no clue as to what had gone before, I made little headway in any of these subjects, but I did write my head off every morning.

Jack Lawson had a room on the Quai de la Tournelle. I don't remember what his putative occupation was but most of his energy was going into writing a play. Before and after dinner in the evenings I'd read him parts of *Three Soldiers* and he'd read scenes from what was to turn into *Roger Bloomer*.

He and Kate Drain were either just married or on the edge of getting married so she was usually part of the audience. She was a handsome strapping girl from Oregon with the finest brown eyes and level brows you ever saw. Her father was famous in the

A.E.F. as "Colonel Drain of the Tanks." Like everybody else she wore some quasi-military uniform.

I was absolutely intoxicated with Lawson's dramatic style and swore he would turn out the greatest playwright ever. We ate well and drank well and loaned each other money when we ran out. We listened to the chansonniers at the *boîtes de nuit*. We raved over Charpentier's opera *Louise* and suffered at the Comédie Française. We led a fine life.

Robert Hillyer turned up from time to time. He was a First Lieutenant and had a marvelous job carrying dispatches around Europe. Dudley Poore, like me, was a lowly private, only in the Post Dispatch Service, so we had to find hidden drinking places to meet Lieutenant Hillyer lest the MP's catch him frolicking with enlisted men.

Somewhere around the Verdun sector I'd met a French doctor named Lucas-Championnière, who invited me to visit his family when I reached Paris. They came from the unreconstructed gentry of the Vendée, from a race of royalists who didn't believe the French Revolution had come to stay. His mother, known to me as Mme. Bibi, was a hearty redcheeked French countrywoman who made me think a little of Mme. Leconte. His sister Germaine, a quiet girl with lovely hair and eyes, lived for music. She had much the same tastes as I had but much more information. Soon I was seeking her out at the concert halls.

Paris was full of music that spring. Les Six were just beginning. Erik Satie was the rage. Debussy and Ravel were everywhere. When I managed to get myself invited to tea Germaine would play Milhaud's songs on the piano. Together we cultivated a mania for *Pelléas and Mélisande*. She'd sing and I'd mumble the words as we went up the stairs at 52 rue de Clichy: "*Toute ta chevelure, Mélisande, est tombée de la tour.*"

Paris really was the capital of the world that spring of the Peace Conference. It looked as if every man or woman in the United States who could read and write had wangled an overseas job. Relief was the great racket. Those who couldn't disguise themselves as relievers came as journalists or got attached to government commissions. Mme. Leconte's became an American hangout.

I've forgotten who first brought Griffin Barry around. He was a small rosyfaced man who knew everything and everybody. At that time he worked for the United Press. He was the insider incarnate. There was hardly anybody he hadn't been to bed with. Griffin was a radical, full of the lingo of Mabel Dodge's salon in New York. Love must be free. Everything must be frank; talk, talk, talk. He was the future Greenwich Village encapsulated. Griffin was immediately intrigued at uncovering our nest of literary doughboys, red enough to set the Seine on fire.

It was Griffin who introduced Bob Minor, a big opinionated Texan, whose charcoal cartoons we had all admired in the *Masses*. Bob Minor was just on the edge of becoming an active revolutionist. He dropped tantalizing hints about the hazards of the Russian revolution and the German underground and Jack Reed's adventures. He was already a little too deaf to listen to anyone else's notions. With Minor came Mary Heaton Vorse with her charming look of a withered Irish rose. In fact in the course of a month Griffin brought down every three-barreled name out of the mastheads and bylines of the big circulation American magazines. They loved the cheapness, the good food, the feeling of being really in France.

Tom Cope and I were heartbroken. We had lost our quiet hideout. We were intolerant of big names anyway.

Griffin Barry was a catalyst. It was Griffin who produced the Ewers. "Trilby" Ewer was about to become Foreign Editor of *The Daily Herald*, the English independent labor newspaper. We got along. I raved about Spain. He began to hold out hopes of a correspondent job in Madrid when I emerged from the army. It was through Ewer that I got a typed copy of *One Man's Initiation: 1917* into the hands of Allen and Unwin in London. They showed interest. Somehow I obtained a leave when the courses closed at the Sorbonne to go to London. I've forgotten how I raised the several hundred dollars guarantee Allen and Unwin insisted on from the author before they would publish a book by an unknown soldier.

Back in France I found the Sorbonne detachment dissolved. I

was shipped to a depot in a hellhole called Gièvres. In spite of imploring messages to Major Scott, who was deep in the work of writing the peace treaties at the Hôtel Crillon, begging him to pull strings to speed my discharge, I found myself once more lost in casuals. Gièvres may not have been hell but it made me understand the concept of limbo. Our daily task was moving scrapiron from one side of a railroad track to the other. When it was all piled up we were told to move it back across the tracks again.

Day followed day and no sign of my discharge. The Quartermaster Sergeant claimed no knowledge of my service record. To be a man without a service record is one of the worst fates that can befall a private in the U.S. Army.

I might well be in Gièvres to this day if I hadn't gone AWOL. After a lot of fancy dodging from train to train to avoid the MP's I made my way to SOS headquarters in Tours. There a Top Sergeant, a prince among men, led me through a maze of red tape until he discovered in a filing case a reasonable facsimile of my service record. He made out the orders. After another breathless trainride I sneaked back into the barracks in time for next morning's roll call. I presented my papers to an astonished C.O. and walked over to the railroad station with my discharge (honorable, by God) in my hand.

Good old Tom Cope had loaned me a gray suit, one of his best silk shirts and a pair of bright blue socks. I went to the public bath in Tours and had a long relaxing soak in a huge brass tub fed by swanshead spiggots. I hid my O.D. uniform, and the hated puttees that were always coming undone, under a pile of soggy towels in the corridor, and sauntered out a civilian. The tree-shaded streets of sunny Tours were honied with the smell of flowering lindens. Sinbad might be in bad, but it was as a free man that he was commencing his travels.

In those days I had a fair head for liquor but architecture intoxicated me. The blues and the purples and reds, like the colors of greenhouse anemones, of the stainedglass windows in the apse of Tour's creamy gothic cathedral went straight to my head. On the way to Paris I stopped off in Blois and Vendôme and stared lovingly at every snuffer-topped tower and every ogive arch. Waiting for trains I sat writing verses in the station buvettes. I was in Paris in time for July 14, la Fête de la Victoire.

CHAPTER 3

Sinbad

Toward the end of July Dudley Poore and I accomplished a rendezvous at San Sebastian. After a term at Cambridge he also had managed to get his discharge in Europe. When a Spanish consulate refused to visa his passport because the border was closed on account of labor agitation, he waded across the Bidassoa into Spain.

With our army discharges in our pockets we were in no mood to fuss with international red tape. If I remember right we lunched triumphantly that day off a mess of tiny eels at a seaside restaurant in the direction of Fuentarrábia.

The weather was bright. The wine was cheap and good. The sea was fresh to bathe in. After the army slum everything we ate seemed delicious. Shipping our suitcases ahead of us, walking where we could, hopping buses and diligences, riding on the hard benches of third class coaches, we made our way through the Basque country. At last we would get our fill of Spain.

Always in sight of the sea we made daylong walks around the green flanks of the hills of Guipuzcoa. We liked the Basques. On the trails we consorted with muledrivers who filled us up with wise sayings and with wine out of their botas. We marveled at the clarity of the Castilian the countrypeople spoke in the Montaña de Santander. We were struck with awe by the rampant great shapes of the buffalo in the cavepaintings at Altamira. We almost knocked ourselves out climbing breakneck passes between the Picos de Europa. We delighted in the talk of the shepherds in the dark Asturian valleys. When our legs would carry us no farther we sat by the roadside and sketched.

In Madrid we found Arthur McComb. We gorged ourselves on Goya and Greco. We made excursions with Pepe Giner. I walked about Segovia one moonlight night with Antonio Machado, whose poems I was already trying to translate into English.

Machado was a large shambling creature in a wrinkled suit shiny at the knees. His derby hat was always dusty. He gave you the feeling that he was more helpless than any child in the daily business of life, a man too candid, too full of feeling, too awkward in a scholarly sort of way to survive; "Machado el bueno," his friends called him. I never think of the aqueduct or the Romanesque portals of the tawny churches or the fairytale silhouette of the Segovia alcazar without hearing the cadences of his verse. Etched in moonlight the city unfolded as we walked about it like a poem Antonio Machado might well be writing at that moment. He was a great man.

In Madrid I drank a sentimental beer at the Oro del Rhin in memory of Roland Jackson. Roly had enlisted in the artillery and was killed during his first few days at the front.

Sitting at the same table where Roly and Lowell Downes and I had planned our hairbrained expeditions I could still hear Roly's deep voice. "Suppose I drank beer with my enemy?" he asked the night we argued about how to abolish war. He lay back in his chair with his long legs stretched out across the floor so that the waiter tripped over his grimy sneakers, and laughed as he stared at the ceiling. "And gave him what he wanted, wouldn't he maybe give it back to me?"

As the correspondent for a labor paper I wasn't much of a success. Though I was thoroughly interested in syndicalism and socialism and trade union matters, I was continually distracted by scenery and painting and architecture and the *canto hondo* and the grave rhythms of flamenco dancing. And the people, the people, the infinitely tragical, comical, pathetic and laughable varieties of people.

When I dashed off to Lisbon to cover what was described as a royalist plot to overthrow the Portuguese republic I was arrested at the border. Officials on the watch for subversives wouldn't believe my American passport. My name was *d'Spash* and why couldn't I speak Portuguese? It was my first experience with the difficult little language of my paternal ancestors. I found I couldn't utter a word. I had to pay the passage to Lisbon of a gendarme who was ordered not to turn me loose until I'd been vouched for at the American consulate.

I came away with a more favorable view of early Portuguese painting than of the then republican government. I found the politicians grandiloquent and evasive. Their air of ineffectual benevolence rubbed me the wrong way. The working people seemed unnecessarily grubby and downtrodden and illiterate. A man is intolerant at twentythree.

When no revolution transpired I found it a relief to get back to the haughty idiosyncracy of the Spanish. From beggar to grandee the Spaniards carried their burdens with style.

Needing a spot to settle down for a while to finish a second war novel, I rented a little garden house at the *Carmen de Matamoros,* an English pension, up on the hill in Grenada. There were hardly believable views of the city and the *vega* and the snow mountains beyond. There, in spite of a bothersome bout of rheumatic fever, I just about finished the job. Dudley stuck around to help nurse me.

We procured a physician, a most agreeable man who was convinced I had Maltese fever, and was so out of breath from his long climb up the hill that we never could get much out of him when he reached my bedside. Arthur meanwhile sent recommendations and medications from a German specialist he uncovered in Madrid. At length the disease died off but forever after we referred to the lovely spot as the *Carmen de Matatodos.*

In the spring of 1920 I took ship for New York, not to stay home, I assured my friends, but to find means to finance fresh trips.

New York turned out, for me, to be a number of different cities. There had been Elsie Rizer's and Wright McCormick's city of theatrical boardinghouses and newspapermen's bars. Then there was Jack Lawson's New York that soon began to revolve around Esther Andrews' and Canby Chambers' hospitable apartment in the Village. There was Jack's sister Adelaide's circuit of sketching classes, exhibitions and the Art Students' League. A little later I would discover a different city in the midtown east side.

One of the New Yorks I frequented during the earliest Twenties proved to be an emanation of Cambridge, Massachusetts. Cummings already had his room on Patchin Place. Nagel was painting abstractions on Washington Square. Nagel's stepfather Gaston Lachaise had a studio nearby. Schofield Thayer and Sibley Watson, who as weathy amateurs had moved in the background of the cercle littéraire at Harvard, appeared as gods of the machine behind the *Dial,* which they transferred from Chicago to New York to transform into a first rank literary magazine. Stewart Mitchell, known to us as the Great Awk when he was editor-in-chief of the *Harvard Monthly,* was editor of the *Dial.*

Cummings was the hub. Cummings and Elaine. His Elaine Orr had for a while been the wife of Schofield Thayer. Poor Schofield was too far gone in psychoanalysis to keep a wife. He was being psyched by the great Freud himself. Elaine was living alone in a lovely apartment on Washington Square. She was the Blessed Damozel, the fair, the lovable, the lily maid of Astolot. To romantic youth she seemed the poet's dream. Those of us who weren't in love with Cummings were in love with Elaine.

Cummings and I would occasionally lunch together at a Syrian restaurant he frequented down on Washington Street. We would eat a special clabber known as leben and a marvelous dish made of raw eggplant mashed to a paste with sesame oil. With the thin unleavened bread these made an excellent meal for people who might have had too much to drink the night before.

Afterward we'd roam around the vegetable and flower stalls of the old Washington Market or go to see the fish in the Aquarium down at the Battery. Cummings never tired of drawing sealions. As he walked he would be noting down groups of words or little scribbly sketches on bits of paper. Both of us lived as much for the sights we saw as for the sound of words.

We would go home to work and then would meet in the late afternoon at Elaine's for tea. Nagel would appear, or Slater Brown, or Mitchell and after an hour or so of talk—though she was silent as a mouse nobody ever dared show off too much at Elaine's—we would go out to our Italian speakeasy of the moment—as I remember they were all named Maria's—for supper.

Cummings had a way of looking like a chimp at times. As we poured down the dago red he would become mischievous as a monkey. Nagel was already a bit neurotic. Cummings would tease poor Nagel until the top of his head was ready to fly off. Elaine hardly said anything, but a word from her would heal all sores. Cummings had all sorts of cryptic ways of talking. "Dos d. your w." he would say severely when he thought I wasn't drinking fast enough. When Lachaise and Nagel's mother, who looked like one of Lachaise's nudes with clothes on, were of the party, they'd leave about this time. They didn't like to see young people drink too much.

Somehow we often managed to get hold of good French brandy. After a couple of brandies on top of the wine Cummings would deliver himself of geysers of talk. I've never heard anything that remotely approached it. It was comical ironical learned brilliantlycolored intricatelycadenced damnably poetic and sometimes just naughty. It was as if he were spouting pages of prose and verse from an unwritten volume. Then suddenly he would go off to Patchin Place to put some of it down before the fountain ceased to flow.

His mind was essentially extemporaneous. His fits of poetic fury were like the maenadic seizures described in Greek lyrics. When I first started going to his family's house at 104 Irving Street in Cambridge while we were all in college Estlin would sometimes extemporize on the piano. His father, Dr. Cummings, was the adored center of a huge oldfashioned New England family: Estlin's mother, a grandmother, his aunt Jane, a younger sister, cousins, a widower friend. All heard Dr. Cummings lay down the law with rapt admiration; but when Estlin extemporized on the piano Dr. Cummings had a touching way of yielding the floor to his son. He played like fireworks. He talked the same way.

Those New York nights none of us wanted to waste time at the theater when there was a chance that Cummings might go off like a stack of Roman candles after dinner.

There is a time in a man's life when every evening is a prelude. Toward five o'clock the air begins to tingle. It's tonight if you drink enough, talk enough, walk far enough, that the train of magical events will begin. Every part of town had its own peculiar glow. The Jewish East Side had a flavor that we found particularly romantic. Saturday nights we would foregather at Moskowitz's "Rumanian Broilings" on a street east of Second Avenue.

Mr. Moskowitz was a courtly waspwaisted little man who played the zymbalom while we drank his wine, which drew a faint flavor of the Danube from the shapes of the bottles—though Cummings claimed Mrs. Moskowitz made it of turnips in the cellar. We'd eat gobbets of broiled lamb and drink and chatter and applaud Mr. Moskowitz.

Sometimes we talked about the Russian revolution with Yiddish journalists and poets. These were well-informed and skeptical people. It all seemed very close; wasn't there a waiter at the café across Second Avenue who'd always tell you how Trotsky still owed him seven dollars? Mr. Moskowitz played well. He liked to feel he was an artist among artists. Sometimes he would be so moved by the enthusiasm of our response that he would distribute free wine. Mrs. Moskowitz, a stout practical lady, would come waddling after him, taking the bottles away as fast as he set them on the tables.

Then nearby there was always the classical burlesque show upstairs in the building at the end of the avenue. We claimed that

Minsky's was in the direct line from Aristophanes, and Terence and Plautus. After the circus, which was his favorite show, Cummings in those days esteemed burlesque. We were late getting to bed the nights we started at Moskowitz's.

Though we seemed to be spending an awful lot of time eating and drinking we managed to get work done. Cummings had finished *The Enormous Room.* The *Dial* was publishing his poems and his taut line drawings. Except for the people on the *Dial* whom he considered old friends, Cummings was leary of wasting his days with editors and publishers. He never pretended to be practical about practical matters. He thought a poet should be fed by the ravens, and of course he was.

A number of friends became involved in inducing Boni and Liveright to publish *The Enormous Room.* I don't remember exactly what I had to do with it but I do remember getting in one of those embarrassing crossfires between author and publisher. I thought *The Enormous Room* was one of the best books ever written and begged everyone concerned to see that it be published intact. The publisher had other ideas.

Cummings and I spent a good deal of our time together in antiphonal cursing out of the editorial fraternity. We were fed up with New York and the marts of trade. When I found a Portuguese freighter that would take a few passengers out of New Bedford for Lisbon at a very low rate, Cummings decided to go along. He was pining for Paris and I was hell-bent for Persia.

My experience with *One Man's Initiation: 1917* had hardly been happy. The English printer refused to put it through his press until I'd bowdlerized the soldiers' language; and when it did come out, the publishers, after the first six months, reported the sale of sixty-three copies. No New York publisher would buy the remaining chapters of Bobby's and my G.N., which Jack Lawson's agents, Brandt and Kirkpatrick, were circulating under the title of *Seven Times Around the Walls of Jericho,* and when *Three Soldiers* (after something like fourteen rejections) found a home with George H. Doran, his editors reported that they would have to cut out the smut.

All I'd done was put down the soldiers' talk the way they talked it. I tried to argue with them.

Gene Saxton, who later became a good friend of mine, was begging me not to bleed and die for a few four-letter words. In the end I told them to do what they goddamn pleased with it. I was going to take the advance and get the hell out.

So it was in the mood of shaking the dust of the City of Destruction that Cummings and I, about the middle of March, 1921, met at a dreary lodging in New Bedford called the Elm Gate Inn to await the departure of the S.S. *Mormugão*. New Bedford was full of nostalgia, as if Herman Melville had just left it after writing the first chapter of *Moby Dick,* but we were too impatient to appreciate it.

The *Mormugão* was only twentyfour hours late in sailing but the extra day seemed endless. The first night out her engines stopped with a sudden jolt in the middle of supper. She rolled like a log in the trough of the sea. The wine spilt. Apples shot across the table like cannon balls and a horrible clanking and crashing came from the engineroom. The captain and the ship's officers threw down their napkins and galloped out of the saloon.

Cummings and I sat there with our feet braced, drinking what wine we could reach to keep it from spilling. Soon I had to apply old Dr. Parson's seasick remedy. This consisted of little shots of brandy on the hour and half hour. By gum it worked. Since there was no way of keeping our footing, we crawled, hand over hand, to our cabin and braced ourselves in our bunks.

The ship was rolling scuppers under. Any minute we expected to be called to the boats. We told each other hopefully that maybe she wouldn't start to sink till daylight. In spite of the unholy rumpus we fell asleep and awoke next morning to find the old *Mormugão* steaming placidly eastward.

It turned into a lovely crossing. This time I was delighted with my Portuguese cousins. The food, though a little oliveoily, was good, the wine firstrate, the brandy cheap. The ship's officers treated us with a benevolent politeness we found charming.

Arthur, who had come home from Europe to get married, had given me a copy of Henry and Brooks Adams' *Degradation of the Democratic Dogma* to read on the boat. Cummings and I read chapters by turns. We hated the book, each for a separate reason, Cummings because it offended some Emersonian streak in his early training—already I was thinking of him as the last of the great New Englanders—and I, because it went against the Walt Whitman-narodnik optimism about people I've never quite lived down. We argued stormily as we paced the slanting deck.

When we weren't taking the hide off the Adams brothers we sat scratching in our notebooks in the tiny *fumador.* I was working on translations from the Greek Anthology, and trying to decipher *The Lusiads* without a dictionary; Cummings was making his endless jottings.

The night we made our first landfall in the Azores one of the deckhands was sent in to wake us.

"*Lua cheia esta noite,*" the man said in a tone we found irresistibly poetic.

Indeed, in our wake an enormous moon was settling toward the horizon through driving scud silvery as milkweed silk. The sailor hurried us up to the bow and pointed into the first glow of dawn in the east. The lean pyramid behind a blur of cloud was the island of Pico. In a gust of landbreeze came a smell tangy like nasturtium flowers. The high volcanic cone kept thrusting up into the sky as the east flushed into rose and amber. After that "lua cheia" was the watchword when we saw any particularly breathtaking sight on that trip.

By sunup we were drifting under one bell into the harbor of Fayal. The air smelt of lemon blossoms. The town, with its pink, orange, burnt siena and flat white houses, hung like a piece of stage scenery against the spinach-green hills.

Ashore the streets were full of women in huge stiff black hoods that stuck out so far in front their faces were hidden. The men wore cloaks with many little capes. Everybody was very quiet. A tiny bright rain was falling. We had forgotten it was Good Friday. We peeked into the church set in the middle of the great square that was so like a stage. In the pulpit a blackrobed monk was lecturing with baroque gestures on the *Sete Palavres.*

It seemed a most hospitable town. Everywhere we went men took off their hats to us. We were led about by a delegation of small boys. Good Friday or not, being youthful male strangers we were immediately conducted to the local whorehouse. We explained that this early in the morning we were more interested in tasting the *vinho de cheirão*. As we turned away a portly gentleman in a cloak emerged from the door. He was twirling an unusually luxuriant mustache. A lackey was holding his horse. Before he rode away a girl ran out and handed him up a goblet of wine as a stirrup cup. For some reason the little scene pleased us.

After Fayal all four bunks in our cabin were taken. A gentleman we called the Baron delighted Cummings by producing a little alcohol burner to heat his mustache curler. He was a very pleasant man. He knew native lovesongs from Angola, corrected my pronunciation of Camoëns and, before we parted, inscribed a long poem in my notebook.

At Terceira we anchored out from the mole in a port called Angra do Heroismo. Masses of black steers were swum out to the ship. A rope was fastened round their horns and they were hoisted one by one to the afterdeck. The loading went on long after sunset. In the moonlight the great cattle hanging helplessly by their horns as they swung aboard looked like beasts of the apocalypse.

There were layovers at Ponte Delgada and in Funchal on my ancestral Madeira. The crossing took three weeks. By the time we reached Lisbon we were so at home with the ship's company that it was a wrench to leave the smelly unsteady old *Mormugão*. I couldn't interest Cummings in Lisbon. A New Englander to the core he was repelled by the rankness of the Manueline style. When I tried to rub his nose in the great panels of Nuno Goncalves' São Vicente he said he'd rather look at Rembrandt. At Coimbra some ancestral phobia against popery came to the surface. The students all looked to him like plainclothes Jesuits.

In Oporto instead of investigating the wines we spent our days trying to find a reliable dentist. Cummings had developed an ulcerated tooth. That disrupted my plans for walking him through Estramadura. Poultices cured the ulceration but he didn't feel himself again until we climbed off the train at the Gare d'Orléans in La Ville Lumière.

❧❧❧

That May and June I must have spent several weeks in Paris, though I haven't the slightest recollection of what I did there. Cummings received an advance copy of *The Enormous Room,* and was taken with the horrors most writers suffer at the sight of a freshpublished book. It's always the errors and misprints you see first. He delivered himself of a manifesto which he turned over to me for transmission to Boni and Liveright.

TO WHOM IT MAY CONCERN, it is captioned, and dated *14 mai 1921.*

> I desire that one of two things happen to "The Enormous Room": either
>
> A) it be immediately suppressed, thrown in a shitoir
> B) each and all of the below noted errors be *immediately and completely* rectified without loss of time, fear of money or any-thing-damned-else . . .

There followed a list of omissions, misprints and mistranslations.

> . . . Translation of the French phrases is, at least half the time, very confusing to the reader—it being very important that he should understand that a certain character is *speaking French* and *not English.* I had translated myself as much as was good for the context, and in the MS THERE IS NONE OF THIS NEEDLESS AMBIGUITY. In addition, the translation is . . . but I refrain.
>
> P.S. AS IT STANDS the book is not merely an eye-sore but an insult.
>
> E.E. Cummings

I blush to think that through my neglect this javelin never found its target. Perhaps another version reached the publishers. This one turned up only recently in a batch of old papers in the attic. Certainly I yielded to none in admiration for the book or affection for the author. Sometime that summer I gave due testimony in a review of *The Enormous Room* I wrote for the *Dial.* To this day I believe the book contains some of the best English writing of our time.

❦❦❦

My preoccupation was finding ways and means of getting out to the Near East. It was the only region still highly colored enough to suit my craving for new sights. Before leaving New York I had worked up some commitments for articles with the Sunday editor of the *Tribune* and with the *Metropolitan Magazine.* Now I found Paxton Hibben immensely helpful. We must have met in New York during the preceding winter. He turned up in Paris as secretary of a Near East Relief mission.

Pax was about forty then. Raised in Indianapolis, he had played politics as a Progressive in his youth. He was a schoolmate of Claude Bowers' and a devoted adherent of Senator Beveridge's. He'd spent years in the diplomatic service, worked as a war correspondent, and served as an artillery captain in France during the war. His funniest stories were about his friendship with King Constantine of Greece and how that agreeable monarch smoked two cigarettes at one time to calm his nerves while the British, to make sure that the Greeks should choose the right side in the war for democracy, were bombarding Athens. Everywhere Pax went his career was legendary: astronomic gambling in Mexico City, a duel in Athens, a liaison with a Grand Duke's mistress in St. Petersburg. His stories were wonderful.

Pax promised that if I could convey myself to Constantinople and find him there care the American Red Cross he would try to get me into the N.E.R. What could be simpler? A ticket to Constantinople. The Orient Express.

Ever since as a four-year-old I was taken aboard a sample train of the Transsiberian at the Paris Exposition of 1900 I had dreamed of the great European expresses. I immediately started planning a spy story where the message would be transmitted in a plate of alphabet soup, but I forgot about it when I stopped off in Venice to meet Dudley Poore and the Great Awk. I made a point of looking at all the Carpaccios. The rest of the time we spent bathing with the varicolored throng on the Lido Beach.

For two days on the train east across the Balkans I argued about religion with an Armenian who supplemented his faulty French with excellent Latin.

❧❧❧

I walked into the lobby of the Pera Palace Hotel just in time to see the pool of blood in an overstuffed chair where somebody had assassinated a Levantine diplomat. "Constant" was fantastic that summer. The streets of Pera were packed with White Russian refugees, starving, homeless, desperate except for those few who still had family jewelry to sell and lived high while they could at excellent restaurants kept by their less fortunate compatriots around the Garden of Taxim. Pax, who knew considerable Russian, introduced me to cold cucumber soup there and to Khakhetian wine and to lovely girls whose stories of massacres and miseries he translated for my benefit.

The city was run by all the Allies in conjunction. British, French and Italians vied with each other in military stupidity. The Turks had given up: what little organization there was was in the hands of the local Greeks. If you stepped outside the walls you would be robbed and stripped by the Bashi-Bazouks.

The night one of the Sultan's palaces burned, through the carelessness of the occupying troops, I was out at the old resort hotel at Therapia. A British major was shaking up Alexanders behind the bar. After a winey dinner a British ensign, a hearty English girl and I decided we could see the fire better from out on the Bosphorus. We commandeered a skiff. It was a balmy night. The great flaming building that nobody seemed to be taking the trouble to put out was a breathtaking sight.

We got hot rowing, and decided we needed a swim, so we all plunged in in our underclothes. The water was frigid. The current immediately swept away our skiff. We almost missed catching up with it. Three scared and shivery young people climbed back up onto the dock. Now we knew what Shakespeare meant about the 'icy current and compulsive course.'

A grubby little war was going in Asia Minor. Our Admiral Bristol was trying to make what sense he could of a senseless business. I remember relinquishing my prejudice against brass hats enough to think highly of Admiral Bristol. He felt that if the news could only be published in the American newspapers somebody might try to do something to stop it. I managed to get aboard a destroyer he sent off with a batch of correspondents to interview the refugees.

One port on the Sea of Marmora was crowded to the waterline with desperate Greeks, men, women and children, whose villages had been burned by the Turks. Another was stuffed with Turks in the same plight, only it was the Greeks who had done the raping and maiming and murdering. They all begged to be taken aboard. At any moment they expected the enemy to march in and finish the massacre. The irony was that the Greeks and Turks and their pathetic women and crying children all looked so much alike it would have taken a linguistics expert to tell them apart.

The skipper didn't have the orders and there wasn't any room anyway on a World War I destroyer, so we had to leave them to their fate. We sat with pale faces in the wardroom while the narrow ship lurched through the cross seas at twentyfive knots on the way back to Constant. It was not only the pitching and tossing that had turned our stomachs.

When Pax and his relief group were ready to leave on an Italian steamer *Aventino* for Batum, he wasn't able to convince the N.E.R. management at Roberts College that they should include me in the party, but he did manage to smuggle me aboard at the last moment.

In those days Americans had to leave their passports at the last embassy before entering Soviet territory to keep them from falling in the hands of the Bolsheviki who stole them for their secret agents. With Pax's help I had procured from the representatives of the Transcaucasian Republic a marvelous document written in round Georgian script. The trouble was that before we got ready to sail the Reds had overthrown the Transcaucasian Republic.

When we reached Batum the authorities wouldn't let me land. After I had been biting my nails on the *Aventino* for two days, a young Red army officer appeared who thought it was a great joke to write me out a Red Russian *propuss* on the back of my Social Democratic passport. Americans, almost any American's, were popular in those days, and Pax had probably explained that I was an *amerikanski peesatyel* favorable to their cause.

Batum was full of Red Army troops. There was nothing to eat, but the swimming was marvelous off the pebbly beach. Bathing suits were unheard of. Men and women formed separate naked groups. Being a creature of habit I had to get into my bathing trunks. They looked oddly indecent among the modest naked throng.

The houses I saw were all stripped bare. All furnishings had vanished. I made a great deal out of the theory that the revolution had freed mankind from the tyranny of things. Privately I had long since vowed to keep myself free from possessions. It took me years to learn that when a man lost his property he lost his freedom too.

We were eaten alive by bedbugs in the sleeper on the night train up to Tiflis, but I found the conversation, carried on with whatever *tovarishí* knew a few words of French or Italian or German, enthralling. They were still in the first enthusiasm of the communist experiment. They were making a clean break. Society must be cooperative like a hive of bees, *comme les abeilles, die biene.* Everybody talked about bees. They were laying the foundations: food and schools, peace and freedom for all, except for the damn *burzoi* that were causing them so much trouble. In the summer of 1921 it would have been hard to find a war veteran who wouldn't have endorsed that program.

In Tiflis the relievers had to let me pitch my folding cot in their quarters. There was nowhere else to go. Famine. Terror. About twenty people a day were dying of cholera and twice that many of typhus. Pax seemed to have charge of relations with the *bolsheviki.* When he was invited to dine with the high command he took me along.

The table was laid out on a flat roof with a magnificent view of the snowtipped mountains. These were serious dedicated young men in white canvas tunics. Several spoke French and one man excellent English.

I couldn't help feeling a qualm at what good food we ate—vodka for toasts and the best Georgian vintages, while soldiers were literally—I'd seen them—fainting in the streets from hunger.

At least the soldiers had boots. Most of the civilians went barefoot.

Then there were the ragged groups of "counter-revolutionaries" driven at bayonetpoint into back alleys. They didn't look any guiltier than anybody else to me. War after all, is war, said Pax. I couldn't gainsay him.

After dinner Pax played a trick on me. We had trooped, a little fuzzy from the vodka and wine, down stairways and through corridors of the huge bleak building under the roof garden. I was seated in a row of chairs in a large room. Before I could say Jack Robinson what I'd thought of as a canvas wall rose, disclosing a theater packed with men and women in white tunics.

Speeches, cheers, shouting. Pax made a short talk in French about the aims of the Near East Relief which I'm sure nobody understood and then introduced me as an *amerikanski poait*. Being nothing of a public speaker I couldn't think of what the hell to say until I remembered William Blake's 'Ah sunflower weary of time.'

It was one of the few poems I still could recite. It was that or nothing. The audience must have thought it was an *amerikanski* ode to the revolution because their applause raised the roof. Pax almost turned purple trying to keep from laughing.

Since the N.E.R. wouldn't give me anything to do and I couldn't bear to sit around taking notes on all that misery I had to push on.

Somehow I had made the acquaintance of a Persian doctor. *Sayid* Hassan Tabataba was on his way home from a German medical school. He had a *passeport diplomatique* but was low in funds, and anyway there weren't any passenger trains running south to the Persian border. What little money I had was tucked away in my belt in gold Turkish pounds, but I had changed one in Batum and was such a millionaire in paper rubles it took a whole suitcase to carry them. With the help of our friends from the roof-garden dinner, Pax procured a document which entitled us to passage on a freight train running through Armenia to Nakhichevan.

We were given a freightcar to ourselves. It was the propaganda car but, as it carried nothing but a few bundles of *Pravda* and *Isvestia,* we had plenty of room to set up our folding cots.

Nobody knew how long the trip would take. With a lavish use of my rubles we managed to buy a few loaves of black rye bread which turned out to be full of gravel, and a slab of smoked caviar. Khaketian wine was abundant. The N.E.R. furnished some sardines and a can of alcohol to use in our little stove. At a station down in Armenia we bought six watermelons. Before the train left some Russians I'd become friendly with appeared with a large wooden chest which they begged me to deliver to relatives in Tabriz.

In my notes I labeled the trip One Hundred Views of Ararat, because we were rarely out of sight of the great snow peak. War had ground the country down to cinders. The soldiers on the armored trains we passed had a hungry feverish air. Famine everywhere. Where starving people weren't dying of typhus they were dying of cholera. The flatcars and boxcars that made up our train were packed with refugees, escaping from what? Where bound? Nobody seemed to know. In one station corpses were stacked like cordwood behind the stove. When a woman died in the car behind us her body was left on a red and yellow striped mat beside the tracks.

About once a day squads of the Cheka police would raid the cars looking for counter-revolutionaries. I cursed myself for taking on that damned chest. It was locked. I had no way of knowing whether it was full of the family silver or of compromising documents. All I could do was sit on it and look forbidding. Nobody ever bothered it. They probably thought it contained some particularly valuable Moscow propaganda.

A touching memory has remained of Erivan. The stationmaster said we'd be there at least three hours, so leaving the sayid and the Armenian, looking like a cartoon of the terrible Turk who distributed the newspapers in our propaganda car, to fend off intruders, I set out to see the town.

The streets were empty, stores and windows boarded up. What inhabitants were left were huddled in their houses for fear of the Cheka and the typhus.

As I passed a rather decentlooking house a youngish woman

came out. She was yellowpale with haunted brown eyes. Wasn't I an American? she asked in excellent English.

"Yes indeed," I said.

She smiled wanly.

No, she'd never been, but she had family there. She invited me in and made me sit on a divan in a small parlor that looked like an oldfashioned Turkish corner back home. Five pallid children straggled into the room and looked at me with wide astonished eyes. She said something that sounded like American. They all bowed ceremoniously.

Wasn't I hungry? she asked.

Of course I was hungry. Everybody was.

"I have an egg."

I got to stammering. I was trying to explain that I hadn't really meant I was hungry. I was on the train going through to Persia. There was plenty to eat in Persia and besides we still had several watermelons. I got to my feet. I had to hurry for fear the train might leave without me.

She insisted.

Before I could stop her she had bustled out. In a few minutes she brought me a single warm hardboiled egg in a pretty little blue enamel eggcup. There was a clean napkin but nothing else on the tray. She peeled the egg neatly for me with thin yellow fingers. I had to eat it for fear she'd force it into my mouth.

All the while the children stared at me with round reverential eyes as if they were seeing the priest eat the wafer at mass.

"Without America we would die," she said and evidently said the same thing in Armenian to the children. When I had swallowed the last of the egg I scrambled shamefacedly to my feet. I was near crying as I walked back to the railroad station.

We were four and a half days in that boxcar. Then, in a particularly wartrodden village on the banks of a swift river, the engineer came walking back and said he was ready to take us to Persia. He and the fireman helped us carry our cots and our duffle and the fat portmanteau known as the hippo that I traveled with, and the accursed chest, up to the cab of his engine. Explaining that rolling stock was not allowed to cross the border they unhitched the coal-car and steamed, after a couple of whistles, across the iron bridge that led from Djulfa in the Soviet Republic of Adjerbaidjan to Djulfa in the Kingdom of Persia.

The river was the Araxes.

We dropped off beside a neat undamaged station. There was a small flowerbed in front of it.

"*Avec quelle difficulté,*" whispered the sayid in my ear. That had been his favorite phrase throughout the trip. I was busy distributing my packs of rubles between the fireman and the engineer. We parted almost tearfully. Then hissing steam the engine backed across the bridge again.

The sayid seemed to grow two inches in height. He was a *hakim,* a great man in his own country. Bowing custom officials in black cylindrical caps ushered us into a clean room with a tiled floor. They examined his passeport diplomatique and my dog-eared propuss with reverential care. We were brought water in brass ewers to wash with and left squatting peacefully on a clean rug that had the effigy of some shah woven into it.

A barefoot bearded servant brought slices of watermelon. He looked like a figure on an Assyrian relief. He came in silence and left in silence. When we had eaten that lunch appeared. Mutton cooked with cucumbers and tomatoes and clabbered milk, accompanied by flat unleavened bread like the bread Cummings and I used to eat at the Syrian restaurant. After that came oversweet glasses of tea, five different varieties of grapes and more melons, the best melons I ever ate.

The quiet was a healing balm. A kitten and a very small pigeon kept walking around the edge of a cistern in the hot sun of the courtyard. Neither seemed to trouble the other. When we had eaten our fill water was again brought for our hands, and we dozed off on our mats for a siesta.

The quiet. The feeling of safety. The unregenerate old Persian world may not have been as good copy as the world full of news: revolution and starvation and battle, stinking corpses and the fear of typhus and of firing squads, but it was unimaginably pleasanter.

Next day we took the train to Tabriz. Leaving me at the seedy hotel, the sayid went to the bazaar with several of my gold pounds and returned with great bags of silver krans of all sizes and shapes. Some of them had been made into buttons or cufflinks. He came riding in a dilapidated vehicle drawn by four illfavored white horses which he described as phaeton. Proudly he announced that he had hired it to take us to Teheran.

Little bells jingled continually from the harness. The driver was a grimy character in a fuzzy white wool hat named Karim. Karim had a distressing cast in one eye. His assistant was an obscene broadfaced imp named Ma'amat, who traveled caked in dust with a bag of oats in a sort of sling back of the carriage. They looked like a pair of cutthroats but they turned out to be quite decent fellows.

Before we could leave we had to waste hours looking for the Russian family I was to deliver the chest to. All they gave me for thanks was a suspicious stare; they looked at me as if they expected to find a bomb inside. I never did discover what was in that damn chest.

Thirteen jingling days in the phaeton to Teheran. Persia was more outlandish than I had imagined. The road hadn't been repaired since it was paved with stone by the Shah Abbas in the seventeenth century. The mudwalled gardens with tinkling streams winding among the fruit trees were out of Hafiz or Omar. Men dyed their beards blue or red with henna. They wore bulbous felt hats or gigantic turbans. Their raiment was out of miniature paintings. One lovely morning we met a group of horsemen going a-hunting with hawks on their wrists.

The ride was idyllic except for the noonday heat and the dust and the mosquitoes at night. The sayid said they were malarial. From Tabriz on he dosed himself with quinine. He wanted occasionally to take my temperature but I told him I was too mean to catch malaria. At every *caravanserai* we were regaled with stories of a tribe of brigands known as the Shahsivan. Their swords were so sharp that only yesterday one of them had sliced a traveler through from the shoulder to the navel.

After the things we had been through we could snap our fingers at the Shahsivan. We were now admitting to each other that we'd been scared pissless every moment since we left Tiflis. The sayid who'd been morose and silent on the boxcar expanded into a genial traveling companion.

He even proved to be a good cook. After jingling and joggling all day over roads that were a series of washedout gulleys or dry streambeds or occasionally bottomless sloughs, we would arrive at a *khan* or caravanserai, choose the least filthy room, unroll our rugs and set up our cots. A charcoal brazier would be brought in and cruzes of water. Karim would spread the word of the sayid's medical skills and the maimed and the halt and the blind would crowd around for treatment. The sayid had some medicines and several kits of surgical instruments but he was very short on ether. I occasionally had to act as his assistant. Once I sat on a patient's head while the sayid cut what he called a cold ulcer out of his back.

Payment was in kind: eggs, chickens, small bags of rice, melons. While the sayid fanned the charcoal Karim would kill and pluck the fowl. The sayid's chicken casserole with rice cooked in the chicken fat and bitter oranges was a firstrate dish.

After we had eaten, as the light failed on the dry hills, and camels groaned and horses and mules champed in their stalls, the sayid would move from campfire to campfire in the courtyard, or from brazier to brazier in the rooms built into the protecting mud wall where the more pecunious travelers lodged, discussing what he called *la politique*. Though I couldn't understand what he said, I gathered that he was quite an orator. He was an Iranian nationalist. He preached schools and *fabriques*. Thus would Persia again become a great nation. Pan Islam: Mohammedans from Istanbul to Kitai must unite against the Communists to the north and the Ingliz to the south. He would come back flushed and with a glint in his eyes to translate what he had been saying for my benefit.

Americans must understand, he kept telling me, they must learn to understand Asia. He admired Americans. It was an American missionary who had induced his father to send him abroad to study. The little people of Asia were now ready to enter the civilized world. For help he trusted to American money and German science.

Middays the sun was brutal. The phaeton leapt like a flea from crag to crag following the windings of Shah Abbas's road over an endless succession of eroded purple mountains. The top wouldn't stay up. Our noses burned to the color and shape of goodsized beets. Every few miles we had to stop while Karim and Ma'amat patched broken parts of the phaeton with scraps of old rope. We kept expecting it would fall to pieces like the one-horse shay, but it never quite did.

The towns were dilapidated. It was the philosophical dilapidation of centuries, not yesterday's ruin that had so shocked us in Soviet territory. There was a place called Mianeh, famous in medical history for its white bedbugs that carried a particularly intractable local fever. It was in Mianeh that, above the droning of mosquitoes, we first heard drums beating and frantic voices chanting "Hassan, Hosein."

This was the first day of Moharram, the month dedicated to Hassan and Hosein, the grandsons of the prophet, who were done to death by the evil men of Kufa. These were the first *imams,* the expiatory martyrs of the Shiite sect of Islam. To weep for their suffering, to suffer as they had suffered, meant forgiveness of every sin. Every night from Mianeh on I fell asleep to the drumbeat and the chanting voices.

In Zenjan the people had lashed themselves into such a state that they refused to feed us in the cookshop in the bazaar. The sayid was wearing a European felt hat so they wouldn't believe he was a moslem. We had to send Ma'amat to fetch our food to the khan and when he took back the pottery vessels they broke them on the ground so that no believer should be defiled by eating after *kaffirs.*

In Kasvin we stayed with the sayid's brother, who was some sort of public official and looked very much like him. He gave us a royal welcome and in spite of the fact that Persians don't usually drink in Moharram brought out a pitcher of heavy mahogany-colored wine.

The rooms were large. The only ornaments were the tiles on the walls and the handsome rugs. No woman showed her face. Though servants silently brought in the big brass trays of food it was the sayid's little nephews who actually waited on us.

There was a marvelous quiet about everything. After supper the little boys took me up to my room, laid out my bedding on the floor for me and retired with a series of solemn little obeisances.

It was a night of ferocious moonlight. I was too excited to sleep. I climbed out of the tiny window onto the roof and tried to find some way of getting down to the street. I didn't dare go through the house for fear of straying into the women's apartments. No way. I crawled back in and lay down wishing, for the first time in that trip, that I was back at the corner of Broadway and 42nd Street. I went to sleep listening to the awesome distant chanting. "Hassan, Hosein . . . Hassan, Hosein."

We were escorted out of Kasvin by some officers of the gendarmerie on beautifully groomed horses. Their riders made them prance and curvet as they wished us a pleasant journey. The sayid explained that they showed such dash because their leader Riza Khan had become the most powerful man in Persia. Wherever Riza Khan's power extended travel was safe on the roads.

After the gendarmes had left us he confided in me that he could never marry in the Persian style as his brother had. Persian women were so undeveloped. After knowing the mademoiselles of Europe it would seem like marrying an animal. To the sayid European ladies were aways mademoiselles. There was the daughter of a German colonel who was studying medicine; he hoped she would marry him when he had set up his practice.

The sayid had managed to cure his chills and fevers before we reached Teheran. I paid off Karim and they left me at the Hôtel de France. I had hardly begun to enjoy its quasi-European luxuries—at least there was a bath and sheets on the beds—before the malaria hit me with a bang. The sayid came around like a good fellow to dose me daily with some decoction of quinine *intra venos*. The medical terms rolled with what unction off his tongue! His treatment helped, but my recollections of Teheran are laced with chills and fevers and the nightmare chantings of Moharram.

Added to the fever was lack of funds. I was down to my last gold pound. The bill kept mounting at the hotel. The clerk at the desk began to give me sharp looks and I hurried through the lobby. Between bouts of fever I would go tottering around to the cable office in hope of remittances from America. I had been sending off articles from every post office. Albert Nock whom I knew was a man of his word; he had promised to print my stories in the *Freeman.* Then there were firm commitments from the *Tribune* and the *Metropolitan Magazine.* I learned later that the *Metropolitan* had failed, with a thud. When nothing turned up I had to use my last few krans to cable for two hundred dollars from my longsuffering aunt in New York. A man has to have been broke in a foreign country to understand the sublime pleasure he'll take even in the wording of the cable that reports funds in the bank.

By the tenth of Moharram I was well enough to attend the procession that commemorates the death of Hosein at the hands of the hostiles at Kerbela. Through some pleasant people at our legation I was invited to join the *corps diplomatique.* Chairs had been set out on a flat roof overlooking a square in the bazaar. The European ladies were all dressed up; the men wore Palm Beach suits, Panama hats and boaters. Chatter and chitchat. It looked and sounded like an official garden party in England. We were guarded by a contingent of Riza Khan's gendarmes.

Frantic crowds poured out from the covered ways of the bazaar to converge on the great square. Officers of the gendarmerie led the way, tall weatherbeaten men in astrakhan caps. Their heads were bowed. They walked very slowy. Grooms led their horses behind them. Tears ran down leathery cheeks. There followed standards green and orange and shining brass, the hand of Fatima, the crescent with the mare's tail, then penitents in black beating their breasts. Behind them came a strangely hideous device carried by four men on their bare backs. It was like some enormous candelabrum only steel blades sprouted from it in all directions, each weighed down at the tip by a spiked brass ornament. Then came men stripped to loincloths with skewers and daggers stuck into their flesh, men spitted with lances and arrows to stand for the arrows that killed Hosein's two sons when they ran to the river for water at Kerbela. Their blood seemed to steam in the searing morning sun. After them stumbled two long lines of men and boys in shrouds belted with chains at the waist. They executed a sort of slow snakedance as they crossed the square.

Each man with his left hand held on to the belt of the man ahead, beating himself on his bare shaven head with the flat of a sword held in his right. The lines moved slowly, groaning, beating in time. Blood ran down faces and necks and clotted with the dust on the white shrouds.

It made me ashamed to be looking at this sight as if through a keyhole. I slipped out of my folding chair. The diplomats were staring with such cold fascination down into the square they didn't notice me leave. After a mere two weeks among these people I felt close enough to them to resent staring at their strange penance as if it were a wild animal act at the circus. Resentment comes cheap when you are twentyfive.

I had been told it would be dangerous for anyone in European clothes to be seen on the streets that day. If stares could have killed I would have been dead before I reached the Hôtel de France, though no man made a move. Painting water colors is a soothing entertainment. As soon as I could get my breath I settled down to daubing a set of views of Teheran.

My problem now was how to get home before my money ran out entirely. No more hope of seeing Khorasan or Isfahan or Shiraz. There was a Russian engineer, a thin blond fidgety man, with a pretty Polish wife who sat by my bed with a thermometer during the fever times. He knew about my desperate visits to the cable office, but any American to him was a millionaire just the same. He was offering me a marvelous speculation. He claimed to own a Ford car. We'd get a pass from Riza Khan, who was then mopping up the remnants of the collapsed Republic of Ghilan. We would drive down to Recht on the Caspian Sea. There we would use my dollars from America to buy caviar. We would drive the caviar to Baghdad and sell it to the British at a vast profit. With the proceeds of my share I could buy myself a first-class passage home from Basra.

I might have been fool enough to take him up if it hadn't been for the fever. Anyway it turned out that the Russian didn't own the Ford at all. He made this confession in Dostoevskian form the day half the roof blew off the hotel.

E

Fall in Teheran is windy. Every few days vast wind and dust storms, a little like what Mark Twain used to describe as Kansas spring breezes, lashed the city. This morning I'd been sleeping off my last feverish fit when I was wakened by the rattling of a thousand dishpans. Sand and dust drove into the room from all directions and suddenly the Russian engineer appeared with his wife passed out in his arms. She came to and began to jibber in Russian when he laid her tenderly beside me on the bed.

The ceiling of his room had blown off.

He further blurted out in a flood of bad French that he hadn't been able to buy the Ford. The fellow had refused his note and he didn't have a sou to pay his hotel bill and the hotel was a wreck anyway, and what would we all do? *C'est la fin, absolument, c'est la fin.*

When I got into my clothes I found that one end of the flat tin roof had curled up off the rattletrap building like the top off a tin of sardines. That marked the end of my stay in Teheran. By the grace of God a draft for forty pounds had appeared at the cable office the day before. I was already dickering with an Armenian, a young man in a handmedown British uniform, who actually possessed a model T Ford and who spoke missionary American, to take me to the Iraqi border. So I bade an abrupt farewell to the sayid and to the Russian engineer and his pretty wife.

As soon as we hit the road I forgot about the malaria: travel always did agree with me.

The road followed the trail of the ancient conquerors through Hamadan and Kermanshaw. During the recent war Russian and Turkish armies had fought over it. The British expedition to Baku had advanced over it, rebuilding the road as they went: that was why it was passable. Every village had been burned and half the caravanserais were in ruin. The Armenian and I, for all our bags of silver krans, had trouble getting ourselves one skimpy meal a day.

At Kermanshaw we stayed with the American missionaries. Their compound was full of Lours: lanky men in bulbous brown felt hats. The Lours laughed a great deal. They had fine teeth, a hearty selfsufficient look. They were said to be the descendants of the ancient Medes. I wished there were some way I could find out more about them, but my bag of krans was getting light. Must push on to Baghdad.

After the mountains of Luristan the road began to descend by a series of gigantic steps. We passed Bisitún, the mountain shaped like a hut with a broken ridgepole. On one of its soaring rock faces the great Darius had carved his bragging inscription: *I Darius King of Kings*. All too soon, because I hated to leave so much of Persia unexplored, the hills dropped away and we were looking out over a streaky blue plain.

"The Messpot," said the Armenian. He left me at a place called Kasr Shirin in charge of some Persian gendarmes who promised to deliver me to the railhead.

There seemed to be no road any more. The gendarmes placed me in an extraordinary vehicle that reminded me of the oxdrawn beds of the Merovingian kings, only this was drawn by two mules tandem. It was shaped like a springwagon, only it had no springs. It had a top like an oldfashioned surrey, and was screened with pink curtains. The woodwork was painted with pink and blue and purple flowers. In this we jounced for hours through the saffron and vermilion gulches of a succession of badlands. The gendarme officer and I lay back to back on a thin mattress with our chins resting in the palms of our hands while his riflemen walked beside the mules. I never had a more uncomfortable ride.

At last I was deposited behind coiling strands of barbed wire in a yellow clapboard railroad station that had a peculiarly western dismalness about it. The Babu stationmaster was outraged. My papers weren't in order. He wouldn't accept Persian money for my ticket. I didn't even have the right time. I must go right back where I came from. Unfortunately the Persian gendarmes and their romantic vehicle had long since disappeared behind a cloud of dust.

When an engine and three mustard-colored coaches shuttered against the sun backed into the station I made my way through a flutter of Babus clucking like barnyard hens and set my heavy hippo in the only first-class compartment. Then I went back for my folding cot and musette and striped Tabriz blanket. Brown

hands yanked at me feebly but they didn't quite dare use force.
The afternoon advanced. The sun set in sweltering heat. Muffled in my blanket against the buzzing flies I fell asleep.

I was awakened by a pleasant Englishman offering me a drink of scotch. The train was rumbling slowly through the night. He had ridden down from some oil boring in the region of Mosul. We sat drinking in the dim light. He said all the men who worked for him were Yezedis, devil worshipers. It was a cult that centered around a place named Sheikh Aadi. He didn't know whether this was a village or a tomb. Nobody would tell him where it was. The Yezedis were supposed to be the dregs of some ancient Manichaean sect. They had a sacred book but they were forbidden to read and write. They dropped all *sh* sounds out of their language. The name of Sheitan was sacred. They were accused of promiscuous lovefeasts on certain nights like those the Romans ascribed to the early Christians. They did the lowest possible kind of work, roadmenders and scavengers. The better off had truck gardens. They were supposed to believe in the Gnostic sevenfold emanation of God, but they worshiped the devil in the form of a golden peacock as lord of this world.

We ran out of whiskey and of information about comparative religion at about the same time. Nothing to it but to doze off again. When I woke up the Englishman had gone. I was left marveling like Hamlet at the things there were in heaven and earth.

Next morning after cruising for far too many breakfastless hours over desert of a smooth battleship gray, the train came to a stop in a mess of freightyards and British army cantonments that proved to be Baghdad. Sepoys. Tommies marching in columns of fours. The Hotel Maude of which I'd formed high hopes turned out to be the British junior officers' mess. I was led into a small unfurnished room and told I could put up my cot there.

The food was, even in my hungry state, uneatable. The only alleviation was a shack in the garden on the bank of the yellow Tigris, lettered *American Bar,* where they served Munich export beer.

The Britishers I talked to had been in Baghdad for months and years. They had reached the screaming stage of boredom. Their amusement was drinking beer in the mess hall after supper, singing bawdy songs and throwing beerbottles at the rats.

The rats had taken over the Hotel Maude. I had barely set to work to seek out ways and means of continuing my trip toward the west when I came down with a fresh bout of malaria. I had gotten hold of sheets somewhere for my cot. It was by climbing up a corner of the sheet that a rat climbed up on my chest. When I tried to bat him off he had the impudence to bite me on the lip.

After that I was very careful about tucking the sheet in under me when I turned in. I slept with the little dagger Sayid Hassan gave me as a keepsake when I left Teheran under my pillow. Some boys from British Intelligence broke into my room one night to ask for my papers. In those days intelligence services always broke in on you in the middle of the night. When they flashed a light in my face they found me dripping with fever and thrashing about with my dagger at imaginary rats.

The British were dead set to keep American prospectors for oil out of the Messpot. When they discovered that I wasn't an oil man they became quite friendly. When they examined my Transcaucasian passport they burst out laughing. After that they really were a help. They gave me the name of the British army doctor who was their malaria expert. He knew his business. After a three weeks' treatment of massive doses of quinine, carefully spaced, he cured my malaria so perfectly that it never bothered me again.

The American consul turned out to be an excellent fellow. When I decided, since the cost of a steamship ticket from Basra to Marseilles proved out of sight, it would be more fun to cross the desert to Damascus than to beg a ride in a British army plane, he wired Constant to send my passport to meet me in Beirut and issued me some sort of provisional screed. The most helpful thing he did was to find someone to introduce me to Gertrude Bell.

Gertrude Bell was chief of British Intelligence for the whole Messpot. I already knew her translations of the Persian poets, but I was hardly prepared for what I found.

She invited me to tea. I found her sitting at a thoroughly English little teatable placed under a dusty palm in the date garden that surrounded her villa. There were no other women. The tea-drinkers were young men in uniform, from her staff mostly. The minute I saw her I decided that Queen Elizabeth must have been just like that. She was a smallish plain horse-faced Englishwoman —as I remember her hair was reddish to gray—but there was something very like majesty about her.

She was incredibly learned in the languages of the middle Orient. She knew all the dialects. She had the tribal histories and the family histories of the Bedawi at the tip of her tongue. I could appreciate the stories I'd been told of her arriving in her plane at the encampments of rebellious Arabs and giving them such a tonguelashing in their own dialect that they would fold up their tents and flee.

Baghdad was ruled in those days by a British general, Sir Percy Zachariah Cox who was High Commissioner. He was known to the Arabs as Cokus. All Cokus's information about Arab politics was said to come from Miss Bell. Cokus had a way of inviting local bigwigs whom he considered unruly to tea with him. Before they knew what had happened they would find themselves under gentle restraint on a P&O steamer headed for Ceylon.

People tended to sit on the edge of their chairs when they drank tea with Miss Bell under the rustling palms of her date garden. She must have been told the story of the dagger and the rats because she kept laughing privately to herself while she talked to me. Like most people who know their business she was easy to talk to.

She couldn't have been more helpful. When someone suggested that it was dangerous for any European to try to cross the desert to Damascus right at this moment she said "Fiddlesticks." She went on, as if referring to some rare type of wallaby, "They won't hurt an American." She knew people who would take me. "They aren't all quite on our side," she said, "but they are quite reliable."

The British had an Arab revolt on their hands. The tribesmen claimed they had been cheated. Lawrence had promised them Damascus in return for their help against the Turks, but by the peace treaty Damascus had been awarded to the French. The story going around the campfires was that Lawrence had gone to King George and broken his sword over his knee before resigning his commission in disgust. The British had set up handsome young Feisal of the ruling family of the Hedjaz as King of Iraq but Baghdad was no substitute for Damascus. To complicate matters war had broken out between the Ibn Saud and the Ibn Raschid factions in southern Arabia.

Miss Bell described the situation with some relish, as if it were an unusually intricate chess game, before turning me over to a skinny young captain who obviously spoke good Arabic, to act as guide and interpreter and to take me to see the heads of the various factions. "Tell them they can speak quite frankly," she said. "What they publish in America won't make the slightest difference."

Dawn was the time for formal calls in Baghdad as it was in ancient Rome. I was still shaking a little from a malarial chill the morning I followed Miss Bell's young man through a maze of pitchblack streets into a courtyard where a robed sentry answered our *salam aleikham* with a reassuring "And unto you peace." A steep stairway led up to a dark gallery where I was introduced to a whitebearded personage at the far end of the carpet and to a dim row of whiskered figures squatting along the wall.

Miss Bell's young man and I squatted against the mud wall. Through the arches opposite we watched a faint streak in the east become a yellow glow while we sipped the three traditional tiny cups of coffee.

It became possible to distinguish faces and the flash of eyes under the headcloths. New visitors came in always with the same low greetings. When the muezzin called from a nearby mosque many of them went out on the flat roof to perform their devotions.

There was little conversation besides the continual greetings and the invocation of the name of Allah. When the walls began to glow with rosy light that poured through the arches there were only four of us left sitting on the edges of the red, blue and yellow patterned carpet: the whitebearded dignitary in a silver embroidered gown on a little dais at the end, a pale darkbearded man with a higharched nose and a high forehead under his heavy headband who squatted opposite, and Miss Bell's young man and I. Streaks of kohl along the eyelashes gave a special intensity to the dark man's glance.

His name, if I caught it correctly, was Jassem-er-Rawwaf. He spoke very little; only occasionally made a gesture of assent or dissent with his long thin hands.

The talk between Miss Bell's young man and the whitebearded sheikh became too fast for me to catch a single one of the Arabic words I had been struggling to memorize. All I knew was that bargaining was going on and that I was the subject of it. Suddenly all three rose to their feet. I unbent my stiff legs as best I could. The sheikh and the darkbearded man solemnly pressed the palms of their extended right hands together.

"It's all settled," said my Englishman.

"What's settled?"

"Your journey to Damascus. You must let your beard grow and wear Arab dress and bring tucker for two weeks. Jassem will furnish the camel and the tent and will deliver you safe at the Hotel Victoria in Damascus. Have you twenty gold pounds Turkish on you?"

Forewarned I had brought my meager moneybag along. We all squatted down again and sat in reverent silence while I laid twenty gold pounds in a little pile on the carpet beside Jassem's knees. For some time he didn't seem to notice them. Then he scooped them up and let them drop one by one from his right hand into his left.

He leaned toward me to speak to me directly.

"What is he saying?" I whispered to Miss Bell's young man.

"He's saying the desert air is sweet; in two weeks he'll make a bedawi out of you."

Jassem belonged to the Agail, which I understood to be a confederation of tribes that made a business of running caravans across the desert. According to Miss Bell's young man messengers would have to go and come. It would take time to arrange for my safe passage. That was all very well, but my cash was running low again and my bill was piling up at the Hotel Maude.

An odd event of the waiting period was a visit from the French consul. He had sent word he was inviting me to dinner and picked me up in a skiff after dark. His consulate was just across the Tigris from the Hotel Maude. Before dinner he led me into his office in a mysterious way and, after he had carefully closed the door, whispered to me that it was madness to try to cross the desert to Damascus. The British were just arranging the trip to make sure I got killed.

But why? They'd been very nice to me.

He shrugged. Maybe they thought I knew too much. When I asked him how he happened to know I was going—I hadn't told anyone—he became almost hysterical. He paced back and forth behind his desk waving his arms. The bazaars, everything anybody did was known in the bazaars. He himself was shadowed constantly. The Near East . . . the struggle for oil . . . *la politique* . . .

There wouldn't have been any way of getting my twenty pounds back even if I'd wanted to. After more dreary days of waiting while I spent what cash I had left on an Arab outfit and on canned goods for the journey, I finally climbed into a banged-up model T Ford with Jassem and several other gowned and bearded dignitaries to be driven out to Romadi on the west bank of the Euphrates where Jassem's caravan was encamped.

About half way the driver jammed on his brakes. There was a dead body on the side of the trail. It was a beardless oliveskinned youth who might have been a Hindu because he wore scraps of a British uniform. He lay on his back with a stony smile on his face. We could not tell how he had met his end. In any direction you looked there was only the horizon. The smarting winter wind hissed over the plain between the rivers.

Jassem examined the body gravely and shook his beard and led us back to the car.

As if I hadn't already been waiting three weeks, the rain held us up four days longer in Romadi. The British put me up in their mud fort. I had nothing to do but let my beard grow. Every day I sent out to inquire when the caravan would leave. Always the answer was *bukra insh'allah*. Tomorrow if God wills.

Jassem had furnished me with a magnificent conical tent, striped with crimson like a fuchsia flower and ornamented with pink and blue diamond shapes. I was to be tended by a soiled and obsequious man named Fahad. Furthermore a sort of interpreter was produced, a crookednosed youth named Saleh. Saleh had worked for the British and picked up a few Cockney phrases, each featuring the expletive bloody. Since it had been an Indian army unit Saleh had worked for he had the idea that English and Hindustani were the same language. That sometimes made him hard to understand.

Finally, one early dawn Fahad and I packed my gear and my tent into an enormous pair of tasseled saddlebags and Fahad handed me up onto the back of a riding camel. At first I thought her name was Malek but I later learned it was Rima.

The Agail all stood around anxiously waiting to see if I would fall off when she jerked to her feet. The hobble round her knees was unloosed. Rima grunted and groaned and opened herself up like a jackknife. My head poked up above the low clinging mist into sunlight. She pirouetted on her soft pads and followed the long string of baggage camels away from the flat roofs and datepalms of Romadi over the bare crumbly hills to the westward; and there I sat, jouncing and bouncing to the camel's mincing gait, wearing an embroidered Baghdad gown over my khaki shirt and pants, with a huge headcloth draped over my steelrimmed spectacles, the funniest-looking Arab anybody ever saw.

So far as I could make out the caravan moved, like a migration of birds, without formal organization. Nobody seemed to give any orders. On the march Jassem and the leaders of the Agail kept ahead on their fast dromedaries on a continuous watch for raiders. Then came strings of baggage camels and a Syrian merchant and his wife in their litter and the two dancing girls from Aleppo in their litter and a hearty man named Abdullah who herded twenty skittish mules; and then a great mob of brood mares and young camels that grazed as they traveled. In the rear came a straggle of weak camels and solitary riders who attached themselves to Jassem's outfit for protection. On our flanks for the first few days rode some hardboiled little brown riflemen on ponies, henchmen of the head sheikh of the Delaim, who was our official protector at that point.

Persons of distinction, among whom I was beginning to count myself, astride beasts that moved faster than the packanimals, sometimes rode ahead with Jassem and sometimes dropped behind to stretch legs and rest a while before catching up.

In Romadi the British adviser had introduced me to a foppish young man in an enormous silverbound headdress who was the nephew of the *naquib* (whatever that was) of Medina and a relative of King Feisal's. He had a fishy eye. I guess he hankered after his own sex. I didn't exactly cotton to Sayid Mohamet, but he was very civil. We exchanged gifts. He gave me some particularly good dates and I gave him a can of condensed milk.

Then there was the fat sheikh I had a letter to, who fed me such a good meal in Kubeisa, the desert town which was our first stopping place. Whenever I met the fat sheikh for days after he produced a piece of roast chicken out of his saddlebags. How he kept it fresh I couldn't imagine. Usually in the fat sheikh's company rode a venerable whitebearded gentleman in a green turban who sheltered himself from the sun with a dark blue umbrella. He was on his second pilgrimage to Mecca.

Late in the first afternoon's ride I was invited by Sayid Mahomet and his fawnlike attendants to drink tea. They helped me make Rima fold herself up on the sand of a dry watercourse so that I could climb off to unlimber my cramped legs.

While his cook brought the water to a boil over a fire of wormwood twigs the sayid and his friends tried to explain the problem of safety money. Though the Delaim were levying a tax as our official protectors another tribe was trying to horn in. My presence was causing extra charges. Five, the fingers of a hand, five pounds for each camel they were demanding, and special safety money for the stranger. If not, bang bang, *baruda ketir,* plenty gunplay.

We'd hardly raised the little swellbottom glasses to our lips when over some pebbly hills that blocked the western horizon there appeared a bunch of armed men riding their camels hard. They reined in when they saw us and the wind brought us the gurgling and groaning of their beasts as they dismounted.

The sayid brandished his gun and made big talk about battle but what he did was to climb on his camel in a hurry. The rest of us followed him at a lope after the caravan, saddlebags jouncing and rattling, camels slobbering and snorting as they went. I'd never imagined the camel was such a noisy beast.

That night I was scolded by Fahad and Saleh for having taken up with the sayid. They tried to make me understand they considered him a low fellow. All I could do was laugh and shrug. Not knowing the language gives you a special sort of detachment. My watch had gone to Damascus by the mail plane. I didn't even know what time it was, much less whose private life was reputable and whose was not. "It's charming never to know exactly what's going on," I entered in my journal. "I was never happier in my life."

Once I got the knack of sitting comfortably in my saddle, I found camelriding a great way to travel. Rima's ordinary gait was a fast swinging walk. I would ride first with one person, then another, occasionally looking back at the long string of baggage camels that disappeared in depressions, curved around hills, rose against the sky on summits, trailing like a kite's tail behind us. Larks kept starting up singing from underfoot. The desert was full of aromatic plants that made the air sweet. After our first scare the only excitement was when we jumped a hare that the camel drivers would chase shouting into the thorny underbrush or when somebody sighted gazelles in the distance.

About the eighth day out we camped in a vast shallow valley opposite a row of long black beetlelike structures which were the tents of the Delaim. By this time making camp had fallen into a routine. Fahad and Saleh pitched my round tent next to Jassem's campfire in the lee of a halfcircle of great bales. I later learned these were Persian tobacco to be smuggled into Damascus. The sayid and I and the dancing girls, from whose tent came a faint squalling of babies, and the Syrian merchant's family were the only ones who didn't sleep on mats in the open. Each group of travelers squatted around their fire, in the shelter of their goods banked against the wind. The fires were arranged in an oval, so that the bales and boxes made a sort of a fortification all around us.

It was midwinter. When the sun set a chill came into the air.

Blue smoke spirals uncoiled crisply from the campfires. The mollah would chant the evening prayer and the men would line up barefooted facing the southwest and make their prostrations slowly out of unison. Meanwhile urged on by the wailing *coopalayawp coopalayawp* of their drivers, the camels, after grazing under guard on the hills around, would come shambling into the open space inside the ring of campfires and be hobbled and folded up in rows chewing and bubbling and groaning. Their drivers fed them the extra feed they needed on the march by popping eggshaped balls of mash into their mouths.

We spent five desperate days among the Delaim. The first morning I guessed that something was amiss. Our camp filled up with rawboned whiteskinned nordic-looking men with waxed mustaches who wore flowing robes of white wool. I had been told that they were supposed to be descended from a lost band of Crusaders. From the first crack of dawn tumultuous speechifying went on round Jassem's campfire. The fat sheikh, whose roast chicken had by this time been all eaten, seemed to act in the role of mediator. Jassem, his beard slightly lopsided like Moses's beard in the paintings, sat silent directing the making of coffee with movements of his long hands, and stroking a string of amber beads. As the weather was cold he wore two headcloths, one white and one purple. Even sitting he was taller than the rest and his eagle beak contrasted sharply with the broad faces of the Delaim. The man had authority. Once he showed anger and leaned forward across the fire and said something slow and deliberate that made the whole circle of men quiet down and nod their heads.

When the orators had ridden home after the first day's powwow I tried to discover from Jassem what it was about. He smiled and rubbed his thumb and forefinger together in the thousand-year-old gesture and said gently: *Floos,* money.

The first great rumpus happened that night. I was sitting on my cot reading by candlelight when everybody started rushing about and tripping over my tent ropes. Saleh ran in breathless to get his gun, which he had left with me for safekeeping. Fahad appeared shaking his head in a most lugubrious manner and roughly barred my way when I tried to step out of my tent. My candle had been knocked over so I sat a while in the dark listening to the growing tumult outside. I began to remember a lithograph in the upstairs hall at home of an explorer in a pith helmet being transfixed by assegais: The Unfortunate Death of the Prince Napoleon. Thank God I didn't have a pith helmet.

Not understanding yet how careful the Arabs were with firearms I kept wondering when the shooting would begin. Guns were brandished but not a trigger was pulled.

It turned out that one of Ibn Kubain's men—that was the tribe that was trying to horn in on the Delaim's safety money—had tried to steal the sayid's rifle. The rifle was recovered but heads were broken and there was much bad blood. Double sentries were posted and everybody went heroically to sleep.

Next morning I was awakened long before dawn. The stars crackled in the cold. The camp was a struggling confusion of drivers holding their camels' necks to the ground while the packs were being fastened to their backs. The camels writhed and groaned and waved their snaky necks about. The drivers cursed and yanked and kicked.

I found Jassem crouched over the last embers of the fire warming his hands. He was laughing quietly to himself. I crouched beside him and embarked on a speech I'd been making up out of my vocabularies about how I had run out of provisions and needed to buy food and possibly to establish a credit for the purpose. Still laughing he shook a long finger at me and handed me a last drop of coffee in one of his thimble cups.

Fahad brought Rima. She jerked to her feet and we were off at a jogtrot toward the Dipper. Jassem was trying to shake off his tormentors by striking to the north of the regular caravan tracks. We rode all morning through grassy uplands to a great waterless canyon along a scarcely marked trail that wound down around the face of red sandstone cliffs and then up across the opposite rim to a pancake flat desert. We traveled eleven hours at top speed and made camp in the dark, wolfhungry and dogtired.

Before I had a chance to get up a sentence in Arabic about buying food Jassem had me sitting at his right hand eating with his men. He furnished my grub for the rest of the trip. The trouble was that the Agail ate so very little. A handful of dates and rice was a day's ration for a desert Arab. And it was bad manners to eat more than the next man. Night after night I dreamed of roast goose.

Jassem kept up his forced marches through a badlands country of eroded mesas and stony gulches. I was pretty well worn out by the time he finally gave us a chance to rest and to bathe by camping early one afternoon beside a waterhole in a dry arroyo. Each man retired modestly behind his own separate rock to wash himself.

Bathing when you have been deprived of it for many days becomes an exquisite pleasure. I can still remember the special sense of wellbeing I had that night sitting at Jassem's campfire, watching the moon rise through the fragrant darkgreen smoke of the aromatic herbs they were burning. The coffee tasted unusually good. We sat over it unusually long.

When the wind changed and blew the smoke in our faces they all laughed at me because my eyes watered. Hassoon could hold his face in the thickest smoke without blinking. Didn't we have any campfires in America? they asked me. Some of the Agail had been to America and had come back telling of great cities and much money. The coffee we were drinking came from Santos and they imagined I must live where the coffee came from. They wondered that great ships made of iron should float in the sea. Then Jassem, pronouncing his words very carefully, as for a child, tried to tell me about the Nejd, his country in the dry south of Arabia. All their eyes fastened on my face when I tried to explain how much I liked their life in the desert. Hadn't I better give up the stinking cities, said Jassem, and come to live with them where the air was fit for a man to breathe.

It seemed to me that night that Jassem and Hassoon and Ali and the two little black men who drove the camel colts were the finest people I had ever met. These desert people, more than any people I had ever known, seemed to take a man for what he was. Each man stood up by himself, in the fearful wind, under the enormous sky. What did I care how long it took to get to Damascus? I had more than half a mind to take up Jassem's offer. Would the world of the civilized ever make it up to me for not having lived that life?

When we made camp the next evening, one of the camels that had gone hopelessly lame was slaughtered. The poor camel seemed to know what was coming as he stood tottering in the center of the ring of fires, looking from side to side out of bulging eyes. Then one of the little black men from the Nejd, after his partner had tied his long sleeves behind his back to bare his arms, jerked the camel off its feet and neatly cut its throat. Before the last twitches of life were out of the carcass it was skinned and cut up amid great scrambling and shouting.

Fahad, bloody up to the elbows, came back to our fire staggering under the liver and several ribs. The liver was immediately set on the embers to grill. I remembered that I still had a few onions at the bottom of my saddlebags, so at sundown we made a noble supper of gobbets of camel meat fried with onions. It was like very tough mutton but men who haven't had their teeth in a piece of meat for three weeks aren't particular. For once my Arab friends ate all they could hold.

A couple of days after the feast on camel meat we sighted two little conical mountains to the westward. My heart leapt up at the sight because I thought they were the beginning of the mountains of Syria but it turned out not. In fact these little mountains were nearly the end of us.

I was riding ahead with Jassem. As we jogtrotted toward the mountains Hassoon spied a man on horseback looking out over the plain. There was a cry of robbers, and we pulled our camels up short and rode back full tilt to the main body of the caravan. Far away we could see men on white ponies loping like rabbits down the slope.

The camels groaning and roaring were made to crouch and hobbled in a flash with their loads still on them. The dancing girls and their babies tumbled squeaking out of their litter. The Syrian couple sat groaning in theirs. The rear sections of the caravan halted as they came up until the five hundred camels were all crouched down squeezed tight together in an uneasy square.

The sayid, who annoyed everybody very much by stopping to change into his best Baghdad gown for the occasion, mounted one of Abdullah's horses. Abdullah himself rode the other. The Agail and all the other combatant members of the caravan took up positions on the little hillocks round about.

The Syrian merchant and his son took firm hold of me by either arm and sat me down in the deepest part of the ravine, whether for my protection or theirs I could not guess. The merchant's fat wife lay in a heap at her husband's feet and now and then let out a long curdled shriek.

Eventually I managed to get loose and to scramble up on a hillock above the ravine to see what was going on. The sayid was riding in circles at a gallop with his long sleeves floating behind him. Robbers on horseback, he shouted. Guns many many.

The Agail were falling back from their scouting positions. It was a fine sight to see them girding up their long robes for battle and tying their flowing sleeves in knots behind each others' backs. There was a body of horsemen advancing toward us; nobody knew who they were.

Jassem was quiet and smiling as ever. With one hand he held his gun, with the other he musingly stroked his beard. The purple and white headcloths fluttered behind him as he led his Agail, now loaded down with extra cartridge belts, up into the hills.

I joined the noncombatants who sat smoking on a little hillock, presided over by the hadji. The ancient pilgrim nursed his umbrella and invoked Allah at every breath. We must have been sitting there an hour when a rifleshot and then another rattled through the hollows of the hills. Two men on white ponies appeared on the slope above us riding at a gallop and occasionally shooting. Their bullets whirred over our heads.

We noncombatants broke up in confusion. I have a distinct recollection that the hadji raised his umbrella. I found myself back on the pebbles of the ravine engaged in profound conversation with a Turkish cameldriver, a pleasant man I had been exchanging salutations with ever since Romadi.

What language we spoke I don't know to this day, because he knew no language I knew, but we managed to convey ideas to one another. This Turk claimed that the Arabs were a low and shifty lot. Three times he had been stripped naked and left for dead by the Bedawi. Too many guns, too little law. Neither did he like the war nor the Germans nor Baghdad nor the British. He had been in the Turkish army and had started home to his village near Brusa after the defeat. He had wandered to the most inconceivable places. Everywhere too many guns and too little law. Guns bad. Law good.

Meanwhile the Agail were falling back toward the camels as more men on ponies came loping down from the hills. The attackers rode round and round us, shooting as they rode like the Indians in "Custer's Last Stand," which used to be the climax of Buffalo Bill's Wild West Show. There was an immense amount of powder burned, but nobody seemed a penny the worse.

At last Jassem climbed to the top of the hillock and waved a long white sleeve. The Agail ceased firing. So far as I could make out people began telling one another that the pony riders were friends after all.

The raiders came riding into camp on their loping ponies, riding in pairs, singing alternate snatches of song as they came. Their clothes were ragged and dirty, looped up with cartridge belts. They were cousins it turned out of the Ibn Kubain people who held us up before.

Such a set of walleyed crooknosed squinting scarfaced slitpurses I never saw. They strode haughtily about the camp picking up a rug or a cookpot or any other object that pleased them and carrying it off. Robbers and sons of robbers, Saleh called them.

The next day was spent discussing safety money around Jassem's fire. I was surprised to see several old women of the tribe of our attackers join the group and raise their voices as freely as the men. At last a ransom of five camels, and five pounds Turkish for my hippo was agreed on as the price of protection. I tried to tell Jassem to let them take the hippo. What few wornout clothes I had weren't worth five pounds, but he paid no attention.

The morning after the sons of robbers saw us on our way past the two little conical mountains. Jassem had tried to give them the impression that we were headed for Aleppo instead of Damascus.

Again they sang part songs in triumph as they rode. Everybody in the caravan praised Allah with relief when the sons of robbers ceased protecting us and returned to their tents.

All that day the wind blew hard in our faces. The wind of Damascus, Jassem called it. That evening we saw the mountains of Syria purple athwart the setting sun.

A rainy spell slowed us up. More and more camels went lame from hard riding. My shoes split. The chilblains I had developed on the Italian front came back. Round Jassem's campfire we were on half rations. The only food left was a tiny bit of rice and a concoction of fried dates known as *khastawi* that I found increasingly delicious.

It was remarkable how well I got along on the starvation diet. "Let them take a thousand years to reach Esch Scham," I entered in my diary. "I don't care. I never sat at such fragrant fires with such fine people as the Agail . . . Christ I feel hearty, bearded, Whitmanic. All the bile out of my belly—all the wrinkles planed out of my mind by the great cold purple flint flatiron of the desert."

That didn't keep me from dreaming, the minute I closed my eyes at night, of hot rum punch and *sole bonne femme* chez Prunier and Mme. Leconte's magnificent omelets. The worst thing was the cold "wind of Damascus" continually in our faces. "Feet chilblained, hands stiff with cold," I noted, "but jolly as a lark."

In a rocky defile at the edge of the Syrian foothills we just missed another holdup. Jassem's scouts caught the glint of a rifle behind a rock and Jassem waved his long sleeve to turn the main body of the caravan back into the plain. The scouts reported that these men were not mounted, so Jassem and his advance guard cocked their guns and rode cautiously toward them to see who they were.

They stared up at us sheepishly when they saw the main body of the caravan winding away into the distance on another trail. They wore colored headcloths and looked a motley crew. The ones who didn't squint were walleyed. Most of them didn't even have guns. Not real Druses it was explained, but halfbreeds from the edges of the Druse country.

They asked to see the mad American who was wandering in the desert and when I was produced stared at me critically but amiably. When they were finally bought off with fifteen pounds Turkish and a bag of dates I began to wonder how much more I was costing Jassem than the twenty pounds I'd paid him in Baghdad.

From then on it was the French camel corps and the customs officers along the Syrian border that Jassem had to evade. We were moving through dry mountains interspersed with sand dunes. We advanced slowly because the camels had been several marches without food and were worn out. We were entering populated country. We moved through flocks of sheep and goats. At last one evening we saw blue smoke rising from a distant village. Villagers on donkeys rode out to our camp.

That night the camp was full of comings and goings. There was deep talk around Jassem's fire, and the groaning and bubbling of camels being loaded. The last thing I heard before I went to sleep was the clink of coins being counted from palm to palm.

When I woke before day the caravan had vanished. Camels, bales of tobacco and rugs, little bags of what I had begun to suspect was opium, all the goods had vanished into the blue haze. Jassem sat as usual beside his fire quietly grinding his coffee. As I sipped the last three tiny cups with him he gently insinuated that when I talked with the French officials in Damascus I should not know how many camels there had been, nor how we had come.

I assured him that I had a very bad head for figures.

My entry into Damascus was excruciating. Sayid Mahomet, his cook, and one of the Agail, who went along on foot to care for the animals, started off with me. At first I rode Abdullah's white stallion but the saddle was a clumsy wooden affair without stirrups and hideously uncomfortable to my galled posterior. After we'd crossed the first ridge of hills the sayid took pity on me and let me ride his beautiful dromedary.

As we advanced into the inhabited land the dromedary became

more and more skittish and kept trying to bolt back toward the desert. At last, deliriously hungry, galled, limping, tired to a frazzle, we reached an inn that smelt of roast meat. After six weeks without a green thing to eat a plate of green beans was a marvel. There was curd cheese and kebab. It was hard for me to mind my manners and eat no more than the sayid ate.

We entered the oldest city in the world lolling in a landau. The Agail and the sayid's cook, thank God, took charge of the animals. I'd had enough riding for a while. I could think of nothing but a hot bath, but before going to the Hotel Victoria I had to make a round of visits to relatives of the sayid's, bearded old men in the Scribes' Bazaar, mysterious people in courtyards who seemed to be plotting against the French, a tailor in a tailor shop, the keeper of a café frequented by the Agail. It was all very interesting but I was too tired to care about Hedjazi plans to take over Damascus. All I could think of was how hungry I was and how desperately I wanted a bath.

When we came out of the last café we found a drunken French officer sitting in our landau. The sayid protested. The officer began to abuse him in French, which he luckily didn't understand. There would have been the devil to pay if I hadn't made a speech about how *"les braves alliés"* must stick together, etc. We went off toward the Hotel Victoria singing "La Madelon de la Victoire."

Another hurdle. The Frenchman insisted we have a drink with him. When we drew up to a bar next to the hotel it transpired that it was only for French officers and that Arabs weren't allowed in. I hadn't thought too highly of Sayid Mahomet but I must say he behaved with great dignity. Explaining with gestures that as a moslem he couldn't drink he sat quietly in the cab while I went in with the Frenchman and bolted an absinthe frappé, which was the last thing in the world I wanted at that moment.

Somehow I managed to shake the Frenchman and to exchange the proper farewell civilities with the sayid and at last, after a tumultuous argument with the man at the desk because I hadn't a passport and was disguised as an Arab, found myself alone in a fine oldfashioned highceilinged European bedroom that had a bath and hot and cold running water.

Next morning after twelve hours' sleep and a shave and a succession of hot tubs, I found a French official waiting in the lobby to arrest me. After hours of explanations my passport was uncovered at the American consulate. Also a packet of mail.

The first news of *Three Soldiers.* The damn book was selling. I'd have money in the bank.

Then my troubles really began. All the French officials wanted to know how the hell I'd gotten there from Baghdad. British Intelligence invited me to lunch. I was a nine days' wonder. Before I knew what was happening the consul and his wife were fitting me into a borrowed suit of tails to be taken to a party at the French High Commissioner's.

Thank God they had a sense of humor. The pants proved much too large and had to be tightened by an enormous safety pin behind. The consul and his wife almost laughed themselves sick. All I remember of that party, except for a marvelous moonlit view of Damascus from the terrace, was having to dodge behind a group of potted palms when the safetypin came loose and to signal desperately to Mrs. American Consul to come and fasten me up again.

Back at the hotel I started reading the reviews of *Three Soldiers* which Gene Saxton had industriously collected. Some people wanted me lynched, others were for setting up a statue.

It gave me spots in front of my eyes. It all seemed an invasion of privacy. What did any of it have to do with me? This wasn't me. I was the nameless traveler who'd been sitting by the campfire with Jassem er Rawwaf. Before I knew what had happened I had slid the whole wad of clippings into the scrapbasket.

I did write my friends. I wrote Arthur McComb: "I arrived in Esch Scham lustful after baths and food and warmth. Since then I have done nothing but bathe and eat, hobbling on chilblained feet, extraordinarily sore in the groin from the pommel of my saddle, from cookshop to cookshop in the bazaars where I gorge on pastries made of honey and sour cream, and on extraordinary messes of vegetables stewed in deliciously rankflavored olive oil. Battered but triumphant like the old black bull in the song."

For once I had a bellyfull of travel. "At present," I wrote Robert Hillyer a few days later, "I am bound for the U.S.A. having biJasus destroyed the illusion of geography—No more retching after

Cook's Tours or pinings to join the agile Mr. Neuman in his Travel Talks—All of it is bunk—When the final disgust seizes me I shall retire to the Nejd and have a great quantity of giggling wives in pink nighties. Until that time comes I will content myself with the contemplation of the following truths. There's as bad wine to be drunk in Tiflis as on Eleventh Street, the phonographs squawk as loud in Baghdad as they do in Sioux City, and politics are no more comic in Teheran than in Washington D. C. . . . I am now on my way home, as I said—(curious word 'home' I wonder why I used it)."

The return to the West had its penalties. Rested and clean-shaven, wearing a freshpressed civilian suit, I drove around to see the sights of Damascus before taking the train to Beirut. At the entrance to the principal mosque I found Jassem. He was wearing a new headcloth and a new Baghdad robe. Saleh was in attendance. When I walked up to Jassem with my hand outstretched he looked at me with an expression of incredulous horror on his face. Where was my beard? his hands said. I fingered my smooth chin. Tears came to his eyes as he saluted me gravely. Then with a gesture of utter repudiation he turned his back and, picking up his slippers, walked off across the dusty carpet of the mosque.

CHAPTER 4

La Vie Littéraire

Looking back on it, lunching at the Plaza with Scott and Zelda in the fall of 1922 marks the beginning of an epoch. It must have been in October because it was a crisp autumn day.

New York is at its best in October. The girls all look pretty in their new fall outfits. There's a novel twist to the arrangements in the shop windows. The sky is very blue. The clouds are very white. Windows of tall buildings sparkle in the sun. Everything has the million dollar look.

I walked most of the way up Fifth Avenue. When I found I was late I jumped a bus. In the twenties you could still sit out in the air on top of the Fifth Avenue buses. I arrived breathless at the Plaza. Inside the carpets felt cloyingly thick. The flowers in the flowershop had the look of goldbacked tendollar bills. A gust of expensive-smelling perfume that came out of the coiffeur on the way to the elevator gave me a moment's sickish feeling: I was like a dog about certain kinds of perfume. The elevator man's buttons flashed like gold sovereigns.

Scott met me at the door of his suite. I wondered afterward whether the Fitzgeralds were really living there or whether they hired the suite just for the day to impress their guests. Scott gave me a searching look out of his blue eyes and scolded me for being late.

Immediately he introduced me to an appealing sort of man with curly graying hair and strangely soft wrinkles in his face. Sherwood Anderson had large shadowed eyes and prominent eyebrows and a selfindulgent mouth. He had put on a gaudy Liberty silk necktie for the occasion. When I told him how much I admired his writing all the wrinkles in his face broke into smiles.

Scott and Zelda both started plying me with questions. Their gambit was to put you in the wrong. You were backward in your ideas. You were inhibited about sex. These things might perfectly well have been true but my attitude was that they were nobody's goddamn business. I held them off as best I could until Sherwood got talking about his writing and I could listen and roam around the room and look out the tall windows into Central Park where the leaves were just beginning to turn, and at the skillful elderly waiter and the glittering luncheon table.

Afterward I used to kid Scott about his silly questions. They were like the true or false lists psychologists make up. Even that first time I couldn't get mad at him and particularly not at Zelda: there was a golden innocence about them and they were both so hopelessly goodlooking.

As I remember we drank Bronx cocktails, and then champagne. Scott had good bootleggers. The meal was something like lobster croquettes—Scott always had the worst ideas about food—but everything you ate at the Plaza was good in those days. There was always the creamiest sweet butter to spread on crisp French rolls.

After lunch Sherwood went off to an engagement and Scott and Zelda asked me to drive out to Long Island with them to help them find a house. They had some kind of red touring car with a chauffeur. On the way Scott talked about Sherwood's writing, admiringly but critically.

When he talked about writing his mind, which seemed to me full of preposterous notions about most things, became clear and hard as a diamond. He didn't look at landscape, he had no taste for food or wine or painting, little ear for music except for the most rudimentary popular songs, but about writing he was a born professional. Everything he said was worth listening to.

In Great Neck we picked up a blond beefynecked salesman at a real estate office. He showed us several ritzy mansions. Scott and Zelda made life miserable for him. Nothing pleased them. They parroted his way of saying "gentleman's estate" until I was thoroughly disgusted with them. I tried to stick up for him. The poor devil was only trying to do a little business.

After they wearied of tantalizing the real estate man we dropped him off and went to call on Ring Lardner. I was looking forward to that as Scott and I had been agreeing that nobody handled the American lingo better. The Lardners lived in a big Long Island house like the houses we had been seeing. We were ushered into a long dark livingroom with a fieldstone fireplace. A tall sallow mournful man with a higharched nose stood beside the fireplace—dark hollow eyes, hollow cheeks, helplessly drunk. When his wife tried to get him to speak he stared at us without seeing us. He was literally out on his feet.

We drank up some of his whiskey and started back to town. I've never felt more depressed. Scott kept saying that Ring was his private drunkard; everybody had to have his private drunkard.

On the way back we passed a carnival. Rollercoasters, whirling lights, a calliope playing. Zelda and I clamored to be allowed to take some rides. Scott wouldn't get out of the car but sat there with a bottle of whiskey he had pulled out from under the seat. Zelda and I rode on the Ferris wheel. Carnivals, amusement parks, the flash of colored lights on faces in the dark, the view over misty suburbs twinkling with lights, these were things I liked to try to paint. I tried to explain my infantile excitement to Zelda. She wouldn't listen. Zelda and I kept saying things to each other but our minds never met.

It wasn't that she wanted me to make love to her: she was perceptive enough to know I wouldn't make a pass at Scott's girl. She may have thought it bourgeois but that was the way it was at that time. We'd only known each other ten hours, but for all our misunderstandings the three of us were really friends. At least I felt that way and I believe Scott and Zelda did.

The gulf that opened between Zelda and me, sitting up on that rickety Ferris wheel, was something I couldn't explain. It was only looking back at it years later that it occurred to me that, even the first day we knew each other, I had come up against that basic fissure in her mental processes that was to have such tragic consequences. Though she was so very lovely I had come upon something that frightened and repelled me, even physically.

Zelda kept insisting on repeating the ride and I sat dumb beside her, feeling more and more miserable. She was never a girl you could take lightly. Through it all I felt great respect for her, a puzzled but affectionate respect.

Zelda sulked all the way back to New York. Scott was sulky drunk. It was with relief I said goodbye to them under the gilt Sherman in front of the Plaza. At the last moment they were both charming goldenhaired children again. We parted friends and I think remained so.

For the Fitzgeralds that was the beginning of their Great Neck period, which Scott made *aere perennius* in *The Great Gatsby*. For me it was the beginning of something quite different. They were celebrities in the Sunday supplement sense of the word. They were celebrities and they loved it. It wasn't that I was not as ambitious as the next man; but the idea of being that kind of celebrity set my teeth on edge.

I had come back from the war and the Near East not quite sure whether I wanted most to paint or write but with no idea of making a career of either one. I had a faint hankering after the theater. All I knew was that I wanted to get a lot of things off my chest. As one book led to another the plan to take up architecture gradually faded, but I couldn't abide the notion of setting up as an author. I was damned if I'd let anybody classify me on that index card. At least not yet. I was planning to write novels, but on the side.

Coming through Paris I bought an early copy of *Ulysses* and even shook the limp hand of a pale uninterested man in dark glasses sitting beside the stove in the back room of Shakespeare and Company whom Miss Beach claimed was James Joyce. I read the book at one gulp while laid up with a bout of flu in a tiny inside cabin way down in the third class of one of the big transatlantic liners: parts I found boring and parts I found magnificent. If *Ulysses* didn't accomplish anything else—for me at least—it disposed of the current theory that the English novel was dead.

The first thing I felt, arriving back in New York, was the gap left by Wright McCormick's death. He was killed sometime that spring mountainclimbing in Mexico. It broke up a special triangular friendship between Wright and Ed Massey and me. Wright and I had seen Ed through his first puppyadventures with chorus girls. We had tried to help him make the best of an unsatisfactory marriage. We had overweening confidence in each others' abilities. We were all going to do something terrific: Ed as a playwright and stage director, Wright as a poet and shortstory writer, I in ways as yet undefined. College friendships bulk so large. The people involved are quite out of scale with the rest of the world. When one of those early friends dies your universe is irreparably diminished.

Really to belong to New York you have to have a job there. Scott's Princeton mates, John Bishop and Edmund Wilson, whom I soon met, had editorial jobs. Since I was in funds from *Three Soldiers* and had paid off my debts, I continued by hook or crook to scrape up a living without having to go formally to work for any publication. To a certain extent it made me a fish out of water.

From Elaine Cummings I rented the pleasant airy studio that was back of her place on Washington Square with a separate entrance on the Mews, but if anybody had referred to it as my home I would certainly have been shocked. At the slightest excuse, and particularly upon the occasion of the publication of a book, I bolted for foreign parts. It was during these years that I lost track of the number of times I crossed the Atlantic. I'd go steerage, second class, first class, according to the state of my bank account. Young women I met at cocktail parties liked to tell me I was running away from myself.

That was partly true. Maybe I was running away from them. I never got around to explaining that I was running toward something too. It was the whole wide world. I still had an insatiable appetite for architecture and painting, particularly the work of the so-called scientists of the early Italian renaissance, Masaccio, Piero della Francesca, Pollaiuolo, Paolo Uccello. I wanted to see everything they had ever painted. I wanted to see country, landscape and plants and animals and people: men, women and children in city, town and hamlet. I had to hurry. There would never be time to satisfy such multifarious curiosity. When you are in your twenties it never occurs to you that you may live to be an old man.

New York was a continent in itself. Through friends and acquaintances I picked up I delighted in exploring the creeks and channels and backwaters of the city . . . always as the visitor, the tourist on his way to the railroad station.

At that time I probably felt nearest to being at home with Cummings and Elaine. Elaine's apartment, when I dropped in for tea, was made particularly delightful by the presence of little Nancy. We called her Mopsy. I always did like little girls of three or four but Mopsy at that age seemed particularly entrancing. Cummings was at his most charming in the company of a small child. When Mopsy's bedtime came we would leave her in charge of a nurse and go out to dinner.

Listening I enjoyed more than talking. So long as he lived I never tired of Cummings' conversation. In those days he took pleasure in elaborating certain Rabelaisian episodes involving various friends. Each time he told it the tale became taller. He'd see the joke even if he were involved himself.

There was the famous episode of *le pisseur*. On one of my dashes through Paris, possibly the year after my forty days in the desert, Cummings and Gilbert Seldes, whom we had known from Harvard *Monthly* days, and I ate dinner at the Café de la Paix. Full of wine and François Villon and Cummings' imagery we embarked in a cab for the *rive gauche* in search of a little *boîte* Cummings had discovered there.

In a particularly dark little alley Cummings decided to alight for the purpose of taking a leak. Immediately he was seized by a pair of *agents de police* in cloak and kepi who appeared from nowhere. "Un pisseur" they cried and marched him off to the police station. I followed declaiming in noisy French that the gentleman was America's greatest poet and that we had all served at the front to save la belle France from the *sale boche* and *vive la France* and *vive l'Amérique* etc. etc.

The gendarmes only walked Cummings off the faster. When I tried to follow them into the police station to continue my protestations they pushed me out the door. When I tried to force my way in they threw me out bodily. I was lucky that they didn't arrest me too.

Cummings finally emerged, somewhat shaken, because he remembered La Ferté all too well. In his hand he had a summons to appear in court next day. Before the hour came Gilbert got hold of Paul Morand, the author of the *Ouvert la Nuit* stories we had all found amusing. Part of Gilbert's business in Paris was to arrange for the publication of Morand's articles in the *Dial*. That gave him an in. Morand was an official at the Quai d'Orsay and had no difficulty in getting the charge dropped. Cummings celebrated the occasion with a series of drawings of a horizontal J.D.P. in a battered felt hat being shot out the police station door by the gendarmes. The tale lost nothing in the retelling.

The success of Gilbert's call on Morand made an impression on all of us. It proved there was something in the notion of a republic of letters. Though Cummings preferred to describe himself as *artiste-peintre* he was never bashful about his role as poet. Perhaps because these things sound less embarrassing in French than in English, Cummings' *poête-peintre* pretensions never rubbed me the wrong way as did Scott's brash enthusiasm for celebrity. As Cummings used to say in New York a little later: If you're going to get drunk it's safer to wear a dress suit.

My attitude was somewhat different. Literary invention could never be made really reputable. A writer who took his trade seriously would be sure to get more kicks than ha'pence. He would be lucky if he stayed out of jail. In my revulsion against wartime stupidities, as a priest takes a vow of celibacy, I had taken a private vow of allegiance to an imaginary humanist republic which to me represented the struggle for life against the backdrag of death and stagnation. Figures like Giordano Bruno, Erasmus, Rabelais, Montaigne presided over my republic of letters. Among its latterday saints I classed Shelley, Stendhal, Flaubert, possibly Walt Whitman and Rimbaud.

This isn't the sort of thing one talks about, even to intimate friends, but it is these private dedications that mold men's lives. In this context the number of copies a book sold was neither here nor there. The celebrity racket made no sense at all.

I loved Cummings for his dedication to some similar cult, based, I suspect, in his case on his Greek, a cult that dated back to the earliest Homeric beginnings and stretched forward into prosodies to come. For a while I may even have shared his conviction that the dedicated man should be fed by the ravens, only in my case the ravens proved neglectful.

A phase we had in common of this same private cult was an offhand downunderneath reverence toward the idiosyncracy of the divergent, various, incalculable men, women and children who make up the human race. As Cummings grew older he narrowed it down. Tolerance is not a New England vice. I never shared his intolerance. He had the brahmin's disdain for anyone who didn't live up to certain specifications.

"Dead from the neck up," he called them; but, in some of what seem to me to be his best poems, and in the descriptions of people in *The Enormous Room,* he expressed, better than I was ever able to express them, feelings of mine about men seen in bitter moments at the front, or among the black tents of the Bedawi: the incongruous splendor, the spark of God—how else can you say it?—I sought in every human clod.

Cummings' delight in certain things was contagious as a child's. Christmas tree balls, stars, snowflakes. Elephants were his totem. I would never have enjoyed snow so much if I hadn't walked around Washington Square with Cummings in a snowstorm. He loved mice. He had a great eye for sparrows and all pert timid brighteyed creatures.

The last time I saw him the summer before he died he was entertaining a tame chipmunk. We ate supper on the porch of his father's old hilltop house in the woods above Silver Lake. The chipmunk kept popping through the vines and out onto the brick floor of the porch for peanuts. You couldn't tell whether Cummings or the chipmunk enjoyed the little scene more. They had the same glint in their eyes. They both looked their best.

Then there was the Village proper. Esther Andrews was quite indignant when she discovered I referred to her place as Melancholia Villa. I never could explain exactly what I meant. I guess what I was trying to poke fun at was the tone of repudiation, the nose in the air attitude that always bored me about Bohemians. It was the sort of smug repudiation that put me off Sinclair Lewis' *Main Street*. What right did we have to rate ourselves higher than successful businessmen or the corner grocer or the whitewings who swept the streets for that matter? It wasn't that I accepted their standards: it was that I felt that to challenge a man's notions you had to meet him on his own ground.

It ended by my convincing Esther that I was fond of her no matter what. There was no arguing with the intelligentsia even at that early date. Freud was already the catchall; if you didn't agree with somebody you found he had an Oedipus complex.

Esther had been one of many attractive young women who pour into New York from the Middle West, learn diction at a drama school and yearn for the illdefined glamor of a stage career. When that didn't work Esther took a job with *Women's Wear Daily*. She had ability and a natural flair for clothes and was pretty well paid but she elevated her scorn and hatred of the women's clothing business into a religion. Business was a bad word. She had taken up with a nicelooking young man of Quaker extraction named Canby Chambers who was somewhat younger than she was. Children, family, matrimony were oldfashioned notions. She utterly repudiated the idea of marriage. Everybody must be left free. What good this sort of freedom was to people nobody ever pointed out. Free was free.

Esther was a born hostess. In spite of her scorn of conventional values—convention was the adjective that damned—she was an attractive and warmhearted woman. Esther's and Canby's apartment or later their house on Commerce Street was the nearest thing to a salon I knew in New York. Esther would have hated to hear it called that. I was too young to have known Mabel Dodge's place on lower Fifth Avenue; and Muriel Draper's salon on the upper East Side, a few years later, seemed to me a little too self-conscious to be fun.

Esther's thwarted maternal feelings went into fussing over failures, lame ducks, dead cats. Success was the unforgivable sin. Her friends were advertising men ashamed of their work, writers turning out happyending tales for magazines they despised, newspapermen who proclaimed themselves prostitutes because they had to tailor their stories to please the city editor. In spite of the tone of selfrighteous repudiation there was a certain amount of lively talk and a great deal of cheerful foolery.

Jack Lawson, with his plays and his lady friends and his enthusiasms and *outré* convictions, and his willingness in those days to argue any topic on any side at the drop of a hat, was a three-ring circus. His sister Adelaide roamed in and out in her gypsy way, paying no attention to all the pretentious nonsense talked around her, interested only in putting how things looked to her on canvas.

It was at Esther's I first met Dawn Powell, one of the wittiest and most dashingly courageous women I ever knew. Every conceivable kind of rebellious character turned up there. Griffin Barry filled the air with radical patter. There was a period when Whittaker Chambers, no relation of Canby's, then a spooky little guy on hush-hush missions as a Communist Party courier, flitted in and out.

Esther Andrews' New York was a sort of mirror image of the Fitzgeralds' city of glitter and success. Everything was the other way around. Anybody who wasn't a celebrity was welcome to Melancholia Villa.

They all teased me about leaving my hat near the door so as to be ready to bolt at a moment's notice.

Farther uptown I found drawing rooms where the conversation was less dogmatic. The three handsome Dudley girls were daughters of a Chicago physician. Their great friend, Susan Smith, who had married in Wiscasset, Maine, was the daughter of a Chicago schoolmaster. Somehow, out of the impact of French novels read in their teens and of impressionist paintings devoured at the Art Institute, they had invented a certain style. Life must be a *déjeuner sur l'herbe* painted by Renoir on the banks of the Seine.

They treasured Victorian furniture and bric-a-brac. From Chicago, with overtones out of the Vieux Carrée and the Federal style houses of old State-of-Maine seaports, they brought with them to New York a special private style of decoration. They carried this special style into their conversation and their cookery and their whole way of living.

I don't know which of them discovered Sneden's Landing. Sneden's was a village of stone houses that grew up in the eighteenth century round the western landing of Dobb's Ferry up the Hudson. When I first went out to visit Susan Smith there the whole village was in the hands of the widow of an Italian sculptor who had been an associate of Stanford White's. The place still had a flavor of the New York nineties. Mrs. Tonetti was a lively lady, well off in her own right, and determined to keep Sneden's free from the advancing suburbs for her large family and numerous friends. It was to be an enclave of nineteenth-century elegance hidden away in a fold of the Palisades.

Mrs. Tonetti and Susan and the Dudleys had notions about things that fitted in congenially. Their special style permeated everything. After crossing the Hudson on an ancient motorboat that plied back and forth from Dobbs Ferry it was like stepping ashore in a foreign country. Another pleasant way to reach Sneden's was to cross on the regular ferry from Yonkers and to walk up five miles by a path along the edge of the water. The riverside copses were full of birds. You occasionally caught a glimpse of a Baltimore oriole or a scarlet tanager. Herons flew up from reedy coves. Just for a minute occasionally you were in Audubon's America. When you arrived there were always good things to eat and drink, things to look at, things to talk about. An evening at Susan's black house was an oasis after the strident dusty racket of New York.

Though I still bucked, like a halfbroken colt at the sight of a bridle, at any hint that I was settling down to a literary career, the fact of having published a read and talkedabout novel did bring certain alleviations to my lot. The ladies were much more receptive.

These were the speakeasy days. In some places you whispered your name through a slot in the door. The waiter smiled with sympathetic understanding at your lady friend. From the moment the door clicked to behind you, you had the feeling of being in the Fortunate Islands, where there were no rules and regulations, no yesterday and no tomorrow, no husbands to complain, no private entanglements with other women, only this moment. The memory lingers of certain female perfumes, of certain daiquiris, the meal slowly eaten, the ambrosial wine. The eyes kindling, the knees furtively touching. The hands creeping toward each other across the table. At length you would drift out into the street enclosed like Homeric gods in a private cloud. The French farce aspects of Mr. and Mrs. Smith registering in a hotel, or the tiptoe climbing of celestial stairs, the latchkey quietly turning in the lock. The lips meeting, arms twining, the delights and terrors that neither the greatest poets or the most meticulous pornographers have ever been able properly to describe . . . asterisks still do it better.

I did my best to keep up with everybody I'd ever liked. There were weekend walks with Rummy Marvin and his Yale friends in the Catskills or the Amish country. There were guys I'd known in the army in odd jobs in various corners of the city. There was Fred Bird, who had been one of our gang in the Red Cross, whom I used to drink beer with in Union City. Fred moved on the fringes of ward politics and told tall tales out of school. Jim Parshall, who worked, I think, in Detroit, I met by chance in a speakeasy which years later was to become the Stork Club. Tom Cope, not yet quite retired to an architecture firm in Philadelphia, put in an occasional appearance at Melancholia Villa. In the midtown region I began to see something of John Bishop and Edmund Wilson. They had formed a triangular friendship with Scott Fitzgerald that was of great importance to all of them.

My first well remembered view of Bunny Wilson was characteristic. It may have been Bishop who went around with me to the office of *Vanity Fair,* where they both worked as assistants to Crowninshield, to fetch Bunny out to lunch. Shy as ever, I waited in the hall by the elevator while whoever it was went in. There appeared a slight sandyheaded young man with a handsome clear profile. He wore a formal dark business suit. The moment we had been introduced, while we were waiting for the elevator, Bunny gave an accent to the occasion by turning, with a perfectly straight face, a neat somersault.

It was the elvish side of him I liked, his penchant for sleight of hand—he early became an honorary member of the American Society of Magicians—his skill with puppetshows. Of course I admired his erudition too. As John Adams said of Jefferson: "He was a great rubber off of dust."

Though he never could learn to drive a car he used, in those days, to travel back and forth to his mother's house at Red Bank through the screaming traffic on a motorcycle. Even when he reached a somewhat dumpy middleage, he was an unexpectedly strong swimmer; once when I went out to see him at Red Bank we went into the surf in heavy weather. We had been talking about Henry James' novels as we trotted down the beach. The waves pounded us. Though I was coughing and spluttering and hard put to it to keep from drowning, Bunny kept unreeling one of his long involved sentences in a quiet conversational tone. Except when he was interrupted by a wave's breaking over his head, he didn't miss a single dependent clause. He completed the paragraph, without ever getting out of breath, when we landed back on the beach. He showed no sign of noticing that I was blowing like a grampus.

Conversation in the early twenties had to be one wisecrack after another. Cracks had to fly back and forth continually like the birds in badminton.

One of the most skilled at this exhilarating sport—though no match for Robert Benchley whom I met a little later—was Donald Ogden Stewart. Don made Bones at Yale. After graduating he spent dreary years selling bonds. I guess he'd had a pretty miserable boyhood. He had recently emerged from the state of Ohio with a healthy appetite for the bright lights. His comic writings had put him on celebrity's escalator. Americans in those days liked books that made them laugh. Humor was our great common denominator. Don invented a Babbitty family called the Haddocks. The books sold. He was marrying an attractive and fashionable debutante.

I've forgotten how we met. In spite of a certain obsession with social status, Don managed to be funny about almost everything. We laughed like fools whenever we saw each other.

My lack of social orientation seemed to him deplorable. He was determined that I must meet the right people. Anyway I'm eternally grateful to him for introducing me to Gerald and Sara Murphy.

This must have been in Paris. I had already lost a good deal of my appetite for the Ville Lumière, though I loved the concerts and the galleries and tea with the Championnières, rue de Clichy. Already in the spring of 1922 I was writing Arthur McComb that I knew Paris too well. "Memories grin at me from street corners. I don't know if I'm in this year or last year. One can nearly always go the present, but to meet the past at every turn with its eternal infernal mirror . . . I hate it."

Running into Don Stewart in Paris gave me a freak view of the city through the Madison Avenue comedy of *Mr. and Mrs. Haddock Abroad.* When he took me to call on the Murphys he furnished me with an entrance to something very different from the huddle of literary expatriates round Montparnasse which I already dreaded.

Of course Hemingway was an exception, just as Cummings was an exception. In the private universe I was arranging for myself, literary people generally, and particularly Greenwich Village and Paris exiles, were among the excommunicated categories. Their attitude toward life made me want to throw up. But as soon as I got to be friends with one of them he or she became the exception, unique and unassailable.

Though Don and Ernest and I first began to see a good deal of each other during the period when I first knew the Murphys, I believe I'd run into Ernest the year *Ulysses* came out while he was in Paris working for *The Toronto Star.* There's a dim recollection of eating a meal with him and Hadley at Lippe's before there was any Bumby, and of Ernest's talking beautifully about some international conference he'd recently attended. When he was a young man he had one of the shrewdest heads for unmasking political pretensions I've ever run into. His knowledge of prizefighting and the policeblotter lingo picked up in Kansas City and Toronto gave him a direct vocabulary that pinned his stories down. Everything was in sharp focus. I found his acid estimates of Clemenceau and Lloyd George and Litvinov thoroughly invigorating. We agreed on a restrained heroworship of Liebknecht and Rosa Luxembourg. He must have shown me one of the short pieces that later went into *In Our Time,* because I right away put him down as a man with obvious talent for handling the English language.

Whenever this meeting was we spent a good deal of time reconstructing our first meeting, when neither of us had any idea that the other was to become what we jeered at poor old Sherwood Anderson for calling a "wordfellow." This first meeting must have been at Schio in May, 1918, when Ernest had just arrived with Section 4 of the Red Cross Ambulance in Italy, and I was getting ready to leave Section 1 in Bassano under a cloud. Fairbanks and I used to evacuate wounded to a base hospital near Schio and it must have been on one of those trips that we messed with Section 4. Ernest and I remembered each other dimly.

It wasn't till 1924, when Hem, as most of us called him, and Hadley were living at the sawmill on rue Notre Dame des Champs that we began to play any part in each others' lives. I liked Hadley from the first. Bumby had arrived. This was during one of my fitful stopovers in Paris.

Hem and I would occasionally meet at the Closerie des Lilacs at the corner of Saint Michel and Montparnasse to drink some such innocuous fluid as vermouth cassis while we talked about the difficulties of putting things down on paper. We both were reading the Old Testament. We read to each other choice passages. The song of Deborah and Chronicles and Kings were our favorites.

In Our Time was out and I was trumpeting it abroad. My story was that basing his wiry short sentences on cablese and the King James Bible, Hem would become the first great American stylist.

It must have been in the spring because we sat out on the triangle of garden between the pavements of the two boulevards and I remember being amused by the fact that, in spite of its name, there was an actual lilac blooming in the Closerie.

Then we would stroll back through the five o'clock crowds to the sawmill and help Hadley give Bumby his bath. Bumby was a large, healthy, sociable infant and enjoyed the whole business. He would be tucked in bed and, when a pleasant buxom French peasant woman who took care of him arrived, we would go out to dinner. Helping put your friends' children to bed before going out to dinner with them is a feature of the society of recently grown-up Americans I've always enjoyed. Men aren't ever quite so egotistical with women around. By the same token young men and women can't put on many airs if they have brats to attend to.

Right from the beginning Hem was horribly prone to accidents. I've never known a man who did so much damage to his own carcass. It was sometime during this period that he pulled the skylight in the john on the stairs outside his apartment down on his head and gave himself a concussion and a lacerated scalp it took him weeks to recover from. He carried the scar to his grave.

When it wasn't an accident it was a sore throat. He was like one of those professional athletes who, although strong as an ox, is always nursing some ailment. Hem's boxing was something I kept away from. Having my glasses as an excuse I had no need to compete with him in that department.

I couldn't ride a bicycle either. Hem was mad about bicycle racing. He used to get himself up in a striped jumper like a contestant on the Tour de France and ride around the exterior boulevards with his knees up to his ears and his chin between the handlebars. It seemed silly to me but in those days Hem submitted to a certain amount of kidding.

He had an evangelistic streak that made him work to convert his friends to whatever mania he was encouraging at the time. I did enjoy going to the sixday bicycle races with him. The Six Jours at the Vélo d'Hiver was fun. French sporting events had for me a special comical air that I enjoyed. We would collect, at the stalls and barrows of one of the narrow market streets we both loved, a quantity of wine and cheeses and crunchy rolls, a pot of paté and perhaps a cold chicken, and sit up in the gallery. Hem knew all the statistics and the names and lives of the riders. His enthusiasm was catching but he tended to make a business of it while I just liked to eat and drink and to enjoy the show.

Now and then he would remember that I was a rival wordfellow and clam up, or else warn me sharply that I mustn't do any writing about bicycle races. That was his domain. I would assure him that sportswriting was out of my line, and that besides Paul Morand had done the thing up brown in *La Nuit des Six Jours*. Maybe it was on account of having read Paul Morand that I so enjoyed the show. Although I was trying as hard as Hem to let what I put on the page spring direct from the event, I still suspected that, most of the time, life copied art.

Hem used to make poor Hadley sit there all night, but I would sneak out and make for my lodgings when I got sleepy. Right from the beginning Hem was hard on his women. Yet I'm convinced that he was more of a builderupper than a breakerdowner. He left them more able to cope with life than he found them. Certainly in his younger days, for all his moods and changing fancies, he had an invigorating effect on every one he went around with. During the period when we were on good terms he opened up for me vistas into the sporting life I would never have seen without him.

He was a moody kind of fellow even then. Sorry for himself. One of the things he'd get sorriest for himself about was not having been to college. I used to tell him he was damn lucky. Think of all the tripe he hadn't had to unlearn. Suppose he'd gone to Yale and been tapped for Bones like Don Stewart. He'd laugh and admit that would have been the ruination of him.

Hem had uncommonly good eyesight. The hunter's cold acuity. In those days he seemed to me to see things and people uncolored by sentiment or theory. Everything was in a cool clear white light, the light which pervades his best short stories, "A Clean Well Lighted Place," for example.

He had the same shrewd eye for painting. Maybe Gertrude Stein, who was no bungler in that direction either, helped him develop the knack. He would take in excellence of color and design at a glance. The School of Paris was already full enough of faddism to make a cat sick, but Hem never fell for the shoddy. Whether it was politics or literary work or painting he would take the guff out of a situation with a wellplaced fourletter word.

I well remember his buying Joan Miró's "The Farm"—I think it was the last "objective" painting Miró did—because I had to rush around scrounging up cash. We were all constantly borrowing each others' money. He found he could buy it for two or maybe three thousand francs (damn little in dollars at the current exchange) and was in a fever for fear someone else would snap it up. He brought the picture home to the sawmill in triumph. It remains one of Miró's best. I wonder what it's worth now. Painting was something we usually agreed on.

Hem's enthusiasms were catching. Though I had an ingrained inhibition against gambling he even lured me out to the horseraces. Hem claimed to be winning great sums and one spring I followed him to Longchamps and Auteuil. My eye as usual was more on the show than the money. It was Degas who taught me to appreciate racehorses and jockeys.

We got our tips free from Harold Stearns. Harold was an extraordinary fellow. Having made a reputation for himself by articles in *The New Republic* and other liberal journals and edited one of the first and most successful collections of views on American civilization, he came over to Paris.

In Paris he gave up writing and dropped everything. Even his pursuit of drink and women seemed to lack conviction. There still was a certain sallow charm about him. He remained an entertaining talker. He lived a pathetic barfly life eking out a living selling tips on the ponies to American tourists he picked up in the various ginmills he frequented.

There was some plush steeplechase out at one of the tracks, and Harold gave us the lowdown on a particular little horse that was a rank outsider. Odds thirty to one or something like that. He never charged his friends for his tips and this time he swore by all that was holy that we were going to clean up.

Hem and I scraped up several hundred francs and made for the track. Harold had it fixed up with a stableboy that we were to be given a private view of the horse. It was a pretty wiry little dark bay. The jockey confided in us he was putting all his savings on him. We leered at the horse and patted his nose and talked a lot of wiseacre racetrack talk in French and English. When we got to the parimutuel window the odds were enormous. We were already planning to blow in part of our winnings at a bangup meal at Foyot's.

The horse was a jumper all right but at the water jump he balked, threw his jockey over his head and bolted back round the track the wrong way. He took a lot of jumps backward before he was caught. The race was a shambles. We nearly died laughing. I went back to Paris with my convictions about the folly of gambling much fortified. Next time we went to Henry's Bar Harold pretended not to see us.

Neither of us could afford the loss but we never stopped laughing about it. Hem had either given up his correspondent job or was just about to give it up. He was having a tough time making a living writing. The edition of *In Our Time* that Robert McAlmon brought out in Dijon had earned him acclaim in *rechèrché* circles but no cash. His main source of income was writing smutty poems for a German magazine called *Der Querschnitt.* We got all the fun there was out of that name.

Don Stewart was telling us both that we ought to see more of "people that mattered." He almost put us off the Murphys by building them up as rich socialites. The first time I met them they had an apartment at the top of a very ancient house opposite Nôtre Dame at the corner of rue Gît-le-Coeur and of the left bank quai. They were getting ready to give a party for the entire cast of Diaghilev's Russian Ballet.

Sara was obviously a darling, but Gerald seemed cold and brisk and preoccupied. He was a dandified dresser. There was a sort of film over him I couldn't penetrate. I refused to stay for the party and went off prickly as a porcupine. It was a relief to go back to the *bourgeois à la lanterne* state of mind of rue Nôtre Dame des Champs.

The next time I met Gerald the impression was entirely different. We took a walk together up the quais after lunch. Fernand Léger was with us. It was the first of many marvelous walks. Fernand was a hulk of a man, the son of a Norman butcher. He seemed to me to have a sort of butcher's approach to painting, violent, skillful, accurate. Combined with this was a surgeon's delicacy of touch that showed up in the intricate gestures of his hands.

Gerald, tall and slender, redheaded, Irish as they come, had been studying with Léger, but he was already a painter in his own right. *"Très américain,"* Léger would say approvingly.

The two men set each other off. Beside Léger's visual fury, Gerald's perceptions were rational, discriminating, with a tendency to a mathematical elegance. There was a cool originality about his thinking that had nothing to do with the wealthy amateur.

As we strolled along Fernand kept pointing out shapes and colors. *"C'est bath ça."* Gerald's offhand comments would organize vistas of his own. Instead of the hackneyed and pasteltinted Tuileries and bridges and barges and *bateaux mouches* on the Seine, we were walking through a freshly invented world. They picked out winches, the flukes of an anchor, coils of rope, the red funnel of a towboat, half a woman's face seen behind geraniums through the casement window of the cabin of a barge. *"Regardez-moi ça."* The banks of the Seine never looked banal again after that walk.

So long as I knew him Gerald's mind retained that uncommitted freshness. He left the pretentious bunk of which the "art" world is so full untasted at the side of his plate. Sometimes unabashedly friendly, at other times he had a way of withdrawing suddenly into some black Celtic mood. It was like the closing of a door. Sara was the best possible complement: warm, cozy, humorously concerned with people, with a great knack for the arrangement of furniture or food—if you were a friend of hers you never lacked just the right cushion in your chair before you sat down on it.

I had little taste for the largescale entertaining the Murphys went in for in those days. I was shy and I hated small talk and I didn't like having to answer questions about my writing. I cultivated the pose of sidewalk proletarian to whom riches were vanity. Still I had to admit they spent their money lavishly and well. Nobody organized more amusing affairs. I always regretted missing the famous party they gave to *tout Paris* on a barge on the Seine.

When I got to know Gerald and Sara I preferred dropping in on them when they were alone. Gerald and I had a private bond in the fact that our fathers had parallel careers. Patrick Francis Murphy was raised in South Boston. Impecunious but lace curtain Irish. Mostly selfeducated, he moved the Mark Cross saddlery to New York and made it into Fifth Avenue's great leather-goods store. No more than with my father was making money the be-all and end-all with him. He became a famous afterdinner speaker and shared my father's enthusiasm for the eighteenth-century classics. In fact, they were quite good friends. So Gerald and I understood each others' backgrounds.

I particularly liked the Murphys when they were with their children. I had never had a proper family life and was developing an unexpressed yearning for it. Their three little towheads were constantly amusing. Honoria as a tiny girl had the same special quality she has today and Patrick was one of those children in whom you already see the lineaments of the firstrate man to come. I liked Gerald best when he was, as the children called him, Dowdow.

We were all mad for Diaghilev's Ballet Russe. The ballet would do for our time what tragedy had done for the Greeks. *Le Sacre du Printemps* seemed to us just about the height of what could be accomplished on the stage. Nijinski was already burned out, but we thought the Englishwoman who danced in *le Sacre* under the name of Sokolova carried dancing as far as it would go. Stravinsky's music got into our blood. For months his rhythms underlay everything we heard, his prancing figures moved behind everything we saw.

During the first summer when I saw a lot of Gerald he was friends with two exiled Russian painters. Larionov was a bear of a man who had been a sort of premature *surréaliste* in St. Petersburg before the Revolution. His wife Goncharova was designing the sets for Stravinsky's *Noces.*

When the time came to paint the scenery Goncharova found herself shorthanded. Gerald and his friend Vladimir Orlov, who had been an ensign in the Russian navy and had barely escaped with his life when most of the Orlovs were massacred by the revolutionaries, offered to help. I went along. We spent a week in a loft near the Place des Combats heating up gluepots, mixing paint, mostly white and dark brown, and spreading it on vast odd shapes of canvas spread out on the floor.

It was the first time either Gerald or I had worked with Russians. Everything was confusing. Everybody seemed to be at crosspurposes. Nobody would stop talking long enough to do any work. Everybody argued endlessly about problems that nobody seemed able to explain to us.

The weather was hot. When Gerald and I got into a sweat through sheer impatience we would sneak out to a brasserie where they served excellent beer in glasses the size of goldfish bowls. There we would drown our sorrows. The whole thing was a mess. We were distressed because we were fond of Goncharova. The opening was four days off. The scenery would never be finished in time.

It was. Everybody worked all night for two nights. Nobody got the least bit excited. In some miraculous way everything fell into place. The canvases were tacked on their frames. The vans appeared at the right moment to carry the flats across town to the theater. Opening night everything was in order. The production was magnificent. Ever since I've had great respect for the Russian way of doing things.

I'm not sure whether it was the summer of *Noces* or the summer before that I first went down to Antibes. Gerald and Sara were holding open house for a bunch of Americans at the hôtel de Cap. They had induced the manager to keep it open after the close of the season. The swimming off the rocks was as fine as the swimming off Reid's Hotel in Madeira.

If I remember right Archie and Ada MacLeish were there. My first memory of Archie is his magnificent form diving. Gerald had got me to reading his poetry. Though born in Chicago he had a Scottish charm which was hard to resist. Ada was a dandy. Besides being an accomplished musician—Lord how well that woman sang—and a wit in her own right, she seemed just one of the nicest people I'd ever seen. Don Stewart and his wife; Phil Barry, in the first flush of his career as a Broadway playwright, and his handsome Ellen, sound as a good loaf of bread; and maybe Marc Connelly, another diverting Broadwayite, were there. I remember thinking I'd never seen so many Skull and Bones men together in my life.

Gerald seemed to me the only one who had really lived it down. I reflected on my father's dictum that the women were invariably better than the men. I had to admit that, always making an exception for my particular friends, I liked the girls better than their husbands.

Gerald had the knack of a Beau Nash for making discoveries that later proved fashionable. All I knew about Antibes was that it was where Napoleon landed when he escaped from Elba. Hardly anything had happened there since. The French and moneyed British who frequented the Riviera in winter wouldn't have been found dead there in summer. It seemed too hot to them, but to Americans the temperature seemed perfect, the swimming delicious, and Antibes just the quiet untrampled provincial seaport they had dreamed of discovering. The cult of the sun had barely begun.

By the following summer Gerald and Sara were making their home at Villa America. Sara engaged an Italian gardener and started growing sweet corn. Gerald painted in an outbuilding. They invited their French friends down and before long Picasso was sunbathing at Juan-les-Pins, the Fitzgeralds were renting a villa at Saint Raphael and the artistic-fashionable Franco-American rage for beach life had begun.

There was a little tileroofed gardenhouse known as the Bastide where I stayed whenever I got within hailing distance. It was marvelously quiet under a sky of burning blue. The air smelt of eucalyptus and tomatoes and heliotrope from the garden. I would get up early to work, and about noon walk out to a sandfringed cove named la Garoupe. There I would find the household sunbathing. Gerald would be sweeping the seaweed off the sand under his beachumbrellas. We would swim out through the calm crystalblue water, saltier than salt, to the mouth of the cove and back. Then Gerald would produce cold sherry and Sara would marshal recondite hors d'oeuvres for blotters. Saturated with salt and sun, some in cars and some walking, the company would troop back to the terrace, overlooking the flowers and vegetables back of the villa, for lunch.

One of Sara's favorite dishes was poached eggs with Golden Bantam corn cut off the cob and sprinkled with paprika; home-grown tomatoes cooked in olive oil and garlic on the side. Sometimes to this day when I'm eating corn on the cob I recapture the flavor, and the blue flare of the Mediterranean noon, and the taste of vin de Cassis in the briney Mediterranean breeze.

It was a marvelous life. Fond as I was of Sara and of Gerald's conversation I could stand it for about four days. It was like trying to live in heaven. I had to get back down to earth.

It was different when we were up to something special. We made some good trips into the back country and went sailing on the *Picaflor*. The *Picaflor* was a superannuated racing sloop which Gerald acquired with the help of Vladimir Orlov. Since he was a child in the Crimea sailing had been the passion of Vladimir's life. When he gave up whatever work he did with the ballet Gerald took him on as a retainer to handle his boat. He developed into a professional skipper and a firstrate designer of yachts.

The first time we went off on a cruise we learned that none of us knew how to sail that particular boat. We were headed for Genoa with a gentle following breeze when we thought it would be cute to try out the balloon jib. We sat there mooning and drowsing and enthusing about how beautiful the Mediterranean was by moonlight while the wind freshened by imperceptible degrees until it was blowing half a gale.

Suddenly it seemed like one of those windstorms in Vergil's *Aeneid* when the winds blow from all directions at once. Rain fell in sheets. When we tried to come up into the wind to take in the balloon jib we shipped half the Gulf of Genoa. We so nearly capsized it wasn't funny. The halyards jammed. Vladimir couldn't bear the idea of cutting the jib loose so we went careening on. I got out the chart and we decided we could make the port of Savona by standing on our course.

Gerald steered and Vladimir handled the sheet and I sat in the companionway trying to read the chart by a smoky lamp in the cabin. As we neared the harbor entrance all kinds of red and green lights appeared. Which of them marked the channel? We picked the wrong pair and suddenly found ourselves driven in toward an elbow in the breakwater.

The *Picaflor* had no motor. No room to come about. Vladimir dropped our two anchors and we managed to hove to a hundred feet out from the meanest set of foaming rocks you ever saw.

A lull in the wind let us get in the sails and lash down the boom but there we were halfswamped tossing around in a raging sea. Figures gathered on the breakwater. I couldn't remember the Italian word for tugboat. While Gerald and Vladimir pumped and bailed I tried to find the word in a pocket dictionary. All I could find was *pyroscafo.* It certainly didn't sound right but for what seemed hours I hung in the shrouds drenched to the skin and howled "ayuto" and "pyroscafo" at dim figures round the lighthouse.

Eventually a tug appeared and threw a cable aboard. We had to cut our anchorlines. In a jiffy we were being towed briskly into the smooth well-lighted harbor. We had just tied up to a wharf and were congratulating each other on having come through without a scratch when the tugboat captain reversed his engines and started to run us down. More howls in bad Italian. In veering off the tug carried away our bowsprit.

When next morning Gerald and I went into Genoa on the train to find new anchors, while Vladimir poled the *Picaflor* across to the local shipyard to fit a new bowsprit, I tried to get Gerald's mind off his troubles with tales of my first visit. There was always something a little special about my arrivals in Genoa.

It wasn't too long after that little adventure that Gerald and Vladimir started work on plans for the *Honoria,* which was to be a broad familysize ketch, sturdy and weatherproof enough to take Sara and the children and a couple of friends cruising. After this there were cruises on the *Honoria* whenever I turned up at Antibes. Gerald and Sara were spending their capital. How could they spend it better?

By this time Scott and Zelda were very much in the Antibes picture. Scott, with his capacity for hero worship, began to worship Gerald and Sara. The golden couple that he and Zelda dreamed of becoming actually existed. The Murphys were rich. They were goodlooking. They dressed brilliantly. They were canny about the arts. They had a knack for entertaining. They had lovely children. They had reached the highest rung on mankind's ladder. Fortunatus incarnate.

Scott sometimes found odd ways of expressing his devotion, such as the night when the Murphys invited a lot of rather stuffy French people, including a brace of duchesses, to dinner in the garden. Scott and Zelda got drunk on the cocktails and instead of coming to the table crawled among the vegetables on all fours tossing an occasional tomato at the guests. A duchess who got a blob of ripe fruit down the back of her décolleté was emphatically not amused. Gerald eventually managed to drive the Fitzgeralds out. It was many months before they were invited again to Villa America. In fact they were formally forbidden to cross its threshold.

It was hard to stay mad at the Fitzgeralds. Sara particularly was a woman who never let go a friend. Their exploits were getting so hairraising, like the night Scott drove their Renault up the tracks on the viaduct the electric train used to go up to one of the hilltowns back of Cannes. A trackwalker found them both, blond as angels, peaceably asleep in the car. The car was dragged off before the next train came. They had escaped being killed by a miracle.

Like every other friend of Scott's the Murphys were in a quandary. They were fond of him. They admired his talent. They were concerned about him. They wanted to be helpful but friendship had its limits. They couldn't go on having every pleasant evening made a shambles of.

Like many drunks Scott took a malicious pleasure in making his friends uncomfortable. There was the horrible time when Scott let go a kick at a tray of cigarettes and matches an old woman poked in our faces when we were going into a Paris restaurant. We all scrambled around picking everything up. Gerald made amends with a banknote. The poor woman looked absolutely stunned. It was hard to laugh that off . . . and the time he crawled under the doormat at the casino at Juan-les-Pins. Then he had a disarming way of turning up sober for weeks on end, usually when he had to get to work on some book he had spent the advance on. Nobody could be more sober when he wanted to be.

In spite of the scandalous behavior of the Fitzgeralds, or maybe because of it, Villa America attained a certain *renommée* among the French. The French are the most inhospitable of peoples. Foreigners have as much chance of getting an in with them as they do with the Boston brahmins. Gerald and Sara had the gift of treating everybody alike. The French found them chic.

Americans were rather in style in Europe in the twenties anyway. Dollars, skyscrapers, jazz, everything transatlantic had a romantic air. Gerald's painting when it was shown in Paris seemed the epitome of the transatlantic chic.

Before long Gerald and Sara were having to take evasive action before the onrush of French high society. They enjoyed the painters more than the pernickety men of letters. Léger, with his marvelous knack of making everything he saw, everything he heard, everything he tasted a special composition of his own, was their favorite as he was mine; Sara even got to be friends with Picasso.

Picasso was a small dark closed man. He had none of the offhand geniality that makes Spaniards in general easy to get along with. He was sardonic, earthily cynical in a special Spanish peasant way—the cynicism of Sancho Panza. He seemed to me impenetrable even in moments of relaxation and laughter. He was very much the master bricklayer, the master stonemason, the artisan. He was skill incarnate. It was humanity that was lacking. The Greeks would have called him *deinos* as they did Odysseus. You couldn't approach him or his work—the man and the work were inseparable—without profound admiration for the sly elbow, the cunning fingers, the accurate eye; if he had had the gift of compassion he would have been as great as Michelangelo.

Hemingway was lured down to Antibes but I don't remember ever being there when he was. I know he felt ill at ease there, though he loved Sara Murphy. Fishermen never seem to take much pleasure in swimming. He would have felt silly sunburning on the beach. To enjoy the Villa America you had to fall in with Gerald's carefully staged ritual. Hem was already too much the showman to take part in anybody's else charade.

Hem was by this time a figure in the top valhalla of literary Paris. Ford Maddox Hueffer sought his help in editing the *Transatlantic Review.* He was friends with Pound. He lunched with Joyce. He was taken up by Gertrude Stein. He was contemplating a book about bullfighting for Querschnitt which Picasso was to illustrate.

One of the things that had brought Hem and me together was our enthusiasm for things Spanish. Most of my stopovers in Paris were stages on my way to or from Spain. Hem and Hadley had landed in Vigo when they first brought Bumby back to Europe, and arrived in Paris with marvelous recollections of Campostella and Asturias and the Basque country. Hem's Spanish mania came to a head the hot August days when he first attended the fiesta of San Firmín in Pamplona.

I wasn't in Pamplona the year of the first big gathering there that gave Hem the idea for *The Sun Also Rises,* but I was there the next August. We all stayed at the Hotel La Perla.

Hem was the cynosure of all eyes. There was a hardboiled Englishwoman of title known to us as Duff. Hadley was still married to Hem, but I have a notion that the Pfeiffer girls, Pauline and Ginny, were along. There was an English army officer we called Chink. Don Stewart was there: and Bill Bird and his wife and a young friend of theirs named George O'Neil. So was Robert McAlmon.

The Birds were all right even if they were expatriates, but McAlmon gave me a queasy feeling. There was something disarming about the guy too that made me feel guilty for thinking he was such a heel. Maybe Harold Loeb was along. There may have been more.

Since reading the novel I'm not quite sure which remembered events Hem made up and which actually happened. It was like a Cook's conducted tour with Hem as master of ceremonies. As a show the San Firmínes are terrific. Bands. Processions. *Cohetes.* The arrival of the bulls, the unboxing of the bulls, gallopades through the streets. Every square full of wiry dancing countrymen in blue berets. From every alley the rhythms of Basque fife and drum or the bleating of Galician bagpipes or the rattle of castanets.

Every little group had its skin of wine. So far as I can remember the rowdiness never passed a certain point. Good manners among people who believe in man's dignity are a matter of life and death.

Everybody had to be *muy hombre* with the bulls. You ran in front of them when they were driven to the bullring; you tried to get into the pen when they were being examined by the officials. In the *capea* bulls were let in on the public that swarmed in the bullring.

They were young bulls and not of the fiercest but surrounded by a crowd of Navarrese youths taunting them with jackets and handkerchiefs, they made some formidable lunges. A good many young fellows were hurt though I don't remember anybody being killed that year.

Showing off my ignorance of taurine punctilio to a bullring full of prancing Navarrese wasn't my idea of an agreeable afternoon, but Hem had to be in there with the aficionados. His American compatriots felt they had to show their mettle too. The joke on me was that when I walked off after loudly repudiating the business, I found myself face to face with the bull. He had just jumped the fence and was charging down the passage on the other side of the *barrera*. He looked me in the eye and I looked him in the eye. We called it quits. It didn't take me long to climb the footholds on the wall up into the lower tier of seats. My story was that I was finding an elevated spot to make sketches from.

It was fun and we ate well and drank well but there were too many exhibitionistic personalities in the group to suit me. The sight of a crowd of young men trying to prove how hombre they were got on my nerves. I could enjoy an occasional bullfight as a spectacle but every day for a week was too much.

For Hem it was different. He had an extraordinary dedication to whatever his interest was for the moment. Whether it was six-day bicycle racing or the bullring or skiing or fishing a trout-stream, he stuck to it till the last dog was hung.

He stuck like a leech till he had every phase of the business in his blood. He worked himself into the confidence of the local professionals and saturated himself to the bursting point. Outside of an occasional scientist I have known struggling with a tough line of experiments I've never known anyone with that peculiar stickatitiveness. Some of Hemingway's best writing springs from this quality. When he described the matador's work in *Death in the Afternoon* he knew what he was talking about.

The Spaniards were fine and I was devoted to Hem and Hadley but I couldn't have stood the American part of the crowd if there hadn't been a young woman along. I was discovering the truth of Ben Franklin's old saying: "A man and a woman are like a pair of scissors. Neither one is any good without the other." Between us we built ourselves a sort of private box from which we looked out at all these goings on, in them but not of them.

When she had to go back to her university, I decided that what I needed was a good long walk in the mountains. Chink and young George said they'd come too. They were both sturdy fellows and I was delighted. We got hold of some maps and plotted out a trail through the high Pyrenees to Andorra. Bob McAlmon insisted on joining the party.

The poor fellow seemed to me to have all the wrong ideas. He was planning to be very Spanish and wear *alpargatas.* I tried to explain to him that you couldn't walk twenty miles a day in anything but good stout boots. He compromised on sneakers but he couldn't stand our pace and had to drop out the second day.

Chink turned out to be a splendid fellow. Public school and Sandhurst. Stiff as a ramrod and chary of words, but a good walker who enjoyed scenery, just the kind of reliable man you would want to climb a mountain with. The British change their names as easily as a crab changes his shell. He was then Captain Dorman-Smith, but under some other moniker he made a reputation as a general officer in World War II. Chink had first known Hem in Italy and had gone on trips with him. When I tried to get him to talking about our friend all he'd say was, with a shake of the head, "He was a likely lad." Always in the past tense.

We had mostly good weather. Silence and solitude were a delight after the gabblegabble round the tables under the *portales* at Pamplona. My recollection is of a succession of high passes and the scenery unrolling on either side like the painted panorama they used to unroll during the Rhine music in *Siegfried.* The mountains were green toward France to the north, toward Spain dry and lioncolored. The men we met on the high trails were either *contrabandistas* or customs officers. We made twenty or thirty miles a day. Toward the end of the trip we experimented with little spots of brandy when we began to fag out in the afternoon. We considered the experiment a success.

Plunging down a mountainside into Andorra we lost the road and had to follow the cobbly bed of a torrent. Our only light was from thunderstorms. Rain drenched us. We reached the capital about midnight soaked to the skin. Our teeth were chattering. The town was shuttered up tight. At the only inn we found open, they led us upstairs to an evil-smelling room with three beds.

We were absolutely worn out. Our legs ached. Our feet were sore and bruised. We were desperately sleepy. The minute we stretched out in dry clothes the bedbugs came like shock troops, wave after wave. George and I lay there inert but Chink amused me by jumping out of bed, dressing carefully and sitting up solemnly in a chair for the rest of the night. His attitude was that it didn't behoove an officer in His Majesty's army to suffer indignities at the hands of the natives. I esteemed him for it.

It must have been later that fall—or was it the next?—that Hem read me *The Torrents of Spring*. He began one autumnal afternoon of ruddy sunlight at the Closerie des Lilas. Parts of it were really funny, particularly when he brought in the Michigan Indians—Hem had a way with Indians—but it put me in a quandary. I had played some part in inducing Horace Liveright to publish *In Our Time* in America, and Hem was holding me just a wee bit responsible for a lousy contract he signed giving Liveright options on several books.

Now Scott, who rather fancied himself as a talent scout, and was selflessly generous about other men's writing, was working like a beaver to get Max Perkins to take on Hemingway at Scribner's. Scott had one of his literary crushes on Hem, the sportsman-stylist, the pugilist storyteller. We had decided, talking about Hem one evening, that he might turn into a latterday Byron. Scott was right. Scribner's was the publisher for Hem, but how to get out of the Liveright contract?

I never did understand exactly what Hem was up to in *The*

Torrents of Spring. Was he deliberately writing stuff that Liveright, as Sherwood Anderson's publisher and friend, couldn't possibly print, or was it just a heartless boy's prank? I certainly laughed when he read it out loud but I tried to argue him out of getting it printed, at least right now. I said it wasn't quite good enough to stand on its own feet as a parody, and that *In Our Time* had been so damn good he ought to wait until he had something really smashing to follow it with.

That evening he agreed readily that Sherwood Anderson was the last man whose feelings he wanted to hurt. Sherwood had been very kind to Hem when he was a young fellow working in Chicago, and we both knew how babyishly sensitive he was. I agreed with Hem that *Dark Laughter* was sentimental and silly and that somebody ought to call him on it, but I didn't think it ought to be Hem. Hem had a distracting way of suddenly beginning to hum while he was talking to you.

When we parted that night I thought I'd talked him out of publishing the *Torrents*. I suppose it wasn't any of my goddamn business, but friends were friends in those days. It didn't work out that way.

The last unalloyed good time I had with Hem and Hadley in Europe was at Schruns in the Austrian Vorarlberg. They had discovered the skiing at Schruns the winter before. Gerald and Sara joined us there. Everything was fantastically cheap. We stayed at a lovely old inn with porcelain stoves called the Taube. We ate *forellen im blau* and drank hot kirsch. The kirsch was so plentiful they gave it to us to rub off with when we came in from skiing.

This was all crosscountry skiing. We used sealskins to climb. The great excursion was up to the Madlener Haus on a huge snowfield above the town. This was a sort of ski club with roaring fires and hot food. The people were as nice as they could be. Everybody cried "Grüss Gott" when they met you. It was like living in an oldfashioned Christmas card.

Hem went in for skiing up to the hilt. He practiced and practiced. He had to be tops. Gerald was another kind of perfectionist. It got to be a race as to which of them would get to be the complete skier in four days. They both of them did darn well.

I think I had a better time than either of them though, because I knew from the first I'd never be any good. Too damn clumsy. I'd puff sweating up the mountain trails with my sealskins, enjoying the view. The weather wasn't too cold. The sun was even hot. The snow mountains rippled with blue and purple shadows. You had to be a little careful where you went because there was danger of avalanches in the afternoon. I saw one on our way down from the Madlener Haus and was thoroughly impressed.

Going up I felt fine but skiing down hill I had to develop special tactics because I just couldn't get the knack of turning corners. The best I could do was fall down. When the slopes got too steep I used to sit down on my skis and turn them into a sort of toboggan. Was I razzed when it was discovered arriving in Schruns that I'd worn a hole in the seat of my pants.

Mealtimes we could hardly eat for laughing. Everybody kidded everybody during that week at Schruns. We ate vast quantities of trout, and drank the wines and beers and slept like dormice under the great featherbeds. We were all brothers and sisters when we parted company. It was a real shock to hear a few months later that Ernest was walking out on Hadley. When you get fond of a couple you like them to stay hitched.

My last recollection of Paris literary life is an odd one. Don Stewart and I somehow got mixed up with a *Manifestation Dada*. I believe it was after dining with Louis Aragon and Drieu La Rochelle. Aragon was very much the dashing young poet. He certainly showed talent. Drieu, his best friend, was a tall aristocratic youth, whom I thought at the time was the coming French writer. I liked him particularly; he seemed completely on the level; the aristocratic French are more like the wellborn English than they are like the smalltown French bourgeois or the mercenary Parisians. The men had strangely diverse histories. Aragon ended up an orthodox and respectable Communist Party dignitary, but poor Drieu, like quite a few of his more fastidious compatriots, ended up a Fascist and blew his brains out one fine morning during the German war.

Anyway that night we were all full of beans and wanted to do something outrageous. We joined Tristan Tzara in a glary café somewhere near the Tour St. Jacques. He was surrounded by some mighty odd fish. I've forgotten their names but it was a prime collection of zanies. Everybody was racking his brains to think up something abracadabrating to do. Suddenly Tzara, a sallow Rumanian who looked like a chartered accountant, rose and cried "Follow me." The Dadas jumped to their feet leaving half their saucers unpaid for. Don and I, as so often happens to trusting Americans in the hands of the European literati, found ourselves settling their score with the waiters.

It turned into a game of follow the leader. Tzara, trailed by the rest in a solemnfaced cue, marched about the streets executing a number of idiotic maneuvers. They had a little chant: Dada, Dada. Any other place we would have been arrested but the French in those days were tolerant of anything which would pass as a *manifestation artistique*. We ended marching pokerfaced through a Turkish bath. Fat men sweating in steamrooms or dunking in swimming pools looked up astonished but offered no resistance. The attendants asked "What the hell?" All any of the marchers would say was "C'est le Dada." It certainly wasn't very funny.

When we got back out in the air again, Don and I slipped into a cab and made for our respective hotels. Dada left us feeling just a wee mite squeamish.

CHAPTER 5

Commitment: Uncommitment

During the winter months of 1926 I was messing around in Morocco. It started with a trip down to the oasis of Figuig on the edge of the Sahara where there was an excellent little hotel run by a stout French lady known as Madame Mimosa. The specialty of her cuisine was a kind of underground mushroom she called, with a Comédie Francaise intonation, "truffes du desert."

I was trying to ward off a fresh attack of rheumatic fever. Some doctor had told me it would do me good to toast myself on the sand dunes. I kept picking up a rumor that the disease didn't exist below the Tropic of Cancer; so I was getting as far south as I could.

Christmas I spent absolutely alone roaming round the mud villages of Beni Ounif and watching caravans come in from the Tuareg country. The pink and purple mountains kept beckoning me on. On a great boulder set out on the plain beyond the oasis was a marvelously executed bas-relief of an elephant. The French colonel claimed it was neolithic. I wished I could send it to Cummings who was so mad about elephants.

A little before the first of the year I wrote Arthur McComb that I was "full of melancholy reflections on the falling of hair, the loss of friends, the disappearance of ocean greyhounds . . . It is time I hitched up my pants and mended my ways . . . I might embrace Islam, but that would necessitate a painful operation . . . It's much the same with communism or your own romantic antiquarianism—the nearing of the end of the year always brings on these *idées noires.* It is a ridiculous and repulsive spectacle that one offers, I fear, continuously scuttling about the world from place to place like a cockroach running away from a light. I am assailed by wise adages and knowing saws. The trouble is they are all quite true—rolling stones gather neither moss nor information. Here I am suddenly trying to pick up Arabic. It's undignified. It's obscene . . ."

As soon as the rheumatic joints began to subside, I moved on to Tangier. I was trying to work up an article about Abd el Krim's rebellion in the Riff. His Majesty's consul in Tangier was an astute Englishman of the old colonial school, a key man in British Intelligence, who was known, feared and admired all through Morocco as Mr. Harriss.

Mr. Harriss had lived thirty years in Morocco. He knew so much and told it so well I felt I'd have to live there another thirty years before I could even begin to write about Abd el Krim.

There's something Western about the Moroccans. They aren't too hard to get to know. I became quite cozy with a French professor in Rabat who sure enough had embraced Islam. I laid it to

French thrift. He had two wives, one a pallid lady dressed *à la Parisienne* who entertained his guests in the parlor and the other a darkhued damsel who did the cooking.

In Marakesh I became acquainted with a tall glowering man named Achmet who invited me to dinner in the company of a grizzlybearded philosophical gentleman who turned out to be a tailor by profession. We talked about destiny in bad French. After an excellent meal of couscous and lamb, Achmet, as the custom was in those parts, brought out a pipe of kif.

Hashish was the last thing in the world I wanted to experiment with. My friends drew on the pipe drowsily, expatiating the while on the pleasures of quiet. I puffed on it in a gingerly sort of way and of course felt no effect at all. Why should I?

It came over me with a rush that I didn't want quiet. What I wanted was the racket and ballyhoo of the U.S.A. Rebellions in the Riff weren't any business of mine. Why try to find out about Morocco when I didn't know what the Americans were up to? My business was to report the rebellions of the guys I'd known in the army.

A couple of days later a cable from New York caught up with me. Jack Lawson was inviting me to become a director in a new theater he was helping set up. I snapped at the opportunity.

I somehow wangled a passage on the mailplane. It was my first plane ride. I was the only passenger. I sat on the mailbags facing the begoggled pilot, sheltered only by a canvas flap. God what a cold ride. The plane bucked like a bronco. Rain clouds lashed us. We flew through sleet. Tangier, Malaga, Alicante, Barcelona . . . somehow I managed to reach Cette without throwing up on the mailbags. From then on to Paris by the night train. Through Languedoc nightingales sang along the railroad track.

I reached New York just in time to see one of the last performances of a play of mine. My name for it when I designed the settings for Ed Massey's production at the Cambridge Dramatic Club many months before, was *The Garbage Man* but the lights across the front of the Greenwich Village Theatre spelled out "The Moon is a Gong." When I got to the boxoffice, I couldn't think how to tell the girl in the window that I was the author, so I bought a ticket like everybody else.

The New Playwrights' Theatre turned out to be one of those instructive experiences. Four directors were already operating. Their prospects seemed rosy. Jack Lawson had already made a name for himself with *Processional.* Francis Faragoh, a small tart man with a charming pair of exiled Hungarians for parents, had won critical acclaim for his *Pinwheel.* Em Jo Basshe had some reputation as a coming dramatist; and Mike Gold, who I think had already published *Jews Without Money,* was supposed to bring in the support of the radical organizations. It was Mike, with his Yiddish charm, and his air of the East Side Gorki, who had talked Otto Kahn into putting up the money. The aim was to set up a repertory theater dedicated to revolutionary expressionism in New York.

Europe was full of it. In Paris there was the Vieux Colombier. In Berlin there was Piscator. From Russia came rumors of Meyerhold and Vachtangov.

The critics couldn't see us for dust. The radical organizations didn't feel we hammered close enough to the party line. Rows, hysterics, ideological tugs of war.

The main thing I enjoyed about the theater was designing and helping paint scenery. Another was dealing with the devoted young men and women who had been bitten by the theater bug and were working their heads off for it. But it was not for me. I'd always been a morning worker and everything in the theater happens after midnight. I'd rented an apartment, with a marvelous view of the Brooklyn waterfront, in Hamilton Easter Field's house on Columbia Heights. Week after week I'd get to bed just in time to wake up. Lack of sleep finally convinced me that the theater and I weren't cut out for each other.

During part of that time Hart Crane had a room in the same house. We occasionally ate dinner together with Cummings and Nagel in one of our wop speakeasies. We all liked and esteemed him, but the poor fellow was frightfully disorganized. Though women took to him he never could get over an adolescent addiction to other males. His nerves seemed to be strung wrong. Cummings had a special way of teasing him that made him break out in hives.

Lachaise had a house in the Catskills where we all used to foregather winter weekends. Hart would sometimes turn up there. The better you knew him the more painful it was. Hart had the real poetic gift and a kind of plain personal decency you don't often find in literary people. Hart had all the elements that should have made a firstrate poet and a firstrate man, but somehow they were put together wrong. He never managed to straighten out his private life; he was helpless in drink. I'd occasionally meet him walking home across the Brooklyn Bridge late at night, the bridge he made his own by a poem, much the way Walt Whitman put his mark on the ferry that preceded it.

He would be pretty drunk and I would try to get him to go to bed. Once just to be civil he went up to his room and closed the door. Later I heard him tiptoeing down the stairs again. But usually he'd balk on the steps and dart off in search of some dreary and dangerous adventure on the waterfront. You couldn't get mad at him any more than you could at a refractory colt.

Someone told me that when poor Hart finally met his end by jumping overboard from the Havana boat the last his friends on deck saw of him was a cheerful wave of the hand before he sank and drowned. That last friendly wave was very like Hart Crane.

These were the years when we were trying to revive the *Masses*. The old *Masses*, since its suppression during the Wilson administration's drive to eliminate pacifist sentiment during the first war, had become a kind of labarum to a whole generation of refractory young people. *The New Masses* was organized in an effort to build a pulpit for native American radicalism. We felt that the Marxist Leninist line did not apply to the United States. The Marxist codifiers had long since labeled our heresy American Exceptionalism. Never much of a hand to work with organizations, I justified my connection with *The New Masses* to myself as a means of getting firsthand knowledge of the labor movement. The hardcore dogmatists were already leery of my attitude.

Though I hadn't yet read Roger Williams I was already the Seeker in matters political as he was the Seeker in matters religious.

If I remember right Egmont Arends, a broadminded fellow without a theoretical bone in his body, was still editor when I went down to Boston to do an article for *The New Masses* on the Sacco-Vanzetti case. I was interested because the men were anarchists, and I had a good deal of sympathy for their naive convictions, so like the delusions of the early Christians who thought the world would come to an end in the year one thousand, and because they were Italians. In college and out I had personally felt the frustrations that came from being considered a wop or a guinea or a greaser.

It is hard to explain to people who never lived through the early twenties the violence of the revulsion against foreigners and radicals that went through the United States after the first world war. To young men who had come home from Europe convinced that militarism was the enemy of civilization this reaction seemed to embody all the evil passions that militarism fed on. When we took up for Sacco and Vanzetti we were taking up for freedom of speech and for an evenhanded judicial system which would give the same treatment to poor men as to rich men, to greasy foreigners as to redblooded Americans.

Aldino Felicani, the Italian printer who dedicated his life to heading up the defense committee, seemed to me to be an honest man from the first time I met him. I felt the same about many of his associates. It was impossible to talk with Bartolomeo Vanzetti when I went to see him at the Charlestown Penitentiary, where he was serving time on his conviction in the Bridgewater case, without being taken with the man's aloofness from egotistical preoccupations. It was hard to imagine the gentle and cogitative fishmonger taking part in a holdup, even in a holdup in what he might consider a good cause. Nobody in his right mind who was planning such a thing would take a man like that along.

When I was getting up a pamphlet for the defense committee I went to North Plymouth and talked to most of Vanzetti's alibi witnesses. I came away convinced that they were telling the truth. Young Brini seemed to me particularly intelligent and trustworthy. To me the story that Vanzetti was selling eels that Christmas Eve morning of 1919 was more credible on the face of it than his "identification" by witnesses who thought he was the foreign-looking man with a shotgun they had seen in the winter twilight a good six months before they gave their testimony in the Plymouth court. Vanzetti's indictment along with Sacco's for the murder of Parmenter and Berardelli in the South Braintree holdup the following April seemed to me to be standard frame-up procedure on the part of the district attorney. If the man you are charging has already been convicted of a crime you have won half your case.

Talking to Nicola Sacco behind the green bars of Dedham jail, I found him very much the good citizen which his character witnesses described. Where Vanzetti was reflective Sacco was a simple outgoing sort of man. It seemed barely possible that he might have convinced himself that seizing money from a capitalist paymaster to be used for the defense of his persecuted comrades was a justifiable act in the class war. The spring of 1920 saw the height of the delirium of arrests and deportations of alleged radicals instigated by Woodrow Wilson's Attorney General. All this was brought close to the Boston anarchists by newspaper headlines reporting that on May 3 their comrade Salsedo had jumped or been thrown to his death from the fourteenth floor of the building on Park Row where he was supposedly being put through the third degree by Department of Justice agents.

Writing about these things forty years after it is hard to reconstruct the frenzy of the Palmer raids. Radicals, foreign and domestic, were being denounced and herded into jails by law officers and such civilian organizations as the American Legion all over the country.

The red baiters had their justification too. The butchery of their opponents on which the revolutionaries in Russia founded the soviet power was fresh in people's minds. Such anarchist exploits as the Wall Street explosion, with its toll of dead and wounded and the bombing of Attorney General Palmer's house in Washington, made a mockery of the plea that anarchists and communists were merely philosophical dissenters.

A. Mitchell Palmer's reign of terror accounted for the fact that Sacco and Vanzetti carried guns when they were arrested on that streetcar in Brockton. They thought they were being arrested for deportation. The agent who arrested them admitted that he was under the impression that he was picking up an associate of theirs named Boda against whom he had evidence to justify deportation proceedings. My hunch was, though I never asked him the direct question, that Vanzetti refused to testify in his own behalf in his first trial at Plymouth for fear he might be trapped into giving information damaging to other members of the anarchist group to which all these men belonged. There are still unexplained mysteries. It is even possible that some of Sacco's and Vanzetti's friends were, as Carlo Tresca hinted years later, involved with professional criminals such as the Morelli gang in acts of violence. What stood out clear as day was that Sacco and Vanzetti were not being given a fair trial.

The crux of the Sacco-Vanzetti case, on which all the agitation was based, was this conviction, shared by many people who were not in any way radicals, that the prosecution was a frame-up. Due to an eccentricity, which I understand has been since corrected, in Massachusetts procedure, there was no way of getting a hearing for fresh evidence turned up by the defense after conviction. Judge Thayer refused to admit the Madeiros confession or any other new leads. When the case was argued on appeal before the Massachusetts Supreme Court it could be argued on the record only. There is no question that Judge Thayer and most of the jury thought they were performing a stern civil duty by seeing to it that "the anarchistic bastards" should properly be hanged. The nearest thing to a review of the evidence was by the commission Governor Fuller appointed to advise him on pardon or commutation.

The only one of the three I'd had contact with, President Lowell of Harvard, had seemed to me to be a wellintentioned gentleman of considerable intelligence; I was appalled when he put his name to the report that sent Sacco and Vanzetti to their deaths. Even to this day, when the passions of the hour have cooled, it is hard to understand how a trained historian could have shown so little curiosity about the human background of the case. Like the Supreme Judicial Court, Governor Fuller's three commissioners stuck to the record and the record killed.

From the point of view of twentieth-century history the question of Sacco's and Vanzetti's guilt or innocence is secondary to the fact that the worldwide agitation in their favor proved to be the testing ground of one of the most effective weapons in the war for the destruction of the capitalist order. The Sacco-Vanzetti agitation proved to be the last mighty effort of the loosely organized anarchist movement which grew out of the split between Bukharin and Marx in the First International. The widespread protest that started as a spontaneous expression of anarchist ideals and hatreds ended pretty much under Communist Party control.

In Boston the work of the Defense Committee was hampered by continual patient efforts of the American C.P. to take charge of the agitation. The propaganda schools in Moscow learned an important lesson in international politics from the Sacco-Vanzetti agitation. Griefs and discontents, properly stimulated and directed, were more effective than armies in the world struggle for power.

The passions aroused were allconsuming. Old friends cut you on the street. Just one example. Lowell Downes, Bobby Hillyer's great pal in college days, whom I hadn't seen since Madrid, when he heard I had put my name to a pamphlet defending Sacco and Vanzetti, wrote me from California formally breaking off relations.

This sort of controversy wasn't in my line. For one thing I could never convince myself enough of the rightness of my own opinions properly to take out after my opponents. I could never quite get used to people I thought were friends getting sore at me personally instead of at my reprehensible opinions. I kept remembering a motto lettered over the entrance of the Carcel Modelo in Madrid: "Abhor the crime but pity the criminal."

The ideological rumbles around the Sacco-Vanzetti case and the New Playwrights' Theatre got my head to spinning so I decided to pull out of New York for a while. I craved fresh air and I had to have some sleep.

After a short visit to my halfbrother James down in the Northern Neck of Virginia, I started on a walk through Gotham Pass in the mountains west of Lexington. An early snowstorm hit me crossing Warm Springs Mountain. It was a delight to discover, arriving there footsore, weary and wet, that a little inn was operating in the old Warm Springs courthouse and that you could swim in the mineral pools across the road. Swimming alone at dusk in the warm clear water of the deep pool was an unforgettable pleasure. The octagonal frame springhouse looked as if it dated from the time of Jefferson. Snowflakes drifted in through an opening in the roof. Nobody in the Virginia mountains had ever heard of Sacco and Vanzetti or Marx or expressionism in the theater. If they had they didn't give a damn. What a relief!

By November 1, *el dia de los muertos,* when all the hucksters sell little skulls made of sugar candy, I was in Mexico City. Mexico was still the colonial capital. The buildings you noticed were all colonial baroque. There was Marxism aplenty, but it was the Marxism of Orozco and Diego Rivera, whom you could see at work on their murals in the Secretariat of Education. There were further reminders of the Mexican revolution when some mustachioed colonel who had survived from Villa's Dorados would shoot out the lights in one of the bars on the Avenida Juarez. When you went to dance at the Salon México they frisked you for arms at the door. Pistols and knives were carefully checked on a long table.

There's a marvelous clarity about the light in the Valley of Mexico. Things and people stand out in brutal relief. People tend to become cartoons of themselves.

The Americans I ran into there were mostly radicals but their theories hardly jibed with the picaresque realities of their lives. There was a retired wobbly named Gladwin Bland who was making a pretty fair living from a series of small business enterprises. Gladdy was full of stories, which he told with a certain satirical detachment, of the days when he believed the I.W.W. were really building a new society within the shell of the old.

Howard Phillips, who already knew more about Mexico than anybody you could meet, native or gringo, was launching his *Mexican Life.* Yarns and tall tales abounded. We saw a lot of Mexicans, journalists, literary people and the like, with whom we punctiliously observed the posadas before Christmas and *año nuevo* when everybody at the party greeted the arrival of the new year by kissing everybody else on both cheeks. Over the *copitas* the Mexicans would tell you how they hated all gringos, but you were different.

My friends were all pretty much bound to the city. Except for Sunday excursions to drink beer on the punts at Xochimilco or in the cave behind the pyramids at Teotihuacan I didn't explore the back country as much as I'd have liked. I did get in several days of walking with a young fellow of mostly Indian blood named Xavier Guerrero.

Xavier was a painter of real talent, but he was renouncing his art out of dedication to the Communist Party. We walked around from village to village in the chilly mountains back of Toluca. We ate off the Indians and slept on straw mats wrapped in insufficient serapes. Cold and fleas made sleep uneasy. There was a bare sculptural magnificence about everything: the mountains, the prickly pears, the maguey, the broad darkly molded faces. I sat looking and sketching while Xavier, who ought to have been doing the drawing, spread the gospel of Lenin and Marx among the villagers.

They talked a great deal about *los enemigos*. Xavier kept explaining that los enemigos were the capitalist oppressors, but it occasionally came out that when these people talked of los enemigos they meant the Indians on the other slope of the mountains.

Xavier was as dedicated as an early Christian. I have often wondered what became of him. It seemed to me even then that in the long run he would have done more for his Indian peons whose lives he had such a passion to uplift by painting them than by proselytizing them. Art even if it's worthless does little harm. At its best it furnishes an immense lift to the human spirit. Politics, in our day, has become as destructive as religion was in the fifteenth century.

I got back to New York in March with as many stories in my head as a dog has fleas. Something new had come into my thoughts further to distract me from the theater and from radical agitation. I was trying to organize some of these stories I had picked up in Mexico into the intertwined narratives that later became *The 42nd Parallel. Three Soldiers* and *Manhattan Transfer* had been single panels; now, somewhat as the Mexican painters felt compelled to paint their walls, I felt compelled to start on a narrative panorama to which I saw no end.

The summer of 1927 saw the last frantic struggle to save the lives of Sacco and Vanzetti. April 9th of that year Judge Thayer finally got around to sentencing them to death. My wisecracking friends from midtown New York had been kidding me about my radical frenzies until it seemed to me I must be about as Marx-struck as Xavier Guerrero. Scott Fitzgerald, with whom I had a long session during some short visit of his to New York at about this time, was particularly funny about it, kidding and serious too. He was on firm ground when he begged me to keep novelwriting and propaganda separate. Even a touch of propaganda would ruin my work if it hadn't ruined it already. I can still remember the scornful look on his pale face. His features seemed particularly carefully delineated, like a sketch by James Montgomery Flagg, that day.

All the same Sacco-Vanzetti was becoming the fashionable cause. Picketing the Boston statehouse was the one a day good deed of the literary radicals that summer. I even managed to get hauled in myself.

The joke was it was all a mistake. True to my conviction that I should stick to the position of observer I did not think it was my business to picket or march. When *The Daily Worker*, of all papers, asked me to report the excitements in Boston, I was perfectly willing to send in a daily article. Though I was thoroughly aware of the tension between the Communists and the anarchist defense committee, my attitude, somewhat naive at the time, was that it didn't matter where you published so long as they printed what you wrote. *Litera scripta manet.*

While I was trotting around getting stories from the picketers one afternoon the cops made one of their periodical raids. They pushed me into the paddywaggon with the rest. The cops were quite unmoved when I tried to produce credentials as a reporter for *The Daily Worker.*

Still the police had been told to treat the picketers gently. The ride in the paddywaggon was made delightful by the fact that I found myself sitting next to Edna St. Vincent Millay. Outside of being a passable poet Edna Millay was one of the most attractive women who ever put pen to paper. The curious glint in her coppercolored hair intoxicated every man who saw her. Besides having violet eyes and the loveliest hair in the world Edna Millay had a wealthy husband. We had hardly time to choose our places in the cells at the Joy Street station before Eugene Boissevain was bailing us out. The charge was "sauntering and loitering." I was one of the bunch who chose to stand trial and, months later, when everybody was forgetting Sacco and Vanzetti, had the somewhat barren satisfaction of being acquitted.

Sacco and Vanzetti were dead. The New Playwrights' Theatre, though not quite on the rocks, was proving to be one headache after another. Administration and moneyraising just weren't my dish. It occurred to me this might be a good time to visit the Soviet Union. There wasn't much sense in going just for the trip, but studying the Russian theater, obviously in its heyday, would be helpful in planning new productions, and might give me sidelights on how people lived in a socialist society. I had learned long since that asking direct questions the way Scott did was the last way to find out about anything.

For several weeks in the spring of 1928 I tried to work up a deal for a free passage. I think it was Sam Ornitz who had introduced me to a plausible fellow connected with Amtorg who was looking for a man to feed and care for a shipment of muskrats to Leningrad. Mink and sable were getting scarce in the western provinces of the Soviet Union. The export of furs to capitalist countries was one of the surest sources of valuta. Someone got the idea of importing American muskrats to stock the depleted streams. Why couldn't I feed the muskrats and get a free ride to Leningrad? Maybe the higher-ups decided I wouldn't be the man properly to indoctrinate these capitalist muskrats with Marxist Leninism. Anyway the deal fell through and I had to raise money for the trip by getting an advance on a book contract.

The first night's sleep on an outbound ocean steamship has always seemed the grandest thing in the world. I took a third-class passage on the *United States* of one of the Scandinavian lines to Copenhagen. The crossing was delightful. Everything neat and clean, beer cheap, good plain food; it was an experience eating raw herring for breakfast. I got my first sight of Rockall, that strange outcropping of the earth's crust which stands alone in the North Atlantic some twentyfour hours steaming west of the Pentland Firth. It reminded me of the reproduction of a German painting called "The Island of the Dead" that used to give me chills when I was little in the upper hall of our house at Sandy Point. We passed near enough to feel the groundswell and to hear the growl of the surf. The rock rose, tall as the biggest ocean liner, in reddish slate cliffs that tapered into peaks, white with bird-droppings as a high mountain is with snow. Gulls and gannets whirled about it in an endlessly screaming cloud.

Helsinki seemed dismal when I reached Finland on the steamer from Stettin, after a dash to London and Paris to round up old cronies, and a couple of days of partying in Berlin with van den Arend. Van was just back from Madagascar, where the import-export firm he worked for had suddenly gone broke. In spite of champagne with a peach in it we found Berlin nightlife depressing. Already I was seeing it through the eyes of Georg Grosz. Never liked nightlife anyway. Now Helsinki seemed thoroughly antiseptic. There was nothing to drink and never any darkness and the sea wasn't salt; and of course my Russian visa, supposed to be waiting for me, had not yet arrived.

When after endless days of waiting I finally did reach Leningrad in the company of a Russianborn American named Kittin, who edited a Russian language newspaper in New York, everything seemed breathlessly exciting by contrast.

The summer of 1928 was a good time for Americans in the Soviet Union. Russian governments since time immemorial, have tended, like the oyster, spasmodically to open and close. This was the period of a receptive attitude toward foreigners. The relaxation of NEP was still noticeable. The war to the death between Stalin and Trotsky was at a stalemate. Trotsky was in exile but Stalin did not yet feel himself sufficiently entrenched in power to sweep out Trotsky's adherents. People still dared to mention Trotsky's name. American engineers had been making themselves useful to the regime. There was no anti-American propaganda; in fact individual Americans were more popular than not.

Everything in Leningrad moved against a background of vast Palladian colonnades set up like stage scenery at the end of every vista. Always I was conscious of the iceclear steelgray waters of the Neva pouring past into the Baltic. I stayed at the old Evropskaya Hotel where the rooms still had the air of Stanislavski's settings for the Chekov plays.

Kittin's Russian was a great help. We saw the sights together. At the Hermitage we got so interested in talking to a Kirgiz that we almost forgot to look at the pictures. He was a young fellow just a year out of the nomad tents on the steppe. His brother was a party member and was studying at the university for eastern peoples. He himself was still *byezpartini* [without a party] he said; he wanted to see the world and to decide for himself. He was working as a common laborer in a metallurgical plant, where he made just enough to live on. He was a great reader. It was only since the revolution that there had been any reading among the Kirgiz. He was reading Gorki. He wasn't planning to read anything else until he'd read everything Gorki ever wrote.

The things he liked about the revolution were reading and the new kind of marriage. Before, among the Kirgiz, a man couldn't marry until he had enough cattle or money to buy himself a wife. Here at the plant where he worked, if a girl liked a fellow she would take up with him. If they got very fond of each other or were going to have a baby, then they registered the marriage.

He couldn't wait for us to tell him everything about America. Did we have any nomads, what was our marriage like, how much did a metalworker make? He wanted to go to America, he wanted to see as much of the world as he could so that he could decide what kind of system would be best for his Kirgiz people.

We had hardly sopped up all we could from the Kirgiz before I found myself shaking hands with Etienne de Beaumont and his wife. "*Quelle collection! Epatant. Formidable.*" I'd met the Beaumonts as friends of the Murphys at Villa America at Antibes. They were patrons of the avantgarde arts; and *très américains* perhaps because an ancestor of the count's had accompanied Tocqueville on his famous American tour.

Falling in with the Kirgiz and the Beaumonts on the same afternoon caused me to underline Leningrad's cosmopolitan air in my notes. It was as a gateway between east and west that the Czar Peter built his northern capital. Russian writers I met of the Leningrad school strongly felt the European tie. They didn't conceal their scorn of Moscow.

Stenich, who came to see me at the hotel, was as avantgarde as the Beaumonts. He spoke excellent English. He had translated a novel of mine and was eager for news of the latest by Joyce and Eliot and Pound. His father had been a wealthy businessman of Czech origin but Stenich wrote and thought in Russian. Friends whispered in my ear that he was a firstrate poet. He had joined the Red Guards very young and had commanded a division during the civil war, but he had somehow gotten in wrong with the regime, had been expelled from the Party, and had spent a year in jail. Jokingly he called himself a counterrevolutionary.

Stenich and his friends took me for long walks about the city through the milky northern midnight. He showed us the vast square where the monument was to the October dead and told how it was made on one of Lenin's Saturday afternoons when soldiers and factory workers would tackle some particularly unsightly corner of the city and dig it up into a park. He showed us the streets where he had fought eleven years before, the place where they had held the barricade against a desperate attack from the Cadets. He recalled wistfully the enthusiasms and comradeships of those days.

On the embankment of the shimmering broad Neva opposite the spires of the Fortress of Saints Peter and Paul we came upon the huge black statue of a man on a prancing horse. "That's my favorite Russian in history," cried Stenich, "Peter the Great who brought order out of chaos, the first Bolshevik."

Everybody seemed a little shocked. Stenich ought to have said that Lenin was his favorite Russian. Somebody proclaimed that he preferred Pushkin. Someone else brought up the name of Edgar Allan Poe. Did I know that Pushkin and Poe might have met in St. Petersburg? Excitedly they told me the story. During the period when Poe followed the sea he had sailed up the Baltic on a merchant ship. Poe and Pushkin had met face to face, maybe on this very spot. I suggested that this was a myth based on one of Poe's equivocal statements about his early history. Stenich asked brusquely: How did I know? I didn't! They wanted so to believe the story that I began to believe it myself. I remembered Stenich as the most vivid of the Russians I met in Leningrad. Poor fellow, he did not have long to live. He was rubbed out early in Stalin's purge of Leningrad writers.

It was in Leningrad I first met Horsley Gantt. I was asking some question at the desk at the hotel. Horsley had come to the Evropskaya to meet somebody else. We recognized each other as Americans and fell to talking. Horsley was a Virginian who had first come to Russia as a physician with the Hoover Relief. He had thought of Pavlov only as a great physiologist until he visited his laboratory. He was swept off his feet by the man and by his work on the conditioned reflex. When I met Horsley he was completing what amounted to a seven years' apprenticeship of study and experimental work in Pavlov's laboratory.

He invited me out to breakfast at his lodgings next morning. I don't remember what we talked about but I do remember the strawberries. The Leningrad strawberries are the best in the world. I remember them being big as your fist and fragrant as the French *fraise du bois*. These were the famous strawberries poor Nicky used to send to his wife's grandmother, Queen Victoria, in the days before the thrones fell. Horsley wanted to take me out to meet Pavlov. I fought shy. I couldn't imagine that the great scientist would want to waste his time with a wandering American writer. I've been kicking myself ever since.

I did see his laboratory. "Saw Pavlov's dogs in Leningrad," I wrote Cummings. "Incidentally all his work has been on gland secretions other than the sexual and most of his work on the physiology of the brain has been via the saliva glands of the dog where he can measure the secretions. The whole thing is coming out in an English translation this year (International Publishers) [this was Horsley Gantt's translation]. Everybody says it will annihilate Dr. Watson (John) and make Freud look like 30 cents. Be that as it may. He hates the Soviet government and roars against them in his lectures, and they give his laboratory more money every year. So everybody is happy. Talked to his wife. I imagine he really is a great man, nearly eighty with bushy whiskers and never missed a day in his laboratory all through the war and the revolution.

"People are so hospitable here and so nice it's heartbreaking—and the breadth and emptiness of the country is magnificent . . ."

Horsley took me out on the train to a seedy suburb to call on the prerevolutionary critic, Chukhovski. The censorship had forced him to give up literary criticism. Instead he wrote children's books. His "Krokodil" had been such a success with young and old that it afforded him a sort of sanctuary against the regime. Lenin's enthusiasm for Pavlov's discoveries protected Pavlov in much the same way. I remember Chukhovski as a congenial tall gray man with the airs and graces of a European man of letters of the last century. He talked nostalgically of European wateringplaces, Carlsbad, Wiesbaden, Cannes. They never would let him go abroad. He intimated that he himself was fairly safe but they had so many ways of getting at you. His daughter was in trouble, only exiled, not imprisoned. He feared for his young son. It was not so much what he said as what he didn't say that was heartbreaking.

There had been something familiarly western about the vast nostalgias of Leningrad. Taking the night train to Moscow seemed a leap in the unknown. It rained all the way. When I looked out in the morning I could see nothing but scrubby firs and birches fading into mist. The train was gritty and crowded but traintrips through unknown country are always fun.

There were no tourists in those days. A grim young woman from Voks settled me in a vast room at the old Moscow Hotel. The first American I found myself talking to there was Ivy Lee. What the man who was devoting his life to giving eyeappeal to old John D. Rockefeller was doing in Moscow I never learned, but lacking anybody to talk English with, he used to waylay me in the lobby and tell me tales of his early life. He was a southerner. He had no trace of humor but I couldn't help admiring his dedication to his trade. I was sorry when he left.

Soon I found myself busier than I had ever been in New York. I went to the theater every night. I had a list as long as your arm of people I wanted to see. Mornings I studied Russian. Trying to memorize the forms of the Russian verb gave me a sort of headache I've never had before or since. I was very much taken with the Muscovites I met. I considered myself fairly energetic, but these were people I had trouble keeping up with. They ate more, drank more, talked more, read more, sat up later, got up earlier than I could. Men and women were consumed with an entrancing curiosity about everything under the sun.

Stanislavski was gone but an awfully nice woman who played small parts at the Art Theatre saw to it that I got to plays I wanted to see and translated important scraps of dialogue into English for me. Though she said most of the new plays were so badly written it was just as well I couldn't understand them, I found the acting superb, the settings and direction vivid and uncompromising. Meyerhold's *Roar China* was the production I liked best. The ballet seemed anachronistic and boring. Chekov's plays were still being produced at the Art Theatre exactly as Stanislavski and Chekov had planned them. There was a wonderful new staging of *Boris Godunov*. I've always felt that anybody who wanted to discover what life was like in the Soviet Union could learn more by listening to Moussorgsky's opera than by five years reading of *The New York Times*.

I learned a great deal about how Russian theater people lived from my actress friend. Like Stenich she was nostalgic about the period of war communism. Though actors like scientists had preferential treatment the Art Theatre people came near starving to death. She had never imagined potatoes could be so delicious as the potatoes they roasted over the coals when potatoes were all they could get to eat. Walking home to my hotel after the theater we would often pass a window of propaganda material with a picture of Stalin in the middle. If she was sure nobody was looking she would make a hurried little gesture of shaking her fist at it.

The Kamerny Theatre was doing Eugene O'Neill's *Desire Under the Elms*. It was odd seeing it through Russian eyes, presented according to Taïrov's rather mannered style. Both Taïrov and his wife were warm friends of the Murphys, who had helped them out financially when their company was stranded in Paris a couple of years before. I couldn't get them to talk about much. They were already under critical attack and I suspect they thought I was too close to the Communists to be trustworthy.

The movie producers were more open. Pudovkin was the sort of man you could talk about anything with and Eisenstein was boasting of how much he had learned from *The Birth of a Nation* by that old scoundrel of a capitalist D. W. Griffith. These men were so different from the few American movie people I'd run into, it was absolutely startling. They were men of broad reading, anxious to learn, to take on new impressions.

"The most interesting and lively people I met in Leningrad and Moscow were the movie directors," I told Cummings. "They, as I suppose is natural, say that the theatre is capoot. Eisenstein says that Meyerhold has ruined the theatre by carrying each of his productions so far in a logical direction that it is impossible to go further. Certainly the one Meyerhold show I've seen was damn fine (*Roar China*) but I don't see that it is the end of anything except perhaps Meyerhold's own energy. Eisenstein is worried over the talking movies, because he says he fears they may become an art, and bring all the worst features of the stage back on the silver screen. He thinks the first stage will be allright and simply silly, but then there will be the danger of Moscow-Arting the talkies. Which is interesting because they see almost no American films here—and look upon them with great admiration. Actors and directors make about $25 a week and think they are lucky. I'm wondering what would happen to these people, who are all kids under thirty, if they went to America. I've seen most of the historical pictures and they are superb. Even the bum ones have redeeming features in incidental photography. The great thing is they have little money for elaborate studio work and have to use actual scenes and people and inventive photography. Eisenstein is for some reason not a jew and looks like an ordinary German squarehead. He's extremely gentil and a very interesting bird."

Eisenstein had a curt aphoristic way of talking. We agreed thoroughly about the importance of montage. He may have already been suffering from a damaging amount of conceit as a result of the adulation which surrounded him, but he had one of the most brilliantly synthesizing minds I ever ran into. If he'd been a mathematician, he would have skipped the early stages and started out with calculus and logic.

He had spent a little time in Japan, learned the language, and was up on Japanese art and literature. It was Eisenstein who insisted I go to see the Kabuki Theatre, then making its first visit to Moscow. There was such a scramble for seats my friends had to use all the prestige I had gained in those parts through my efforts for Sacco and Vanzetti to get me in. The show was wonderful, but what impressed me most was how the Russians I knew had read up on Japanese plays.

Somebody took me to see Lunacharski, who was still Minister of Education. With his pincenez and his little goatee he seemed very much the old-fashioned French professor in a provincial *lycée*. We spoke French. I know I am prejudiced against public officials, but I certainly didn't find his conversation very interesting. He was cordial enough; and, when he learned I was planning to meet Dr. Gantt of Pavlov's staff—Pavlov was a name to conjure with—in the Caucasus, arranged for me to join an expedition from Narkompross which was going to explore some of the less frequented parts of Daghestan.

So, armed with Hugo's *Russian Self-taught*, a pocket dictionary, a child's life of Jack London and Pushkin's *Evgeni Onegin*, some kind of propuss given me in exchange for my passport which they insisted on keeping at the Interior ministry, and a wad of rubles, I set out alone for Yaroslavl.

Apart from the gilt onion domes of crumbling monasteries what I chiefly remember there was a giant spadebearded *izvoshchik* out of the chorus of *Boris Godunov* who drove me to the boat. He towered over his spidery droshki and his asthmatic little horse.

He was convinced that I was a German. In German so rudimentary that even I could understand it he confided in me that things were terrible. Every barefoot noaccount in the village thought he was as good as the next man. What Russia needed was a Hindenburg to put every man in his place. Stalin was the man to do it. In all that summer's traveling that izvoshchik was the only Russian I met who mentioned Stalin's name.

The cabman left me at the gangway of the river steamer. I

looked about the decks with some trepidation. The decrepit sternwheeler looked like a Currier and Ives print. Horsley Gantt had told me of his adventures on the Volga the summer before. On his way back to Leningrad after a vacation he reached Astrakhan short of money. He had enough for his fare upriver, but how was he going to eat? He decided to invest his money in watermelons. He stacked his cabin to the ceiling. The trouble was that the water was falling in the Volga, as it usually does at the end of summer. The boat kept running aground. Progress was slower and slower, fourteen days to Yaroslavl. He hasn't just rightly cared for watermelons since.

I had no such difficulties. The five days gliding down the Volga with the current passed almost too fast. I had a room to myself on the upper deck. Marvelous breakfasts were brought me there of tea and black bread spread with sweet butter and caviar. The rest of the meals were mostly cabbage and kasha but not too bad. At the town where Lenin was born I climbed a rickety stairway up a cliff to the Ulianov family mansion. Looking out from the red clay bluff the Volga might have been the Mississippi. The house, obviously the home of a welloff cultured nineteenth-century family, had something of the feeling of a house Emerson might have lived in at Concord.

Astrakhan turned out to be almost as far from the Caspian as New Orleans is from the Gulf. I ran into a Pole who was mate on a merchant ship anchored down at the eight fathom anchorage. He'd spent six months in England and was anxious to exercise his English. He bought us a bottle of vodka in a filthy little cookshack which was operated by a grumpy Tatar and full of bluebottle flies and of the stench of rancid muttonfat. The Pole immediately announced that he was on the edge of suicide. "This bloody Caspian Sea."

Imagine the fate of a fine new steamship launched in the Caspian. It wasn't a sea, it was a bloody trough full of bloody slime. It smelt like a bloody purgative. It was a bloody prison. The north end was so shallow there was nowhere to dock. What was the use of keeping a ship in good shape if you never went into port? The steamers rotted and rusted and so did their crews. The bloody Caspian was one of nature's mistakes.

The bottle was getting low. The Pole seized himself by the hair and shook his head vigorously back and forth. If he weren't a Red he would go back to Poland. He wasn't a Communist but he was a Red and dreamed of a great Red merchant marine. He was rotting and rusting here in this bloody Caspian. How could a great navigator be trained on a sea you couldn't sail out of?

The bottle was empty. The Tatar was closing down his shack. When I left him the Pole went lurching off down the dark street muttering that perhaps this very bloody night he would kill himself, but first he had to have one more bloody drink.

The Caspian sure enough smelt like Epsom salts. We boarded the deepwater steamboat, anchored way out of sight of the low-lying lands of the Volga delta, from a tender. The ship was even more far gone in rust than the desperate Pole had led me to expect. A southerly wind churned the shallow water into a chop. The dingy passengers huddled on deck immediately started, men, women and children, to vomit into the chamberpots they had brought along for the purpose. The sun was hot and the air was foul.

At Makhatch-Kalá instead of taking a swim as I'd intended I had to spend hours standing in line, tortured by flies in the squalid heat, to buy a ticket to Grozny. I don't know when Russian railroad officials evolved the clever idea of never selling tickets until the train came into the station.

At Grozny I found that the expedition I was supposed to meet had already gone up into the mountains of Sheshia. How to take after them? By the greatest good luck I managed to join forces with a French-speaking Russian engineer—I think he was prospecting for oil—who was bound in the same direction. We hired a phaeton. Late that night I found my delegatzia (every traveling group is a delegation) camped in a sort of dasha with French windows. Just as I stepped in the dimly lit room I suffered the indignity of being nipped in the rear by a dog. I turned and found myself facing a shaggy white creature the size of a calf. I shouted, "Down, sir, shame!" and he retired. I don't know why mountain dogs grow so large, but these dogs in the eastern Caucasus were larger than St. Bernards, or even than the enormous white Pyrenees sheepdogs which they very much resembled.

This delegation from Narkompross operated very much like the group of Russians Gerald Murphy and I worked with in Paris when we helped paint Goncharova's scenery. They were picking sites for schools and evidently writing up reports on these remote regions which had almost been forgotten since the revolution. Everything went on in a flood of conversation of which I could follow very little. I never discovered exactly who was in charge. I never could find out what time we were planning to set out in the morning.

There was a schoolteachery woman, several middleaged men, and a ruddycheeked young fellow with noseglasses named Nikolai Semyonovich whom I got to know quite well. They were friendly, but nobody put himself out to help a foreigner. You had to tag along catch as catch can. The country we rode through soon became so strange that we were all foreigners together.

With dismay I discovered that there was another American along. On a trip of this kind the last thing you want is a compatriot.

Anna Louise Strong was a big busty selfcentered spinster from one of the mountain states. One suspected she was the only child of a welltodo family and had been spoiled rotten as a girl. She wore a welldesigned green traveling suit with a split skirt for riding. She wasn't a very interesting woman but she made up for it by enthusiasm. It was a little like the enthusiasm of certain missionaries I had met in various dismal corners of the world, only in Anna Louise it was directed toward the Communist idea.

I couldn't help admiring her courage because it proved a fairly tough trip. Poor soul, her efforts to provide herself with a few creature comforts only managed to irritate the rest of us. Her air mattress made an annoying whine when you blew it up. Since it never occurred to the Russians to put themselves out for her, I found myself in the absurd position of reluctant squire.

From the moment we left Shattoi—these names are all spelled wrong, I never could find them on any map—we were riding up one mountain pass after another. The guides would never take their horses farther than the next valley because it would be inhabited by a different people and they didn't know the language. The Russians were helpless as I was. At every night's stop we had to find fresh interpreters.

The houses were of stone with whitewashed porches, a little like houses I'd seen in Persia, but better. The air of cultivation amazed us all. There were often ruined watchtowers in the distance. As in the Pyrenees the north slopes tended to be wooded with evergreens.

At a place called Khoi we found a feudal castle said to have been built by the Georgians, but the inscriptions were in Arabic. The uplands were sheep country. A shepherd we met on the road had never heard of America. We slept on the porch of some kind of a government house constructed ages ago of nicely squared stones. Huge white shaggy dogs prowled threateningly about us all night.

From Khoi we rode across a pass and down a steep thousand-foot slope into a wellwatered valley with snowmountains to the southward. The slopes were all terraced. Fruittrees filled the bottomlands. The villages were cubist constructions set on cliffs above roaring gorges. This was Daghestan. I felt like Marco Polo.

Botlich, built on a hill between two streams, turned out to be a tiny Damascus. Balconies jutting out over arcaded streets. It was a Moslem town. Muezzins shouted from the stubby towers of the mosques. The horned sheep grazing on the slopes above had the look of being crossed with ibex. The Soviet revolution was represented by a new Workers' and Peasants' Club with loudspeakers, a stage and a movie screen. We bought the best pears I ever ate.

We spent two days in Botlich negotiating for fresh horses. The second night, after we'd all turned in on the roof, the local inhabitants suddenly threw a party for us. Drum, tambourine and accordion started playing in the room below. The Russians were on their feet in a jiffy.

The music sounded Persian. Tall girls appeared in long black dresses that just touched the floor and spun around as if they were on casters. Men and women put on separate dances. Our Russians danced and sang and clapped. There was stewed lamb and vodka and toasts galore. It went on all night.

None of the Russians showed a sign of fatigue when we

mounted our ponies at dawn next morning. We rode past dugout villages like rabbitwarrens where people were mining salt, and down into the deep canyon of a river. The water of that river was salt as the sea.

That night we slept out in a drizzle on a high mountain shelf near an astonishing ancient bridge that hung hundreds of feet over the floor of a narrow canyon. Our blankets of the local wool were so greasy that the rain never soaked through.

Next day the going was muddy. Along the way we met an old grizzly man who had never heard of Moscow. Vladykavkhass yes, but the name Moscow made no impression.

In the afternoon Nikolai Semyonovich nearly lost his horse in a quicksand while we were bathing in a mountain lake. I had never seen a proper quicksand before. The sight was impressive.

At Gounib, perched on a rocky crag, high among the clouds, we slept in beds and ate stewed mutton and mutton cutlets at the Cooperative. Mutton was the only meat available in the entire Caucasus; we were glad to get it. Although it was early September the peaches for which Gounib was famous were not ripe yet. At a village on the way I had managed to buy some apricots locally canned. "To appease Anna Louise," I entered spitefully in my journal. "Very nasty but she liked them . . . Heaven preserve us from all women with three barrelled names."

From Gounib we walked up to a fantastic stone village named something like Rugdjá that had been Judaist during the great proselytizing period—wasn't that the sixth century?—then converted to Islam, then Judaist again, and at some later period forcibly re-moslemized. A girl in the market offered us ears of steamed corn. The Russians wouldn't eat it; said maize was only fit for horses—but it tasted like home to me.

The ancient stone houses opened on arcades. Their doorways were beautifully carved in what seemed Persian designs. Through them we got glimpses of massively ornamented dressers and sideboards. We saw wooden ploughs and harrows made of sharp stones set in a plank. The tools had a neolithic look. Every other man was named Izrafel.

All through Daghestan we kept being surprised by the high style of culture. Somehow this country had escaped the civil war.

There were beautiful villages of cubeshaped dwellings. At Chokh we drank tea in a room handsomely decorated with lilac and pink bands. Finely drawn hammers and sickles in black on white formed a frieze around the top. Food being a rarity the good meals were what we most remembered. At Burshi they produced the usual mutton stewed in clabber, but they served it in handsome copper dishes with hot unleavened bread and ripe tomatoes. From then on the pickings were slim.

We labored across a really high pass through snowfields where we surprised a flock of ibex that bolted off with their horns held flat to their backs. The going got so steep we had to drag our ponies by their halters over the crumbly snow. More passes, and then green valleys and a busride, and we were climbing out into the bustle of Tiflis.

I've forgotten where I said goodbye to the delegatzia. I was sorry to leave them. They had proved excellent traveling companions, energetic and fanatically curious about peoples, languages, architecture, history, everything we ran into. Nikolai Semyonovich was the student out of every Russian novel I ever read. We had long conversations in bad French and worse German, sprinkled with an occasional Russian or English expression. The poor fellow had done well at the University, attained something equivalent to a Ph.D., but his career was about to be ruined because he had the wrong class origins. His people were Moscow merchants or something like that. A committee was at work on the class origins of all the students. When they came to him he'd be out. That would be the end.

Whether his fears were real or imaginary, Nikolai Semyonovich was on the verge of a depression. When I got back to Moscow someone told me he had killed himself rather than face the committee.

Next morning I set off on another bus, back across the Caucasus by the Grusinski highway, to meet Horsley Gantt. He had come by train from Moscow to what was still called, as in Tolstoy's early stories, Vladykavkhass. I was insatiable for mountains. After all that riding I wanted to walk. We decided we would go back up to

Kasbek, which I had just been through on the bus, and start walk ing there. Kasbek was a resort town and was reputed to have a comfortable hotel.

Our plan was to walk across country from the Grusinski to the Ossetine highway. We figured we could do it in a couple of days. Horsley had Leningrad friends with him, an American named Brown, a young Russian named George, and his sister Seraphima. They made faces at the idea of walking so we left them to come up with our knapsacks and blankets in a cart called a *lineiki.* You sat on rough boards back to back and dangled your feet above the rocky road. In their charge we left a collection of pastries and cakes of chocolate we had managed to purchase as reserve rations for our walking trip.

Horsley ran the two-mile in college. He started off at a clip that made me puff even though I was in pretty good training from the Daghestan trek. Halfway up he decided his shoes didn't fit, so he pulled them off and walked barefoot. Though he admitted he hadn't walked barefoot since he was a child in Nelson County he came along at a good pace up the pebbly road. To me, it was a phenomenon as surprising as the high bridge in the Daghestan mountains. When we reached Kasbek after roaming in the twilight through a Georgian castle known as the Castle of Tamara, Horsley's feet, which I'd expected to be a bloody mess, showed hardly a bruise.

The Hotel Francia was a disappointment. The beds were made of wooden boards. Thank heaven we had our blankets. The Georgian proprietor, a voluble fellow with an untrustworthy look in his eye, who was tireless in his complaints about the Communist regime, did turn out some firstrate skewers of shashlik.

We climbed up to the glacier that hangs from the steep snowfields of Mt. Kasbek above the valley, and, on the way back, sweaty and footsore, were led by a little shepherd boy who refused a tip to a deep pool of natural sodawater. This is the Narzan that is bottled in these parts and shipped all over Russia. The water was cold. The bubbles tingled on your skin. We came out ready to lick our weight in wildcats.

We picked a place called Zaramag on the map to head for on the Ossetine road, but nobody could tell us how far it was or how the road went or whether there was any road at all. Finally the hotelkeeper produced a whiskery character who looked like a cartoon of an Albanian bandit who claimed he knew the way to Zaramag.

The bandit had another of those springless carts, drawn by two shaggy ponies. We set out up the road toward Tiflis, our friends jouncing in the cart, and Horsley and I walking ahead. At Kobi, up near the divide, we stopped at a wonderful little posthouse straight out of Gogol. There was a cloth on the table and a polished brass samovar with a flowered porcelain teapot. A pleasant woman in a clean tunic brought out little cakes like American corn muffins and sweet butter to eat with our tea. George and Seraphima had confessed to having gobbled up all our pastries and chocolate on the road up to Kasbek, so I scooped their share of the corncakes, which of course they wouldn't touch, into my knapsack.

Above Kobi our bandit turned west off the macadam road along a trail that followed a sulphurous yellow stream through a valley of steaming hotsprings. We had been told to spend the night at a place we thought was called Tib. "Tib?" we kept asking our bandit. He'd nod his head and point up the valley. It was almost dark before we reached one of those villages of cubical houses linked together by walls and turrets that made me feel we were slipping back into the eleventh century. Was this Tib?

A stout man was discovered who spoke good Russian. This wasn't Tib. It was something that sounded like Tjeb. How far was Zaramag? "Ah, Zaramag!" He waved his hand vaguely toward the mountains. He ushered us into a nice bare room with rugs on the floor. He rubbed his hands and bowed a great deal. He would kill a sheep in our honor. He would order shashlik to be prepared. Squatted on the rugs we waited hour after hour. It was midnight before a dish was brought in piled with chunks of mutton so tough that, hungry as we were, we couldn't chew it, let alone swallow it. We curled up and went hungrily to sleep.

From then on the problem of food was never out of our heads. All we had were the corncakes from Kobi and Horsley's packet of tea. Our host at Tjeb told us that we had to cross a high pass to Zaramag. Our bandit announced he was afraid to go farther.

George and Seraphima decided to backtrack to the Georgian road where they could catch a bus to Tiflis. Horsley and I rented ponies to carry our packs from the son of the head man of the village and pushed on.

The mountains were like the Pyrenees but wilder, huger. We passed walled village after walled village with small ogival gates. There were crenellated castles on the hills. Century after century seemed to be dropping away from us.

We crossed a steep shaley pass that brought us face to face with a ring of huge silent snowpeaks that we didn't know the names of. After wandering through a maze of gorges we crossed another divide and at dusk came down to a broad stream lined with trees, paths, sheepfolds, and a village. Was this Zaramag, we asked excitedly. Our guide shook his head. Was it Tib? He shook his head again. We never did find out what its name was.

We slept in the house of a widow who was a relative of the guide's. There was nothing to be had to eat. When we asked for hot water for tea, the widow explained politely that she could only afford a fire once a day. But tomorrow she would point out the path. We would find everything we wanted in Zaramag.

Our guide meanwhile was explaining he'd never been to Zaramag in his life. He must start home that night. His father would be missing him. He assured us we would find fine meals in Zaramag.

Next morning we started out over the mountain with our packs on our backs. We chewed on my corncakes as best we could but they finally got so hard I broke a tooth on the last one. I have forgotten how many days we walked. When we finally sure enough reached Zaramag it was in a pouring rain. Zaramag was, to put it mildly, a disappointment.

The schoolmaster unlocked the schoolhouse for us to sleep in. Food? No, he had no food, but he did bring us a gasoline stove to boil water for tea. The village was a sprinkling of brokendown frame houses and some stone buildings mournful in the rain. We scoured the place. In a store we found a bag of stale hard candy and five eggs. We hurried back to the schoolhouse to hardboil the eggs. We had barely finished this sumptuous meal when the village officials came to call.

We hoped they had come to invite us to dinner but instead they brought us literature about the mineral wealth of the region. They wanted news about Zaramag published in America. When exploitation of the mines was accomplished they assured us that there would be fine restaurants in Zaramag. We went to sleep hungrier than ever.

Still we were on the high road. Next day was clear. With our packs in a twowheeled cart, we started up the Mamison pass on empty stomachs. At a sodawater spring below the road we met a carter who spoke English. He was an Ossetine, a very cheerful man who had been in Canada during the Yukon goldrush. Now he was back driving a cartload of wheat over the pass to Vladykavkhass. No he hadn't brought back any gold. It was just as well what with the revolution. He was a fine man; I should have liked to have talked to him more, but we were going in different directions.

On top of the pass we got one of the most magnificent views in the world over the valleys of Georgia, and, what was more to the point, food. On the last loop of the road we had smelt something cooking. In a windowless stone building we found a sort of Old Dan Tucker stirring a kettle of soup that simmered over a hearth of glowing coals. Yes he'd sell us some soup. He kept this as a resthouse for carters and muleteers. It was mutton soup with barley in it, hot. No soup ever tasted so good.

After that the road was all down hill. Horsley recovered his scientist's interest in the sensations of hunger.

We tried to match our impressions of the Communist experiment. Pavlov's violence against the regime, he told me, came from his being the son of a priest. He resented the persecution of the church. He admitted that Lenin gave him every facility for his work, but he never admitted that Lenin was right.

Horsley himself lacked interest in politics. At home he had never even registered to vote. He agreed with me that as an experiment in human organization communism was of interest: but all his thoughts were for science. In your lab you could perform your experiment, report the findings. Other men could repeat your experiment to check the results. You were on firm ground there.

I insisted that much of my sympathy for the Soviets was based on their pacifist foreign policy. Wars were the ruin of civilization. Lenin's policy had been a policy of peace. Finally I came up with the theory that neither communism nor capitalism had the answer. From the point of view of developing a humane civilization it was fifty-fifty between them.

Horsley's interest had switched back to the sensations of hunger.

That night we slept supperless again, in a new frame house, on the floor, because we were afraid of what occupants there might be in the bed the family hospitably vacated for us. Our feet were so sore we could hardly put them to the ground. In the early dawn we started out in a pony cart along the banks of a clear splashing river that looked like a trout stream through lovely country densely wooded with giant cedars. When we reached Oni the bus we had hoped to catch had left. No other for two days.

Oni was a market town. The hotel wasn't too filthy. There was an actual restaurant where you could order variations of pilaff and shashlik off an actual bill of fare. There was good Georgian wine. After being halfstarved for a week having a full belly was a very special sensation. The day was hot. We bathed in the river and toasted ourselves in the sun.

Kutaïs turned out to be a stucco town with tiled roofs and cypresses that had an Italian look. People looked almost gay. A band played in the park. There were dramatic performances and recitations and speeches and red flags everywhere. We never discovered just what was going on. It was some kind of fiesta, but everything took place in Georgian. The hotel had a nice garden and wouldn't have been too bad if there had been any way of escaping the stench of a too centrally located waterless closet.

Horsley departed for Batum and I waited for the train for Baku the next day. In the evening alone in an untidy restaurant I tried to note down my impressions. Here I'd been traveling around without interference. Nobody had even asked for my papers. I'd been exposed for three months to Soviet life in the raw and what had I learned?

Details, details, but how to generalize from them enough to form a political creed? Were the Georgians inveterate small proprietors or was it just the two or three innkeepers with whom I'd carried on painfully inadequate conversations? Were the Ossetines procommunist because they were poor or because they were intelligent? Was all this poverty and hunger part of the clearing of the ground for magnificent new constructions, or was it the result of oldfashioned ignorant centralized oppression? Was the waiter with a dirty apron who had just brought me my supper happier now than he would have been under the Czar? Was he a better waiter, a better citizen, did he have more opportunity to study languages—he had told me he was trying to learn French—to play chess, to make love to his wife and raise clean healthy brighteyed children?

As if he had read my thoughts a sallow man with large dark treacherous eyes brought over a bottle of wine and sat down in the chair facing me. He began asking me questions. Where was I from? What was I doing? What did I think? Over several glasses of wine we struggled with our mutual incomprehension over my Russian dictionary. Finally we settled on slogans. Hurrah for Soviet power. Americans were rich but good. Up the international working class. The man seemed satisfied.

When after wading again through the tremendous reek of the waterless closet I got back to my room, I tried to note down what we had talked about. Even with the definitions in the dictionary it was obvious that the words meant different things to each of us. It wasn't that it was hard to understand foreign languages, it was that language was hard to understand.

"Let's stick to facts," I wrote, "but one man's fact is another man's fiction. A fact must mean the same to an Esquimaux or a Milwaukee banker or an Andaman Islander. Stink fits that bill. Stink is a fact. Cable that home Mr. Amerikanski Peesatyel."

Back in Moscow in October I had trouble finding a room. Fadyeev and his wife kindly put me up in their large apartment. Fadyeev was then a youngish fellow with a crew cut and a pleasant breezy manner which at home we would have associated with the West. He came from far east—Siberia. He had written a successful novel and was enthusiastic for the regime. His wife was high up in the Gay Pay U. They had a cheerful comsomolska for a maid and lived simply but well. Their apartment was near a Red Army barracks. Every morning I was waked up by the magnificent deep singing of the regiment marching out to drill. In those days the Russian soldiers always sang as they marched.

Fadyeev's friends could speak freely about all sorts of topics. No danger of having what you said reported to the Gay Pay U. This was the Gay Pay U. I must say I liked Fadyeev. After I left Russia he became a leading proponent of Stalinism in the literary world. When Khrushchev denounced the monster and pulled his corpse out of Lenin's tomb Fadyeev killed himself.

I enjoyed these autumnal weeks in Moscow. The drizzle and sleet were just beginning to give way to snow. I managed to keep warm because I had inherited several suits of magnificent fleece-lined underwear from a lively bunch of American explorers who came through on their way home from hunting Siberian tigers for the Museum of Natural History.

I saw a great deal of Sergei Alimov and his wife Masha. Alimov was a grand fellow who'd lived in Australia and made a name for himself by writing some songs that were favorites with the Red Army. His songs gave him a certain immunity. He could say things nobody else would dare to say. Though he was a fervently patriotic Russian I got the impression he couldn't care less about Marxist ideology. There was always plenty of smoked whitefish and good bread and wine and vodka at the Alimovs, and talk about everything under the sun. Before I left Alimov and his friends tossed me in a blanket, which among the Russians, as among the Esquimaux, is considered a compliment.

It was the season in Moscow. There were marvelous concerts. Though it wasn't open to the public it was fairly easy to get in to the great collection of French impressionist paintings some Moscow merchant had made. More new plays were opening than I could possibly get around to. I visited kindergartens and schools, army theaters, amateur theaters, factory theaters, the theater in the institution for reeducating prostitutes.

It was hard not to catch fire from the enthusiasm for social betterment you found everywhere. Among people who sided with the regime there was a universal sense of participation. Many of the partyliners were dedicated people. I liked what I saw of the efforts to dispel anti-Jewish prejudice, to give cultural autonomy to the subject nationalities like the Sheshians and the Ossetines and all the various unimagined ethnic groups I had run into slogging through the Caucasus. And always there was the stimulus, in spite of the painful difficulty of the language, of the Russian mind. I got the feeling that, in spite of the destruction of so many talents in the liquidation of the old educated and governing classes, the Great Russians still comprised one of the world's major reservoirs of brains.

Like most westerners I've known who stayed any length of time in the Soviet Union I had my jitters too. Days and weeks go by without your being conscious of the Terror and then suddenly the iron fist shows through. I spent an evening with an Englishman and his Russian wife in a stuffy apartment full of bricabrac and veneered furniture. He'd come to Russia to work for the Communist cause. Now he was desperate to get out. It had become a nightmare. They would never let his wife leave. She had the wrong class origins.

He talked about the way the Communists repressed the sailors' revolt at Kronstadt—the Kronstadt story had given me the creeps since I first got wind of it—the incorporation of everything worst in the old Okhrana into the Cheka. "There's no cruelty like Russian cruelty, not even Chinese," the Englishman said.

I tried to argue with him. My point was that the Terror was fading. Most of the old Chekists had been shot. I told him about how freely I'd been able to travel, how easily people talked. My theory then was that the Russian revolution was entering a liberal phase. My parallel was France under the Directorate and Consulate. Napoleon's rule was iron but there were no massacres like Robespierre's.

It was all right for me to talk that way, the Englishman said; I could get out. He and his wife were trapped. Sooner or later they would come for them. They always came at night, no arrests were ever seen, no one ever dared tell.

I've often wondered what happened to them. Within five years Stalin had proved him right and me wrong.

***

Before I left Moscow I had the wind up almost as badly as the Englishman. The Interior Department kept putting off returning my passport from day to day. In spite of the fact that I seemed to be approved of by the Communist publications and was being treated to enough farewell parties to keep my head spinning, I kept wondering whether I had dropped some injudicious remark that might have been reported.

At last the passport was produced. I procured a Polish visa, a railroad ticket to Warsaw.

My Art Theatre actress friend brought the whole company from the Sanitary Propaganda Theatre she coached in one of the big factories to see me off. These were fifteen- and sixteen-year-old boys and girls, blueeyed, friendly, curious. They grabbed your hand with a hard firm grasp. They put on little skits to show in the factories about the dangers of syphilis, about cleaning your teeth, about proper food for children. "Tell us," she asked me as I stood beside my sleeper in the steaming trainshed waiting with desperate impatience for the train to leave, "are you for us or against us? They want you to show your face."

How could I answer? The train was already moving. I jumped aboard.

How could I answer that question? I liked and admired the Russian people. I had enjoyed their enormous and varied country, but when next morning I crossed the Polish border—Poland was not Communist then—it was like being let out of jail.

CHAPTER 6

Under the Tropic

Some of the best times in those years were with Hem and Pauline in Key West. The time that stands out was in late April and early May of 1929.

I arrived, I guess it must have been on the Merchants and Miners boat, worn to a frazzle. I'd almost lost my mind trying to work with the New Playwrights. A theater is a cooperative enterprise. Particularly if you are the author of the current play you feel responsible for a lot of fine people who have lavished days and nights of time and effort on a production. Even off Broadway they have to be paid. I had reached the point when I was putting in my own hardearned money to keep the damn show running for a couple of extra weeks.

Jack Lawson and Francis Faragoh, who had families to support, had already taken the king's shilling and enlisted in the Hollywood movie studios. The party line dominated *The New Masses* and was on its way to take over the experimental theaters. It was a wearing daily struggle to keep out of that straitjacket. I didn't so much need a rest as to get back to consecutive work on some narratives I was trying to organize. When I went aboard the boat in New York I had already sent in my resignation to the board of directors. I was shaking the dust of the theater off my feet.

Hem had been writing enthusiastic letters about vast schools of amberjack and Spanish mackerel and how high he was living on stonecrab and crawfish. Charles Thompson had caught an eight-foot sailfish. The Marquesas swarmed with snipe. He said the Gulf Stream was much better than when I'd been there the year before, "like passenger pigeon or buffalo days."

Hem needed some good fishing and hunting. It was that winter that Dr. Hemingway, his old man, shot himself.

I've forgotten whether I first told Hem about Key West or whether he found it on his own. I had been talking it up to my friends ever since I first saw the place in the course of a walking hitchhiking trek down the Florida peninsula. Dead tired, thirsty and horribly hot I had found myself in a small railroad station. A train came in. I asked the conductor where the train was going. He said Key West and I said fine and by some miracle I had the cash for the fare. I'll never forget the dreamlike crossing of the Keys on the Old Flagler viaduct.

In those days Key West really was an island. It was a coaling station. There was shipping in the harbor. The air smelt of the Gulf Stream. It was like no other place in Florida.

Cayo Hueso, as half the people called it, was linked by carferries with Havana. Cigarfactories had attracted a part Cuban, part Spanish population. The cigarworkers were interesting people to talk to, wellinformed and often surprisingly wellread. Handrolling cigars was skilled work. They had a habit of hiring somebody to read to them at each long table while they worked. They listened with avidity not only to the Socialist newspapers, but to the nineteenth-century Spanish novelists and to translations of Dostoevski and Tolstoi. They were people who had their own ideas about things.

The Englishspeaking population was made up of railroad men, old Florida settlers, a few descendants of New Englanders from the days when it was a whaling port, and fishermen from such allwhite settlements as Spanish Wells in the Bahamas. There was no trace of a cracker drawl in their speech. One remembered that Key West had been northern territory all through the Civil War.

There were a couple of drowsy hotels where train passengers on their way to Cuba or the Caribbean occasionally stopped over. Palms and pepper trees. The shady streets of unpainted frame houses had a faintly New England look. Automobiles were rare because there was no highway to the mainland, only the viaduct that carried the singletrack railroad. The navy yard was closed down. The custodian used to let you go swimming off the stone steps in the deep azure water of the inner basin. You had to watch for barracuda. Otherwise it was delicious.

Spaniards ran good little restaurants well furnished with Rioja wine. Nice colored nurses were available. Since Hem and Pauline had produced two small boys by this time, Patrick, soon to be known as the Mexican Mouse, and Gigi, whom Hem for some reason referred to as the Irish Jew, this was a great advantage. Nobody seemed ever to have heard of game laws or prohibition. The place suited Ernest to a T.

Hem always did have a gang of people with him. I remember he wasn't alone when he came down to see the steamer dock that sunny afternoon. He just gave me time to leave my bag at the Overseas Hotel and to change out of my store clothes and then we all had to go tarpon fishing because the tide was right.

Charles Thompson, whose people owned the chief hardware and marine supply emporium, was taking us out in his motorboat. His nice wife Lorine was along and Waldo Pierce with his beard and his sketchpad and his paintbox.

Waldo came from Bangor, Maine. He was an enormous man

with bushy whiskers who looked like a Neptune out of a baroque Roman fountain. He was a classmate of Jack Reed's at Harvard. His legendary feat was jumping overboard from a cattle boat the two of them shipped on from Europe soon after they got out of college. Off Sandy Hook Waldo decided he didn't like the tone of the third mate's voice; swam ashore; bought himself a first class ticket and met the cattleboat when she docked on the other side. One story was that they had Jack Reed in irons for having done away with his buddy. Waldo was an enormously fluent painter. He had a Renoir sort of palette. He never stopped painting or sketching and he never stopped talking, either.

I liked everybody aboard but the only one I really had eyes for was Katy. Katharine Smith had grown up with the Hemingways. Their families went to the same summer resort in Northern Michigan. Hem and her younger brother Bill had been inseparable as boys. She called Hem Wemmage and treated him affectionately-condescendingly as a girl does her younger brother. When Hem worked in Chicago before going to Italy in the Red Cross, he lived as one of the family in a sort of cooperative apartment run by Katy's elder brother, Y. K. She had been a friend of Hadley's and had known Pauline and her sister Jinny at the University of Missouri. They were all very thick. From the first moment I couldn't think of anything but her green eyes.

It is hot in April in Key West when the trade wind drops. We trolled back and forth between the wharves and an old white steamboat that had gone on a reef in a hurricane. She had lost her stack and the engines had been taken out. Waldo painted a picture of her that still hangs in the upstairs hall at Spence's Point. When Charles took his boat up into a bight away from the town, an unbelievable sweetness of blossoming limes came out along with the mosquitoes from among the mangroves.

Hem had brought along a couple of bottles of champagne which perched on the ice that kept the mullet fresh in the bait bucket. The rule was that you couldn't have a drink until somebody caught a fish. The sun set in a wash of gaudy pinks and ochres. We kept fishing on into the moonlight. I'm not sure whether we caught any tarpon that night, but we certainly had one hooked because I remember the arc of dark silver against the moon's sheen on the water when the fish jumped.

The tarpon seemed only to bite when the tide was low and the water warm in the channels. When they stopped striking and we had finished the champagne Charles said with a yawn that he had to go to work at the store at seven o'clock next morning and headed us in to the dock.

If we hadn't pulled in a tarpon I was probably just as glad because catching tarpon always seemed a waste to me. I hated to see the great silver monsters lying in the dust on the wharf. They aren't fit to eat. About the only use is for mounting. Some people make knicknacks out of the dried scales. Sheer vanity catching tarpon.

We went to the Asturian's for a bite before going to bed. Frenchfried yellowtail and bonito with tomato sauce were his specialities. It was a delight to be able to chatter amiably on all sorts of topics without tripping over that damn Party line. No taboos. Everybody said the first thing that came into his head. After the ideological bickerings of the New York theater Key West seemed like the Garden of Eden.

Hem was the greatest fellow in the world to go around with when everything went right. That spring was a marvelous season for tarpon. Every evening Charles would take us out tarpon fishing and we would fish and drink and talk and talk and talk far into the moonlit night. Days, after Hem and I had knocked off our stint—we were both very early risers—we would go out to the reef with Bra.

Bra was a Conch. That's what they called white people from Spanish Wells in the Bahamas. His real name was Sanders. Hem, who had gotten to be a Conch right along with him, talked Captain Sanders into taking us out. Nobody had heard of a party boat. Fifteen dollars was considered a fair price for the day.

Fishingboats were still smacks whether they had sails or not. They carried a livebox built into the boat amidships to keep the fish alive. Key West had an iceplant, but at the fishmarket down at the wharf they would scoop up your yellowtails with a net out of a big vat when you bought them. Another great tank was full of green turtles. Shipping sea turtles was an important industry.

There was endless fascination in the variety of creatures you pulled up off the reef. Never much of a sports fisherman, I liked going along, just to be out on the varicolored water. I always announced that I fished for the pot. Although as competitive as a race horse, Hem wasn't yet so much the professional sportsman as to spoil the fun. Such was my enthusiasm for the great pale moonstruck snappers known locally as mutton fish that Katy got to calling me Muttonfish. It stuck for a while as a nickname.

We were married in August in Ellsworth, Maine. One of the nicest letters we got was from Hem who had spent the summer following the toros in Spain. He said he was happy as hell to hear "you citizens" were married. I'd written him that I was finishing the first volume of what, to my surprise and shock, had turned out to be a trilogy. "Trilogies are undoubtedly the thing—look at the Father Son and Holy Ghost—Nothing's gone much bigger than that."

This was one of the few references to religion in our correspondence. Ernest had become a Catholic in order to marry Pauline, and by some hocus-pocus had managed to have his marriage to Hadley annulled

He went on to summarize the lives of our friends: Don Stewart had been ruined by signing a twenty-five-thousand-dollar contract and by meeting the Whitneys. "Am relying on you to avoid that—sign nothing—shoot as soon as you see the whites of a Whitney's eye." John Bishop was ruined by marrying a girl with an income. "Keep money away from Katy." Eternal youth had sunk the Fitzgeralds. "Get old, Passos. Age up Kate." Old Hem had been ruined by his father shooting himself. I was to keep guns away from Katharine's old man.

I had to correct the proofs of *The 42nd Parallel* before we could leave on the triumphal tour I had been planning, to show Katy old haunts in Europe and to introduce her to old friends. I wrote Hem to pray for me in my battle for the four-letter words. Leaving that battle a draw, we managed to get aboard the French liner *Roussillon* on November 23.

I had never been happier but misfortune was striking down my friends. Canby Chambers was laid low by infantile paralysis during the previous summer. He recovered but was paralyzed from the waist down for the rest of his life. Before we sailed the bad news reached us that little Patrick Murphy had tuberculosis.

In Paris we found the Fitzgeralds living somewhere near the

Etoile. This was the first time we saw Scottie. She was a bright cute little girl, what my mother's friends used to call an oldfashioned child, in charge of a maneating English governess who gave us both the creeps. Scott was drinking and Zelda was far from being in her right mind; she was obsessed by the idea of dancing in the Ballet Russe. She was a lovely ballroom dancer, but with the best will in the world, it was impossible to start training for the ballet at her age. For anyone who was fond of the Fitzgeralds it was heartbreaking to be with them.

Katy and I rode the *bateaux-mouches* in the ruddy winter sunlight. We lunched at Sceau-Robinson, and made a round of the cafés with Blaise Cendrars, whose poetry I was much smitten with at the time, and the white Samoyed dog that was his inseparable companion. Cendrars was as diverting as his writing, but I was getting further away from the *vie littéraire* with every passing year.

Jeanne Léger fed us the best *blanquette de veau* anybody ever ate. Jeanne was the much soughtafter model Fernand had married in his salad days. They didn't live together, because Jeanne, though a most attractive woman and a marvelous cook, had a *béguin* for the dreariest little boyfriends, but they lived up to the rest of the obligations of matrimony in a curious formal French way.

Hem and Pauline and Ginny Pfeiffer turned up from Spain and we all went up to Montana Vermala, near Sierre in the Swiss Alps, to spend Christmas with the Murphys. Gerald and Sara were handling their disaster in high style. The theory was then that if Patrick were kept at the proper altitude he had a chance of conquering the disease. The Murphys were determined nobody should feel sorry for them.

Dorothy Parker was there, making her usual funny cracks with her eyes full of tears. We skied and laughed our heads off over cheese fondue and the magnificent local white wine evenings in front of fire. We were all set on keeping the Murphys cheered up. For a while it worked.

After that Katy and I spent a week with Cendrars in a chilly old inn in the walled and battlemented town of Montpazier in the Massif Central. They cooked wild goose and venison in a huge oldfashioned chimney and we had truffle omelets every noon for lunch.

Cendrars had lost a hand in the war. It was hairraising to spin with him around the mountain roads. He steered with one hand and changed the gears on his little French car with his hook. We visited Les Eyzies and every other prehistoric cave within reach. Cendrars took every curve on two wheels.

Somehow we survived, and made our way south through Languedoc to Spain. I think that it was in Cadiz we got aboard a small Spanish steamer named the *Antonio Lopez* which transported us in a leisurely way via the Canary Islands to Havana. It was a delightful journey. We had a large stateroom on deck. I amused myself with watercolors and by making an English translation of Cendrars' *Le Panama et Mes Sept Oncles.*

The only other Englishspeaking passenger was a State Department man named Loomis. Mr. Loomis was an old Africa hand and a good storyteller. He had enough nightmare tales about murder cults in the Republic of Liberia to make your flesh creep. He took a dim view of civil liberties there. We were attracted to Mr. Loomis because when we asked him why he had hired two staterooms he answered: "'I got to have some place to keep my shoes, don't I?"

By the middle of April we were back in Key West catching dolphins and kingfish in the Gulf Stream with old Hem on Bra's boat.

That fall I joined Hem in an elk hunt out near Cooke, Montana. Pauline's Uncle Gus furnished the cash for the trip. Uncle Gus was a small nostalgic man, the big wheel in Hudnut's in New York. Stiff with money and having neither chick nor child as the saying was, he lavished attentions on his smart pretty nieces. Ernest fascinated him. Hunting, fishing, writing. He wanted to help Ernest do all the things he'd been too busy making money to do. It was Uncle Gus who financed the first African safaris.

We went out with packmules from an outlying ranch and skirted the edges of Yellowstone Park. While I was along, the elk, which have a particularly acute sense of smell, tended to get wind of us and to make off into the park where they were safe. Too nearsighted to handle a gun, I occupied myself with the scenery and sighting bears, and beavers in a pond, and watching Hem operate as a hunter. He never smoked: his sense of smell was acute. He'd smell a bull elk almost as soon as the elk would smell him.

Hem already had the ranch hands under his thumb. They thought he was the most wonderful guy they'd ever met. He had the leadership principle all right. It occurred to me that he would make a firstrate guerrilla chief. Added to that was the sense of topography that military tacticians have. He knew what the country in the next valley would be like before his horse scrambled up over the rimrock.

Driving back toward Billings in Hem's Ford roadster he spilled us out into the ditch. It was a narrow road and he was dazzled by the lights of an oncoming car. Everybody blamed me with my bad eyesight but I swear Hem was at the wheel. Of course we had been drinking right much bourbon. The car turned wheels up. The rest of us crawled out from under but Hem had a severely fractured arm and was in the Billings hospital for weeks. It was typical of a certain side of Hem's character that when Archie MacLeish took the trouble to go all the way out there to see him, Hem told his other friends that Archie had just come out to see him die.

This was the period of the Great Depression. It didn't affect me very much personally. Katy owned the Provincetown house where we made our headquarters, and I scraped up what money I could for trips. I used to tell people I had been just as broke before the stockmarket crash as after it. My books could hardly have sold less anyway. It was what I saw of other people's lives that brought home the failure of New Era capitalism.

My political theory then was that the Communist Party U.S.A. had a nuisance value. Being an independent with no axe to grind it was up to me to support such of its objectives as I approved until the American public became aware of how much was amiss with the land of the free. I kept writing Hem and other skeptical friends that I was just about to renounce radical entanglements, but the temptation would arise to join in one more piece of do-goodery. The commies are tireless when they think they've got somebody on the hook.

In the fall of 1931 the Communist labor operatives instigated a committee of writers to investigate the abuse of the miners in the soft coal region in Harlan County in eastern Kentucky. Theodore Dreiser consented to serve as chairman.

From my youth I'd had great admiration for Dreiser. It was the ponderous battering ram of his novels that opened the way through the genteel reticences of American nineteenth-century fiction for what seemed to me to be a truthful description of people's lives. Without Dreiser's treading out a path for naturalism none of us would have had a chance to publish even.

The first time I met him he made me think of an elephant. It was something about his nose and the way the skin wrinkled about his eyes. He was pachydermic yet sensitive, standoffish, opinionated; but slyly alert and subject to a sudden flush of understanding when you least expected it. He was curious about what I was up to. I occasionally ate an uncomfortable lunch at his invitation at his hotel at Broadway and 72nd Street in New York.

He had no smalltalk and neither did I. Since he didn't eat lunch he would sit there, in the rather mustyseedy hotel sitting room, watching me while I ate. He was obviously happier talking to women than to men. Neither of us would find much to say. I would sit there abashedly munching the tasteless food and go away with the feeling of having performed a reverential duty.

It turned out that the easiest way of reaching Harlan County by train was through Cincinnati. On the train from Cincinnati to Pineville I found Dreiser in the company of a most attractive young woman. Her manners, the way she did her hair, her neatly tailored gray suit all gave off that special Chicago chic I so appreciated. It did seem odd though that Dreiser should bring a ladyfriend along on this particular expedition.

Apart from that Dreiser handled himself magnificently. He behaved so much like an investigating senator that people around Harlan County thought he was a senator. I'd never understood the meaning of the word "depression" until I began to poke around in those mountains. Miners were living in the most abject misery.

The Communists had organized the National Miners' Union—"National" was the identifying ticket on Communist organizations in those days—and fomented a strike in dozens of small mines that were hardly workable anyway. God knows there was plenty to strike about. The local authorities had responded with strike-breakers and deputy sheriffs. There were dynamitings and gun-battles in true mountain style. The situation was complicated by the fact that the I.W.W. was also at work and a few A.F. of L. organizers. True to form the Communists spent as much time undermining their rivals as helping the miners.

Dreiser, in taking testimony, really tried to get all sides of the story. His great word was "equity." He kept explaining that he was trying to reestablish equity in the treatment of the miners. The law enforcement officers refused to cooperate or to testify. Their stance was that we were foreign agitators and to hell with us. That included newspaper reporters. The Harlan County sheriff started proceedings off by serving Bruce Crawford with a $50,000 suit for slander for an article he had sent out through some press association.

I was as much delighted by the language the miners used as I was distressed by their indigence. Their speech had the lilt of Elizabethan lyrics. The speakin's brought back the campaign that elected Andrew Jackson to the Presidency. The way their eyes looked out of lean mountaineer faces made me think of the Bedawi in the Syrian desert. The coaldust in the eyebrows and lashes gave a little of the same burning look to the eyes as the khol the Arabs use. These were fine people; I desperately wanted to help them.

All we accomplished was a volume for the record called *Harlan Miners Speak*. The Communist effort disintegrated. A number of the leaders ended up in jail. The Communists, who had the best defense organization, were leary of helping wobblies or A.F. of L. men; in the end the miners were left with the dirty end of the stick.

The sheriff's deputies in Pineville played a lowdown trick on Dreiser. They had noticed the comely young lady in the hotel who certainly was not the great man's wife. When she went into his room late one night they stacked a row of toothpicks against the door. Finding them undisturbed in the morning they arrested him at breakfast for infringing some local ordinance against fornication. I did not see the trial but I was told that in court Dreiser confounded everybody by declaring that he was an old man and impotent. Nothing immoral could have happened. What a strange man!

On the way home I began worrying about what Dreiser meant by "equity." Like so many of his words it was a hard one to corner. Years afterward I wondered if it wasn't this haziness of definition that led him into the Communist camp at the end of his life. Equity must have come to mean to him taking away from the rich to give to the poor. Since it was becoming obvious to anyone who would take the trouble to study the Soviet Union that liquidating the rich wasn't making the poor any better off, I never could understand what the strange old pachyderm had in his mind.

The Harlan County authorities paid a number of us the compliment of indicting us under the Kentucky criminal syndicalism statute a few days after we left for New York. Earl Browder, who then headed the Communist Central Committee, tried to talk me into going back to stand trial. I refused.

Something about Browder's sneering tone in using the word "liberal" threw me off. Of course "liberal" was a cussword in the commie lingo of those days. Although I felt the Communists were performing a useful function in casting light on the miseries of the Harlan miners, I was repelled by their offhand treatment of the arrested men and of their "liberal" apologists. Browder made it all too clear he took a good deal of satisfaction in treating us all as pawns in the game. I never did like Earl Browder. I told him I'd wait quietly at home until they came to extradite me. Nothing happened.

A few years later I had a chance to enlarge on what I had tried to tell Earl Browder when I was invited to address a writers' congress in New York. This was the period of the popular front and leagues against war and fascism. This congress was a move to line up writers of what was then called proletarian literature. Some of the professors had been putting that label on my stuff and I had been thinking of how to take evasive action. I had in mind Cézanne's remark to Vollard that so delighted Cummings. *"Écoutez un peu, Monsieur Vollard, je ne veux pas qu'on me mette le grappin dessus."*

Since I considered public speaking a temptation of the Evil One, I sent the piece in by mail to be read at the meeting. Of course nobody paid the slightest attention to it; it's silly ever to try to explain anything. Malcolm Cowley brought out what I meant when he quoted me as having exclaimed: "Writers of the world unite, you have nothing to lose but your brains." I hope I really said it. *Si non e vero e ben trovato.*

Soon after Franklin D. Roosevelt was inaugurated I came down with a fresh bout of rheumatic fever. Dr. Gantt, with whom I cemented a friendship on that hungry walk through the Caucasus, had come home to the Johns Hopkins Medical School to set up a Pavlovian laboratory and to work with Adolph Meyer, the Swiss psychiatrist who was in charge of Phipps. I had brought Katy to Baltimore to have her tonsils out and crawled into her hospital bed as soon as she vacated it. I lay there for painful weeks reading *A la Recherche du Temps Perdu.* Proust is just the thing to read when you have a fever. I never had the patience when I was up and about.

My friends rallied round. Ernest sent me a grand out of Uncle Gus's contribution to his African hunt. Gerald and Sara furnished passage on the Italian Line so that I could convalesce at Antibes. Horsley marshaled the medical talent.

Scott was living in Baltimore because Zelda was being treated by Adolph Meyer. He used to come around and to sit bleakly fidgeting in my hospital room. I was trying to talk him out of the notion that he was high and dry on the rocks. In fact I felt so strongly that he had his best work ahead of him that I didn't want him to publish *The Crack Up.* How easy it is to give your friends bad advice; it turned out to be one of his best books.

Actually Scott was meeting adversity with a consistency of purpose that I found admirable. He was trying to raise Scottie, to do the best thing possible for Zelda, to handle his drinking and to keep a flow of stories into the magazines to raise the enormous sums Zelda's illness cost. At the same time he was determined to continue writing firstrate novels. With age and experience his literary standards were rising. I never admired a man more. He was so much worse off than I was that I felt I ought to be sitting at his bedside instead of his sitting at mine.

For several winters after that Katy and I made a point of spending as much time as we could at Key West. It wasn't quite under the tropic but it was mighty close to it. No doctor's prescription was ever pleasanter to take.

The railroad had folded and now you arrived by carferry from a point below Homestead on the mainland. There were three separate ferryrides and sandy roads through the scrubby keys between. It took half a day and was a most delightful trip, with long cues of pelicans scrambling up off the water and manofwar birds in the sky and boobygulls on the buoys, and mullet jumping in the milky shallows.

Hem and I kept planning a trip to Bimini, but it always had to be put off for some reason or other. The first time we started out we had hardly reached the purple water of the Gulf Stream when old Hem shot himself in the leg—in the fleshy part, fortunately—with his own rifle trying to shoot a shark that was making for a sailfish somebody had alongside and was trying to gaff. We had to turn back to take him to the sawbones at the hospital. Katy was so mad she would hardly speak to him.

Hem's leg had hardly healed when a package arrived for him from Oak Park. It was from his mother. It contained a chocolate cake, a roll of Mrs. Hemingway's paintings of the Garden of the Gods which she suggested he might get hung at the Salon when he next went to Paris, and the gun with which his father shot himself. Katy, who had known her of old, had explained to me that Mrs. Hemingway was a very odd lady indeed. Hem was the only man I ever knew who really hated his mother.

It was on the first of Hem's *Pilars* that we finally made it to the Bahamas. The big money fishing camp at Cat Cay had gone broke in the collapse of the first Florida boom and was still closed down. There were a few yachtsmen and sports fishermen about but the tiny island of Bimini proper was very much out of the world.

There was a wharf and some native shacks under the coconut palms and a store that had some kind of a barroom attached, where we drank rum in the evenings, and a magnificent broad beach on the Gulf Stream side. There was an official residency and a couple of sunbeaten bungalows screened against the sandflies up on the dunes. Katy and I occupied one of them for a week to give Hem more room on the *Pilar.*

We had gotten to calling Hem the Old Master because nobody could stop him from laying down the law, or sometimes the Mahatma on account of his having appeared in a rowboat with a towel wrapped around his head to keep off the sun. He had more crotchety moments than in the old days, but he was a barrel of monkeys when he wanted to be. Life still seemed enormously comical to all of us. Nobody ever got so mad that some fresh crack didn't bring him around. We drank a good deal but only cheerfully. We carried things off with great fits of laughing.

If I'm not mistaken this trip to Bimini was the first time the Old Master really went out after tuna. He'd been reading Zane Grey's book about catching great tuna on the seven seas (and a surprisingly wellwritten book it is) and wanted to go Zane Grey one better.

We had caught a few smallish yellowfins along with some rainbowcolored dolphins on the way over across the Gulf Stream from the upper end of Hawk Channel. It was in the spring of the year and the wiseacres all claimed that the tuna were running.

Katy and I were delighted with the island. We never tired of walking on the beach and watching the highslung landcrabs shuttle like harness racers among the fallen coconuts. We did a lot of bathing in the comfortable surf on the great beach. Hem was scornful of our shell collection.

We got hold of an agreeable storytelling Negro with a small sailboat who took us sailing over the marly waters of the Great Bahama Bank and fishing for bonefish in the shallows between the coral heads. The Mahatma used to kid us about our taste for going out in rowboats together, said people did that before they were married, not after.

The Bimini Negroes were great fun. They made up songs about every incident of the day. Every little job like hauling a boat ashore was a choral event. It was the first time any of us had heard

> *My Mama don't want no peas no rice*
> *no coconut oil*
> *All she wants is handy brandy and*
> *champagne.*

They immediately made up songs about old Hem. I wish I remembered the words. All my recollections of that week are laced with the lilt of those Bimini songs.

Anyway while Katy and I were unashamedly sightseeing and sailing and rowing and dabbling in folklore—all occupations frowned on by serious fishermen—the Old Master was cruising the deep. He'd brought tuna rigs along and was trolling with that implacable impatient persistence of his.

We were ashore when the Old Master first tangled with his great tuna. It had been hooked early in the morning by a man named Cook who was caretaker at Cat Cay. It must have been an enormous fish because as soon as it sounded it ran out all the line. Cook's hands were cut to shreds when he turned it over to Ernest, who came alongside with the *Pilar* in the early afternoon. Hem went on playing it from Cook's boat and sent the *Pilar* in to fetch us so that we should see the sport. I've forgotten who was at the wheel but we cruised alongside while the battle continued.

Among the assembled yachtsmen there was a gentleman who had a large white yacht named the *Moana.* William B. Leeds, of a family famous in the international set, had invited the Old Master aboard for drinks a couple of days before. The Old Master had come away charmed by Bill Leeds' hospitality but even more charmed by the fact that Leeds owned a Thompson submachine gun. Just at that moment a submachine gun was what the Old Master wanted more than anything in the world.

From a boy he had been fond of firearms but now he was particularly interested in a submachine gun as a way of fighting the sharks. Bimini was infested with sharks that season. They even bothered us bathing on the beach, but particularly they had an exasperating way of cutting off a hooked fish just as you were about to get him into the boat. The Old Master tried potting them with his rifle but unless you shoot him right through his tiny brain a rifle bullet doesn't make much impression on a shark. The night before he fought the tuna he'd been trying all sorts of expedients over the rum collinses to get Leeds to part with his submachine gun. He kept suggesting that they match for it or that they cut a hand of poker for it or shoot at a target for it. I believe he even offered to buy it. But Leeds was holding on to his submachine gun which he told me later had been given to him by the inventor's son who was a good friend of his.

It was late afternoon by the time Katy and I got out to the scene of the battle. By dusk the tuna began to weaken. The Old Master was reeling in on him. Everybody was on the ropes but the tuna was still hooked. We were very much excited to be in for the kill. There was a ring of spectator boats around, including Leeds with his machine gun on the launch from the *Moana.*

It was getting dark. The wind had dropped but a nastylooking squall was making up on the horizon. In the last gloaming the Old Master inched the fish alongside. Nobody had seen him yet. One man was ready with the gaff. The rest of us, hunched on top of the cabin of the *Pilar,* peered into the water with our flashlights.

We all saw him at once, dark, silvery and immense. Eight hundred pounds, nine hundred pounds, a thousand pounds, people guessed in hornswoggled whispers. All I knew was that he was a very big fish. He was moving sluggishly. He seemed licked. The man with the gaff made a lunge and missed. The silver flash was gone. The reel whined as the fish sounded.

The Old Master's expletives were sibilant and low.

The fish took half the reel; then the Old Master began hauling in on him again. He didn't feel right. Somebody suggested he might be dead. Bill Leeds had been keeping the sharks at bay with his machine gun, but now he laid off for fear a ricochet might hit someone. The Old Master reeled and reeled.

The stormcloud ate up a third of the starry sky. Lightning flickered on its fringes. Most of the small boats had put back to shore.

Leeds from his launch was inviting us to take cover on his yacht but the Old Master was doggedly reeling in.

At last in a great wash of silver and spume the tuna came to the surface ten or fifteen yards astern of the boat. The sharks hadn't touched him. We could see his whole great smooth length. The Old Master was reeling in fast. Then suddenly they came. In the light of our flashlights we could see the sharks streaking in across the dark water. Like torpedoes. Like speedboats. One struck. Another. Another. The water was murky with blood. By the time we hauled the tuna in over the stern there was nothing left but his head and his backbone and his tail.

Getting Katy and me aboard the *Moana* was a real victory for Old Hem. He'd been trying to cotton up to Leeds on account of that machine gun, and maybe too because he thought Leeds was so stinking rich. Katy had taken a scunner to poor Leeds and declared she'd rather die than go aboard his yacht. There was an oily and rather pimpish old Spaniard in the party whom we called Don Propina. We'd both taken a scunner to him. Anyway Ernest won. The squall blew up so hard there was nothing for it but to take refuge on the yacht. We climbed up the gangplank in the first horizontal sheets of rain and sat wet and shivering under the ventilation ducts in the saloon. To serve us right for being so snooty we both caught colds in the head.

Leeds hospitably put us up for the night. We turned in early, so we never knew exactly how it happened; but when we shoved off from the yacht in the lovely early morning sunlight the Old Master had the submachine gun affectionately cradled in the crotch of his arm.

It must have been a loan because Bill Leeds wrote me later that he didn't make Hem a present of the machine gun until a couple of years after when the Old Master was leaving for the civil war in Spain. Leeds agreed that what we saw was a preview of *The Old Man and the Sea,* though the tales the Canary Islander told Hem in Havana certainly played their part. Nobody ever had much luck trying to trace a fish story to its source.

Nineteen Nineteen hadn't sold any better than *The 42nd Parallel.* What with my rheumatics and enforced winter trips I was running into debt. When I got a bid from Josef von Sternberg to work with him on a Spanish picture he was getting up for Marlene Dietrich I accepted the dare. Everybody I knew had taken a whack at Hollywood. Even Gerald Murphy had spent a month there on the invitation of King Vidor. I had to see what it was like.

Flying out to Los Angeles for some reason you had to change planes at Salt Lake City. The end of the trip was in an old Ford trimotor that seemed to flap its wings like a buzzard. It was the roughest flight I ever had. I felt pretty rocky when I staggered off at the airport.

Von Sternberg was something. Of course he was born Joe Stern in Brooklyn, but he exuded a faint—only hinted at—flavor of Austrian nobility with such gusto that I found myself playing up to it. I'd never been to Vienna either, but we spent as much time talking about the Ring and wine festivals in the old days and the Spanish riding school as we did about Pierre Louÿs' silly *La Femme et le Pantin,* which he was trying to turn into a vehicle for Marlene. Since singing German ballads was what she did best he was determined not to let her sing.

It was an instructive few weeks. The whole thing turned out a mess. When I took sick (rheumatics again) at the hotel, Marlene, who was just the nicest German hausfrau you ever met, sent me flowers. Francis Faragoh insisted on moving me to his house. My old companions of New Playwrights' Theatre days who foregathered there in the evening to play poker amused me by putting aside a tithe of their winnings for the Party. Communism for the highsalaried screenwriters had become a secret solemn rite.

When Katy arrived after a painful period attending to her father's funeral in Columbia, Missouri, I was already convalescent. I'd had my fill of Hollywood. Perhaps I was lucky that my contribution to *The Devil Is a Woman* was made from a bed of pain, because if I'd known more about what was being screened I would certainly have put up a fight. We embarked on the United Fruit boat through the Panama Canal to Havana, and before long were taking up our residence in a pleasant house, known as the Brown bungalow, which Pauline had rented for us in Key West.

It was probably the following spring that Hem and Waldo and I rented Bra's boat to go out to the Dry Tortugas. These are the westernmost islets of the string of coral islands that make up the

Florida Keys. We'd made the long choppy trip across the banks hoping to catch up with one of the schools of big king mackerel that move east and north out of the Gulf of Mexico in the spring. We hadn't caught many big fish.

Waldo set up his easel at one of the embrasures of the vast stone fort and painted. I had my cot and notebook in another shady nook. The sun was hot and the tradewind cool. The place was enormous and entirely empty. We kept expecting to meet poor old Dr. Mudd coming out of one of the tunnels. No sound but the querulous shrieking of the terns. The water was incredibly clear, delicious for swimming. We saw no shark or barracuda, only a variety of reef fish: yellowtails, angelfish, searobbins, all sorts of tiny jewellike creatures we didn't know the names of swarming under the coralheads. A couple of days went by; it was one of the times I understood the meaning of the word halcyon.

Ernest had brought along Arnold Gingrich, who was just starting *Esquire*. The man was in a trance. It was a world he'd never dreamed of. He was mosquitobitten, half seasick, scorched with sunburn, astonished, half scared, half pleased. It was as much fun to see Ernest play an editor as to see him play a marlin.

Gingrich never took his fascinated eyes off Old Hem. Hem would reel in gently letting his prey have plenty of line. The editor was hooked. Sure he would print anything Hemingway cared to let him have at a thousand dollars a whack. (In those days it never occurred to us anyone got paid more than that. We lived outside of the world of agents and big time New York lunches.) Ernest was practicing up on skills he'd later apply to high literary finance. He got Gingrich so tame he even sold him a few pieces of mine for good measure.

Bra meanwhile was spending his time dredging up conches. Tourists had appeared in Key West. Bra had discovered to his amazement that tourists would buy the great rosy scalloped shells. He had the whole bow of the boat piled up with them. The night before we started back to Key West he made us one of the best conch chowders I ever ate. That with fried yellowtail seasoned with a brine and lime concoction he called Old Sour, made a royal feast. We washed it down with a little too much Bacardi rum.

We were tied up to a pier across from the fort. While we were eating and drinking, a couple of Cuban smacks that had been fishing in deep water for red snapper came alongside. They were a ragged sunbaked friendly crew. We handed around tin cups of Bacardi. Hem's Spanish became remarkably fluent. From out of his beard Waldo produced that mixture of French, Italian, and bastard Castilian that had carried him for years through the Mediterranean countries. Bra, who disdained foreign tongues, made himself friendly with shrugs and grunts. Gingrich sat speechless and goggleeyed while we climbed around each other's boats jabbering like a band of monkeys.

There were feats of strength, tales of huge blue marlin hooked and lost, of crocodiles sighted in the Gulf and rattlesnakes twenty feet long seen swimming out to sea. Night fell absolutely windless. There was no moon. Our friends pushed their boats off, anchored a few hundred feet out and turned in. We moved out from the pier to catch what breeze there was. The stars looked big as Christmastree ornaments, clustered overhead and reflected in the sea. The three small craft seemed suspended in the midst of an enormous starstudded indigo sphere.

It was hot in the cabin. Weighed down with heat and Bacardi we lay sweating in the narrow bunks. Sleep came in a glare of heat.

We were wakened by a knocking on the deck. It was the elderly grizzled man who was skipper of one of the smacks. "Amigos, para despedirnos." Redeyed, with heads like lumps of lead, we scrambled on deck.

He pointed. Against the first violet streak in the east we could see a man on the bow of the smack shaking some liquid in a large glass carboy. They were sailing for Havana with the first breeze. They wanted to honor us with a farewell drink before they left.

Everybody climbed up on the narrow planking of the pier. Of course there was no ice. It was a warm eggnog made with a kind of cheap aguardiente that smelt like wood alcohol. Obediently we brought out our tin cups. We were hung over. We felt squeamish. It made us retch. We couldn't insult our amigos. We expected to die but they were our amigos and we drank it.

It was then that Ernest brought out his rifle and started to shoot. By this time it was silvery gloaming. You could feel the sun burning under the horizon. He shot a baked-bean can floating halfway to the shore. We threw out more cans for him. He shot bits of paper the Cubans spread out on wooden chips from their skiff. He shot several terns. He shot through a pole at the end of the pier. Anything we'd point at he would hit. He shot sitting. He shot standing. He shot lying on his belly. He shot backward, with the rifle held between his legs.

So far as we could see he never missed. Finally he ran out of ammunition. We drank down the last of the fishermen's punch. The amigos shook hands. The amigos waved. They weighed anchor and hoisted the grimy sails on their smacks and steered close-hauled into the east as the first breath of the trade lightened the heavy air.

We headed back to Key West. There was an oily swell over the banks on the way back. What wind there was settled into the stern. Bra's conches had begun to rot and stank abominably. The punch set badly. Our faces were green. Our lips were cold. Nobody actually threw up, but we were a pallid and silent crew until we reached the lee of the first low patches of mangroves that lay in the approaches of Key West.

The troubles that arise between a man and his friends are often purely and simply the result of growing up. People who continue to be happy together, a man and his wife, say, manage to cultivate between themselves a private region of perpetual childhood. Growing up means the exclusion of so much.

Take your profession. Very few people choose their careers. In some way the career chooses them. A career means the cutting off of all the wonderful other careers you might possibly have followed.

Playfulness goes by the board. Invention and discovery in later life grow mostly out of the application of hunches and aptitudes developed in childhood play. The people who accomplish things in the world somehow manage to keep that childhood playfulness alive inside them, but for most of us it survives, if at all, inside of a prickly shell.

As a man matures he sheds possibilities with every passing year.

In the same way he sheds friendships. In an age like ours when political creeds drive men to massacre and immolation, political opinions become a matter of life and death. Differences which, when men and women were still in their twenties, were the subject of cheerful and affectionate argument brew recrimination and bitterness when they reach their thirties.

In a time when the meaning of political slogans turns topsy-turvy every few years, anyone who tries to keep a questioning mind, matching each slogan with its real-life application, each label with the thing itself, has to put up with having old friends turn into unfriends and even into enemies.

Add to that the special qualities of the *genus irritabile vatum.* Men of letters suffer from conceit more than ordinary men. They are an egotistic lot. Friendships between them are precarious. They are a little like bulls that way. The bull that was friendly and playful as a calf will gore the guts out of you at the drop of a hat when he's grown.

Ernest and Pauline bought themselves a lovely highceilinged old stucco house in Key West. Pauline was as much fun as ever, Gigi and the Mexican Mouse were as cute as you'd want, but things got rocky between Ernest and me more often than they used to. It may have been as much my fault as his. Katy and I laid it to the literary gaspers. The famous author, the great sportsfisherman, the mighty African hunter: we tried to keep him kidded down to size. We played up to him some at that, particularly nights when he had a sore throat and would retire to bed before supper and we'd all bring him drinks and eat our supper on trays around the bedroom. We called it the *lit royale.* I never knew an athletic vigorous man who spent so much time in bed as Ernest did.

There were times when the clouds cleared and everything was like in the old days. Those long winey lunches we had with Claude Bowers at Bottin's in Madrid.

I'd known Claude Bowers as a boyhood friend of Pax Hibben's at Sheila Hibben's marvelous dinners in New York. Now Claude was ambassador and a professional politician and everything Hem and I tended to distrust; but he was also no mean historian and a candid and openminded companion. He loved to duck the diplomatic palaver and to sneak off from the embassy and to meet us at Bottin's, an ancient Madrid eatery then unknown to Americans.

Claude had a good head for Spanish politics—and for Spanish wine—but he never could get his tongue around the language. Goya's paintings remained "goyos" to him. Hem would expatiate on the bulls and the painting and the Spanish character. I'd display what I knew about the politics. It was in the early days of the Second Republic. All my friends were republicans. All my hopes were in the flowering of the nineteenth-century Spanish idealism that had so moved me when I first knew Madrid. We never could teach Claude the verbs but his comments on the politicos were shrewd and discerning. Hem had no stake in any of it. His partisanship was in various toreros. These lunches were the last time Hem and I were able to talk about things Spanish without losing our tempers.

Katy and I arrived in Key West one fine day and found that some damn sculptor had done a bust of Ernest. A plaster cast of it stood in the front hall. It was a horrible bust. Looked as if it were made out of soap. We let out a roar of laughter when we first saw it. We couldn't imagine that Ernest could take it seriously. That winter I developed the habit of trying to ring it with my panama hat when I stepped in the door. Ernest caught me at it one day, gave me a sour look and took the hat off the bust's head. He was grouchy for the rest of the day. Nobody said anything but after that things were never quite so good.

CHAPTER 7

The Little Cockroach

During a stopover in Madrid sometime in the twenties Pepe Giner got me into the royal palace to see one of the court functions. It was set hideously early. We met at sixthirty in the morning at a café on the large square next to the palace. Pepe had engraved passes. We were late; we rushed past the mounted guards in the court. A uniformed usher with a silver chain dangling across his vest hurried us up a small winding stair and squeezed us into a line of people standing with their backs against the wall of a narrow tapestry-hung corridor. The bitter morning light of Castile poured in from a window opposite.

Before we could catch our breath the procession was upon us. Alfonso XIII walked fast, a step ahead of the mass of uniforms, medals, colored ribbons, fancy swords, monocles and mustaches of the grandees of Spain and the chokers, sunbursts, flashing stomachers of the ladies of the court. They all had the ghastly look of people routed out of bed too soon. Don Alfonso passed so close his epaulette almost brushed our chests as we dug our shoulders into the tapestry behind us to make room.

In that light the modeling of the king's face stood out startlingly clear; there was the thin waxy nose between dead eyes and the jutting wolfjaw of Velasquez's portraits of the Hapsburg kings. It was not the poised haughty set of Philip IV's features; more the halfwit leer Velasquez saw in the face of Carlos II, "the bewitched," who brought the great line of the House of Austria so feebly to a close and left the throne open to the French Bourbons.

Alfonso was very much the international playboy in his habits, what the Spaniards call a "señorito." It was probably a hangover that gave his face that waxen look. Maybe he hadn't been to bed at all. He was obviously in a hurry to get the boring ceremony over. The face was gone in a flash but the afterimage remained. If I hadn't looked so hard at the Velasquez portraits I don't suppose I would have seen it quite that way.

When Katy and I reached Madrid on one of my convalescent journeys we found that Pepe Giner had been appointed one of the curators of that very palace. Under the republic it had to be called the Palacio Nacional.

No one could have been better qualified. He led us up the great marble stairway to the throne room with its gilt lions and its crowding black busts of Roman emperors. This was all the work of the Bourbons. Pepe showed off the ceiling that Tiepolo painted for Philip V with such enthusiasm that at last I began to appreciate the magnificence of these cloudy abstractions of government and power bathed in cool empyrean light. Up to then I had hardly condescended to look at the later Venetians.

Tiepolo fitted our mood that day. We were full of hope that the new republican power in Spain would develop in some such cool light of reason. The rest of Europe was up to its neck in power gone mad, strangling on it. In that morning's papers we had read of Stalin's purge. In Berlin Hitler was proclaiming a thousand years of National Socialism while Mussolini ranted military glory up and down the Italian peninsula and Nazi mobs threatened the liberal institutions that had seemed so well established in Vienna.

It was very quiet in the National Palace. We were the only visitors. While he pointed out the ormolu and the tapestries and the ancient clocks, Pepe, in his humorous, selfdeprecatory tone, described the departure of the last of the Bourbons.

Don Alfonso had passed a bad quarter of an hour when, after a period of riots and general strikes against the monarchy, Ramón Franco's planes appeared in the sky over the palace. Ramón and Francisco Franco were two young army officers in the forefront of the protest against the inefficiency and corruption that had brought about the military disasters in Morocco. Ramón was the ace Spanish aviator, idolized in the airforce. His brother Francisco was then just another officer, as impecunious as only a *gallego* can be. The planes merely *circled* over the palace. When it came to dropping his bombs Ramón Franco lost his nerve. It was the sight of the children playing in the square outside, Ramón told the sympathetic Portuguese who interned him when he took refuge in Lisbon; he had intended to destroy the palace and make an end to the Bourbons forever.

Don Alfonso was profoundly shocked. Although more at home with a roulette-wheel than with problems of statesmanship, he was not a bad sort. He tried sincerely to promote the development of a more constitutional monarchy in the English style, but when elections were permitted the Spaniards overwhelmingly voted republican. Students began yelling "Muera el rey, viva la republica" as they ran out from under the sabers of the Civil Guards on the cobbled streets of Madrid.

One fine April day Don Alfonso suddenly decided he'd had enough. Maybe he was sick of everybody telling him what to do. He burned a number of state papers in his office that afternoon and strode through the palace to the room where his wife, the Englishwoman, was having tea. In no uncertain terms he told her he was through. He was leaving for France. The queen could take time to pack up her things and bring the children by train. He was driving to Cartagena that very night. A battleship was waiting. He had friends among the naval officers he could trust. She would meet him in Biarritz. So he sneaked out of the palace under cover of darkness as stealthily as a defaulting bank cashier.

The people of Madrid woke up next morning to find themselves, to their great surprise, a republic. The only act of unreasonable violence they committed was the upsetting of the handsome equestrian statue of Philip III in the Plaza Mayor, which Pepe and I always admired as we walked through on our way to eat at Bottin's. While he was taking the inventory of the royal possessions Pepe came upon the crown of Spain in a green baize bag stuffed into an old clothes closet.

As he told us the story he showed us the rooms where each episode had taken place. It made us feel as if we had seen it happen.

I was paying for our trip by writing some articles about the second republic; "The Republic of Honest Men" it was called in the liberal press. I managed to get an interview with Manuel Azaña, the Prime Minister, already slated to replace the more conservative Alcalá Zamora when he should retire from the presidency.

During my early days in Madrid Azaña was president of the Ateneo. The Ateneo was one of those musty institutions that grew out of the early nineteenth-century enthusiasm for the arts and sciences. It had a very good library and I used to work in the readingroom days when my room at the Pension Boston was too chilly. Its advantage over other libraries was that you could smoke. There was a waiter who brought you coffee and would even go out for sandwiches if you wanted.

Since it was out of the sheltered conversations of the college professors and doctors and lawyers and journalists who made up the clientele of the Ateneo that most of the enthusiasm for the republic stemmed, it was quite fitting that the president of the Ateneo should become president of the council of ministers.

Azaña's office was in a fine Beaux Arts style building near the Cibyle fountain on the Castillana. As I waited in the ornate lobby I felt the choking in my chest that comes from the breathedout air of government bureaus, the feeling of being cut off from the real world where men and women worked and suffered and enjoyed themselves. *El señor presidente*—of the council of ministers—couldn't have been more civil. He spoke modestly and simply; he had a good sense of history.

Spain had come through the war prosperous on the whole, with a magnificent gold reserve; it would be the business of the republic to spread that prosperity among all classes. Education, hospitals, opportunities to rise in the world. "We don't want any more of our good people emigrating to America."

At that point an elderly attendant in a lustrous uniform brought in a tray of glasses with a cut glass pitcher. On the saucer beside each glass was an *azucarillo*. An azucarillo is a bananashaped cake of spun sugar that has been used in Spain since the eighteenth century to take the curse off drinking plain water. You put it in your glass and pour the water over it and watch it dissolve. Though sweetened water is the last thing I enjoy drinking I complied with the ceremony.

When Azaña had finished his little speech I brought up Stalin and Hitler, the Fascist movements in France. Would the Pyrenees form as good a bulwark against the murderous hatreds that were sweeping Europe as they had against the sensible liberalism of the nineteenth century? He declared himself to be quite confident; Spain had escaped the uncivilizing influence of the war; there might be some advantage in being a backward country.

I left him feeling profoundly unhappy. That afternoon we walked through the workingclass sections on the slope behind the Plaza Mayor. The Socialist Party was celebrating a street fair. Literature was being distributed at prettily ornamented booths. There were cookshacks and booths of homemade toys where cartoons of the various politicos were on sale in the form of jumping-jacks. It was all very innocent and very amusing. One booth displayed a placard: *Limonada Socialista.*

Unamuno laughed his head off when I told him about it. This was the last time I saw Don Miguel. With his parchment skin and his narrow domed forehead he was getting to look more like Don Quijote than ever as the years went on. I couldn't get him to talk about the republic he'd done so much to bring about. He merely asked plaintively: "Where are the great men?"

Then he turned to twitting me on my ignorance of Portuguese. He greatly admired Portuguese literature. His mental development had been as much nourished on Camoëns, particularly the sonnets, as on Cervantes. This surprised me as I'd thought of the author of *El Sentimiento Trájico de la Vida* as being the most Castilian of writers.

Before I left he told me a funny story about beggars. Don Miguel professed great respect for the techniques of Spanish beggars. He had asked an old man whom he'd seen every day for years outside of a church he frequented why he always used the same singsong complaint. "Of course," the old beggar answered, "there are other schools, perhaps you prefer *los naturalistas*."

This time we wanted to see Spain by road. As there seemed to be no way of renting a car we bought a tiny secondhand Fiat which we labeled "the Cockroach." The country never seemed lovelier than on that trip. At the Escorial we spent a lot of time in the private apartments of Philip II. They are still just as he left them. You come out of the bare plaster rooms, furnished handsomely but modestly for a royal personage of the time, saturated with the personality of that narrowly devout, hardworking man who invented the bureaucratic system that held together the Spanish empire in Europe and the Americas for two centuries. He meant well too. When he gloried in the burning of heretics he thought he was serving God and man. How much evil, I kept thinking, can be accomplished by the doers of good.

We walked through Segovia, again by moonlight. In Avila it was as if Santa Teresa, another of Spain's great characters, were still living there. We discovered for the first time the magnificent valley of the Ebro where the cliffs and defiles are on a scale to rival the Colorado Rockies. We almost choked on the abundance of buildings and carving that needed careful looking at in Compostella. At Pontevedra on the Atlantic coast of Galicia we came upon the annual fiesta. I've never seen such astonishing fireworks, all fabricated by the local *pirotecnico,* or such disregard of life and limb as when the red, purple and yellow decorations—the colors of the republic—festooned around the crowded plaza went off in a delirium of flowerpots and pinwheels.

In Santander, on the way back we heard Pepe Giner's cousin, Fernando de los Rios, who represented Granada in the Cortes, address a socialist massmeeting in the bullring. It was a great occasion. The men of the trade unions had come with red- and gold-lettered banners and with their wives and children and basket lunches and bottles of wine. Schoolchildren in white dresses with red bows sang the *Internationale.* Listening to Don Fernando's speech it was a pleasure to follow his classical use of the conditional and the future subjunctive, but very little of it could have sounded practical to the eager miners and mechanics and farmers who had come in buses and mule carts and on bicycles and on foot from all over northern Spain to hear him.

He was greeted with shouts of *"viven los hombres honrados."* Somebody opened a box of white pigeons with red ribbons round their necks. They were supposed to fly up into the empyrean to symbolize the reign of peace and goodwill that was to come, but the poor pigeons must have been in their box too long in all that heat. Instead of flying they dropped to the ground. All through Don Fernando's speech one of them flopped helplessly about in the center of the bullring. That summer I kept seeing signs and portents.

A sign and portent that was certainly not imaginary was the hatred in the faces of the welldressed people seated at the café tables on the main street of Santander as they stared at the sweaty Socialists straggling back from the bullring with their children and their picnic baskets and their bunting. If eyes had been machine guns not one of them would have survived that day. I jotted in my notes: Socialists innocent as a flock of sheep in the wolf country.

I was pridefully extolling the virtues of the little Fiat to Katy, and taking flattering unction to myself over my success in correcting slight malfunctions of its simple little motor when—fortunately while we were traversing one of the few level stretches on the entire trip—a pin dropped out of the steering gear and we went hurtling off into a meadow. We weren't even shaken up but I admit we were shocked.

Two sturdy Asturians who came along genially picked up the little cockroach and loaded it into their truck and deposited us at a repair shop in a neighboring town. When I tried to pay them they refused. We'd do the same thing for them, they said. But their truck wouldn't fit into my Fiat. I got them laughing over the disparity of sizes and did manage to get them to take a few pesetas to make up for it.

The mechanics were the nicest people in the world, but they did take a long time—several days in fact—to straighten out the steering gear. We had to cut short our trip, and besides we didn't have quite the confidence in the little Fiat on the hairpin mounain curves that we had had before.

We arrived at the Hotel Alfonso in Madrid with only a few days left before we were to meet the Italian boat we had passage home on to Gibraltar. To make things worse I took to my bed with a relapse into last spring's rheumatic fever. We put ads in the papers "*Cochecito á vender.*" I had dreamed of getting back most of what I'd paid for the wretched cockroach. Various customers arrived and were interviewed from my sick bed, while Katy made them welcome with glasses of sherry.

They all balked at the price until a young army lieutenant appeared, resplendent in red and blue dress uniform. *Qué muchacho más simpático.* The cochecito was lovely. The price was lovely. He produced credentials. All he asked was to be allowed to try the little car out on the road. He would be back in an hour. What could be more reasonable? I gave him a note to the garage. He retired after eloquently wishing me a rapid recovery.

An hour passed. A day passed. No lieutenant. We called the garage. No cochecito. We called friends. We called the police. The police sent over a very nice young man in plain clothes with whom I had a long conversation about the baroque in poetry, Góngora to be exact. He took down all the specifications most carefully in his notebook and retired after several glasses of sherry. I never felt like a more perfect damn fool.

Another day passed without news. Then there came a call from the aficionado of Góngora: Good news. The cochecito has been recovered by the police. It is reposing at this very moment in the courtyard of *Gobernacíon* on the Puerta del Sol. Bravo. I was profuse in thanks and congratulations. What a magnificent police force they had in republican Madrid.

I had hardly hung up before a fresh army officer was ushered into the room, a captain this time. He professed to be extremely embarrassed. The lieutenant was his brother. I must excuse him. His brother was a little mad. His mania was taking out cars on approval and not bringing them back. The captain respectfully requested that I refrain from bringing charges. His brother was already under restraint in a *casa de salud.* What could I do? The car had been recovered. We poured out more sherry and the captain vowed eternal brotherhood.

As soon as I could hobble, I was over interviewing the police at Gobernacíon. We had found another buyer, at half price. We wanted the car. The police were extraordinarily polite. The cochecito was quite safe. They took me to see it in a rear courtyard. It was swathed in chickenwire so that nobody could touch it.

Couldn't I take the car now? I had a buyer for it. I was leaving for Gibraltar next day. The chief inspector pronounced himself afflicted by this news but the car would have to remain there as evidence until the lieutenant who had stolen it was apprehended. *No hay remédio. Es la ley.* Back at the hotel we called more friends. The aficionado of Góngora appeared for another delightful literary conversation. The lieutenant was nowhere to be found. No lieutenant, no cochecito. The idiotic series of incidents began to seem to me as illustrative of the human predicament as the misadventures of the Knight of the Doleful Countenance seemed to Unamuno.

We took the night train to Gibraltar. The last we saw of the cockroach it was still encased in chickenwire in the courtyard of Gobernacíon.